FIND AND DESTROY

FIND AND DESTROY
Antisubmarine Warfare in World War I

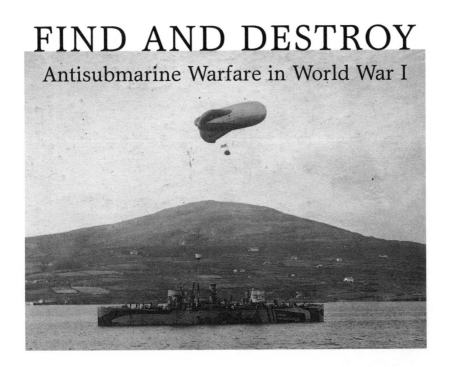

DWIGHT R. MESSIMER

Naval Institute Press
Annapolis, Maryland

Naval Institute Press
291 Wood Road
Annapolis, MD 21402

Library of Congress Cataloging-in-Publication Data
Messimer, Dwight R., 1937-
    Find and destroy : antisubmarine warfare in World War I/Dwight
R. Messimer.
        p. cm.
    Includes bibliographical references and index.
    ISBN 1-55750-447-4 (alk. paper)
    1. World War, 1914-1918—Naval operations—Submarine. I.
    Title.
    D590 .M47 2001

                                        2001030007

Printed in the United States of America on acid-free paper ∞
08 07 06 05 04 03 02 01   9 8 7 6 5 4 3 2
First printing

Distributed internationally by Chatham Publishing,
99 High Street, Rochester, Kent ME1 1LX
United Kingdom

To Yvonne, who has the priceless attribute
of being absolutely reliable

Contents

Preface

I have been interested in submarines and all aspects of submarine warfare since I was a child, and I read every book on submarines in World War I and World War II that came my way. But one thing bothered me. Everything I read about World War I made it clear that for most of the war the British did not have an effective antisubmarine capability. They were in the same boat I was in when I went fishing with a sharp stick. I could stab at the water all day and never get anything. So how did the British sink so many U-boats and why did the Germans lose the war? The answers to those questions involve politics, organization, and technology.

All the translations from German documents are my own. I did not convert the foreign naval ranks to English because I think using each country's rank designation lends flavor to the text. Appendix A lists equivalent ranks. I converted metric measurements into feet, yards, and miles because I think that most Americans can visualize feet, yards, and miles better than they can visualize meters and kilometers. If someone tells me the water is 100 feet deep, I can visualize it—it is deep. But 30.3 meters take some imagination and math for me to get back to what I best understand—100 feet. Appendix B lists gun caliber equivalents. The maps were drawn by hand; therefore, they should not be used for navigation.

Acknowledgments

There are several people who deserve specific recognition for the generous help they gave me. My longtime friend, colleague, and mentor, Charles Burdick, Ph.D., with whom I spent many hours discussing this project, offered advice, support, and ideas until the day he died. I will always owe him an unrepayable debt. John Bullen, Ph.D., of the Imperial War Museum, directed me to valuable sources on British weapons and countermeasures. His help made my experience with the Imperial War Museum very pleasant. Paul G. Halpern, Ph.D., author of *A Naval History of World War I* (Naval Institute Press, 1994) and other excellent World War I naval histories, gave me good advice on sources and shared his insight. I am indebted for his generous help. David McNeil, Ph.D., chairman of the history department at San Jose State University, translated the French naval documents for me, and smoothed the way for my grant applications. His cooperation in scheduling and providing time for research were contributions beyond measure. Tim Mulligan, Ph.D., the specialist in captured German and related records at the National Archives, searched among copious files to locate the relevant records dealing with the Germans' antisubmarine operations in the Baltic and the Helgoland Bight. I very much appreciate his efforts.

Introduction

During World War I, antisubmarine warfare (ASW) involved more than just destroying submarines, although this aspect receives the most attention because it is the most dramatic. The tactics and technology of ASW during World War I, however, must be viewed within the context of the political, economic, and military circumstances that created both the submarine menace and the Allied ASW response.

In the literature on the 1914–18 submarine war, both German and English speaking authors focus on the so-called "lost opportunity of 1916," when Hermann Bauer withdrew the German fleet's U-boats from their anti-shipping role. I contend that the real lost opportunity occurred in August–October 1914 when the U-boats failed to interrupt Britain's cross-channel troop transports and supplies and believe that is when the Germans lost the war. Bauer's actions in 1916 and the Germans' indecision until January 1917 only made the situation worse.

If the real lost opportunity occurred in 1914, then the most effective antisubmarine weapon of the war was not a weapon at all. It was politics. The Germans' fear that departing from the narrow restrictions of the 1909 Declaration of London would bring the United States into the war more effectively blunted their U-boat weapon than any ASW weapon or tactic developed before the autumn of 1917.

Beyond the role of politics there were technological and tactical developments that worked directly to defeat the U-boats. Allied, primarily British, ASW is examined in detail because, from the start of the war, the British were more heavily involved in the ASW campaign than the French or the Russians. Britain's geographic position, and the fact that in 1914 Britain possessed just under half the world's merchant tonnage, made the waters around Britain the most important theater of operations. Once the United States entered the war, the U.S. Navy threw its resources into the ASW campaign. Backed by America's industrial capacity, this resulted in a significant contribution.

Weapons and techniques used by the British were used in exact or similar form by their allies and enemies. All the European belligerents used fishing boats for minesweeping and antisubmarine patrols. They all used mines, laid antisubmarine nets, and, with the exception of the Turks, developed some kind of depth charge. All the Europeans developed hydrophones for detecting submerged submarines, although the British, French, and Americans took this form of technology farther than anyone else. And the Germans took a page right out of the British book and used decoys, so-called Q-ships, in the Baltic.

Germany, Austria, and Turkey deployed ASW on a far smaller scale than did their enemies. After all, in World War I the large-scale use of submarines was essentially a German monopoly. There is an expression among submariners that there are two kinds of ships—submarines and targets. In a comparative sense the Germans offered few surface targets to the British with the result that the British had little incentive to use their submarines in a major anti-shipping campaign. There was incentive, however, to develop antisubmarine weapons and tactics.

Before the war both Britain and Germany paid little heed to the threat the submarine might pose to commercial shipping. As a result not much was done to develop an ASW capability. During the first three years of the war the British made very little progress in developing a serious ASW capability. Britain's neglect of ASW was due largely to British complacency that was reinforced by Germany's haphazard anti-shipping war up to February 1917. When the situation finally became so serious that the British could not ignore it, they undertook to create an efficient, overwhelming ASW capability.

Antisubmarine warfare has three goals that are complementary and to some degree overlap one another: destroy submarines, restrict the submarines' access to their operations areas, and shield merchant ships from attack. The British accomplished those goals through continuing technological advances that combined with a more efficient organization and the convoy system defeated the U-boats. A critical shortage of U-boats, the

Germans' failure to significantly advance the U-boat's performance, and the failure to adopt a more efficient tactical organization crippled the German response to British ASW advances.

Not until June 1917 did the Germans place any large orders for U-boats because of the myopic view that the war would end soon. Until the introduction of the U-117 series in March 1918, the U-boat's designed capabilities with regard to depth limits and maximum underwater speed remained unchanged. Equally serious, German organization failed to meet the changing conditions as the war expanded. Throughout the war Germany had no central command that could direct all the U-boat flotillas in a single, concerted operational plan. Given the global nature of the conflict, centralized control was essential to an efficient anti-shipping war. This shortcoming became particularly serious after the Allies adopted the convoy system in 1917.

For the greater part of the war, the German anti-shipping war was marked by frustration, confusion, and indecision resulting from the debate over whether or not the war would be fought according to the Prize Regulations or as an all-out unrestricted campaign to starve England into surrender. The central issue in the debate was the German civilian government's fear that a departure from the Prize Regulations would bring the United States into the war on the side of the Allies. By the spring of 1917, when German determination collided with Allied technology and organization, Germany's legacy of limited production, poor organization, and disagreement gave the winning edge to the Allies.

FIND AND DESTROY

PART ONE

War, Politics, and International Law

August 1914–January 1915

1

The Prize Regulations

Consider this situation. A nation, almost entirely dependent on seaborne trade, has a powerful navy with which to protect its trade. The nation finds itself at war with an enemy who relies almost exclusively on submarines. The nation with the large merchant fleet and navy, however, has no antisubmarine weapons. Would it not seem reasonably certain that the nation using the submarines would quickly sink its enemy's merchant fleet?

Although overly simplistic this is essentially the situation that obtained between Great Britain and Germany in 1914. So the question is: How did the British manage to defeat the U-boats? Or, in other words: How did the Germans manage to lose? The answer is that it was not easy in either case. The situation illustrates that there is more to the study of antisubmarine warfare (ASW) than simply examining the technology and weapons used by the surface forces and the tactics employed by the submarines. Equally important are the political issues that establish the parameters within which the war was fought.

At the beginning of World War I neither side fully understood the power of the submarine as an offensive weapon. And it is equally true that no one had any idea about what methods would be necessary to counter the submarine. As a result the opening months of the war were marked by both sides overestimating the other side's capabilities and the threat those assumed capabilities represented.

At the start of the war Britain's Admiralty operated on the idea that the Germans would not conduct a submarine war against shipping. This belief was based on existing international law and what was perceived to be the submarine's design limitations for anti-shipping operations under the law. The relevant international law was the 1909 Declaration of London, which was an attempt to protect neutral nations' maritime rights and international seaborne commerce during war.

In brief, the declaration allowed belligerents to stop any vessel at sea, and board and search it for contraband. If contraband was found, the vessel could be seized and sent in to port. If for reasons bearing on the warship's safety that were not possible, the vessel could be sunk. But Article 50, in part, said, "Before the vessel is destroyed all persons on board must be placed in safety."[1] In practice, that meant taking the crew and any passengers aboard the warship for safe delivery ashore.

The navies of the eight nations that drew up the 1909 declaration incorporated its seventy articles into their own naval regulations and called them the Prize Regulations. Under international law the Prize Regulations were binding on each nation's naval officers. The British believed that submarines, because of their relatively small size, the absence of deck guns, and their perceived poor sea-keeping qualities, would be unable to comply with the Prize Regulations, and therefore did not constitute a threat to merchant shipping.

The Germans held the same view and entered the war with no intention of conducting an anti-shipping campaign with the U-boats. In fact, the Germans had equipped only the U-21 and U-25 with deck guns, and during the first six months of the war they deployed their U-boats as reconnaissance and torpedo units of the High Sea Fleet. The U-boats' assignment was to attack units of the Grand Fleet. In that role the U-boats created a threat that caused Adm. Sir John Jellicoe, commander in chief of the Grand Fleet, to temporarily evacuate Scapa Flow and move the fleet to more secure anchorages on the east coast of Scotland.[2]

While the U-boats searched for the Grand Fleet the British focused their efforts on transporting the British Expeditionary Force (BEF) across the English Channel to France. Britain's primary concern during this time was that German surface units, possibly even the entire High Sea Fleet, would pass through the Dover Straits and attack the cross-channel transports.[3]

To protect their cross-channel traffic against a German raid, the British and the French joined forces to close both ends of the English Channel. In the center was the Channel Fleet under Vice Adm. Sir Cecil Burney, with three battle squadrons based at Portland. A joint British and French force composed of torpedo boat destroyers, destroyers, and submarines held the Dover Straits, and across the straits' northern entrance were the destroyer HMS *Firedrake* and twelve submarines. North of that line, seaplanes and airships patrolled between North Foreland and Ostend. Beyond the air patrols were the 1st and 3d Flotilla destroyers based at Harwich. A joint British and French cruiser force held the other end of the channel. If the Germans tried to force their way through the Dover Straits, they would have to fight their way through successive lines of warships.

The important point here is that the British and the French were prepared to defeat a surface attack on their troop transports, which were legitimate military targets. But what would they do if submarines attacked the transports? Antisubmarine measures and defenses were essentially nonexistent at that point in the war, and the only countermeasures available to the British and French warships, whether guarding the Grand Fleet or the cross-channel transports, were deck guns and ramming.

Until 20 December 1914 the British had no specific organization charged with the responsibility for antisubmarine measures. Instead, defense along Britain's east coast was under the command of Rear Adm. G. A. Ballard, the Admiral of Patrols, who had his headquarters at Harwich. His command included several destroyers and a few light cruisers charged with the responsibility of protecting the British east coast from attack "by lightly escorted raiding forces."[4]

There was also the Auxiliary Patrol composed primarily of fishing vessels—trawlers and drifters—and assorted other small craft that played an important role during the war. By 1 September 1914 there were 250 trawlers and drifters in service, although most were still unarmed. These small vessels swept mines, carried out antisubmarine patrols, and watched for German minelayers, which at that time were all surface ships.

Despite the defending forces' weak antisubmarine capability, the U-boats did little to interrupt the cross-channel flow of troops and supplies. Between 12 August 1914, when the British began their maximum effort to transport the BEF to France, and 15 October, when the German army entered Ostend, the U-boats had the ability to seriously disrupt the

BEF's passage to France. Neither the British nor the French could have done much to prevent it. During that critical period, however, the U-boats sank no troop transports or merchant ships carrying war supplies. Beyond causing the British to worry about the potential damage the U-boats could do, they accomplished nothing. Why did the Germans miss that golden opportunity?

Part of the problem was that the German army, the people who actually ran the war for Germany, ignored the need to interdict the British cross-channel supply lines. The only mission the German army assigned to the navy was to guard the army's right flank. Sir Julian S. Corbett, one of the authors of the official British history of the naval war, suggested that "[t]he Germans believed they could make an end of the few Expeditionary Force divisions in their first rush, and it was obviously better for them if the Expeditionary Force exposed itself to that rush."[5] Korvettenkapitän Hermann Bauer, who commanded the U-boats assigned to the High Sea Fleet, said that the Army expected to encircle both the British and French armies in northern France.[6]

Another part of the problem was that the Admiralstab in Berlin and the High Sea Fleet command at Wilhelmshaven were preoccupied with the idea of fighting a decisive fleet engagement. With that plan in mind the High Sea Fleet deployed its U-boats on picket and reconnaissance duties and sent them into the North Sea to reduce the Grand Fleet to manageable proportions. Operating according to that plan Kapitänleutnant Otto Hersing in U-21 torpedoed the light cruiser HMS *Pathfinder* on 5 September 1914. Seventeen days later Kapitänleutnant Otto Weddigen in U-9 sank the old British cruisers *Aboukir, Hogue,* and *Cressy* in just one hour. Although spectacular, these German successes made no material contribution toward reducing the Royal Navy's fighting strength and did not inhibit the flow of men and supplies from Britain to France.

The loss of four cruisers, however, did cause the British to adopt special antisubmarine measures. Following the loss of the three *Cressy*-class cruisers, the Admiralty directed underway British warships to frequently change course and speed to make a torpedo attack more difficult. The directive proved to be very effective in keeping the U-boats from sinking British warships. But the British reaction to Weddigen's successful hat trick was of small consequence compared to the negative effect the German civilian government's policy had on U-boat operations. This is the third, and probably most important, reason that the Germans missed their golden opportunity in 1914.

The civilian government under Theobald von Bethmann-Hollweg and the Admiralstab, headed by Adm. Hugo von Pohl, were committed to fighting the war at sea under the terms of the 1909 Declaration of London. Those terms, as spelled out in the German navy's Prize Regulations, prohibited a torpedo attack on any merchant vessel, including British merchant ships, unless the U-boat captain could positively determine that the vessel was carrying troops or war material. How was that to be done?

Under the government guidelines fair targets were limited to warships and enemy merchant ships on which the commander could see what were either troops or military equipment on deck. The U-boat captain also had to take the ship's location as well as its heading into consideration before he could make an attack. The government's guidelines required the U-boat commander to be absolutely certain before he torpedoed any merchant ship. U-boat commanders quickly learned it was impossible to make an absolute determination by looking through a periscope.

The U-boat captains did not fully recognize the Prize Regulations' inhibiting effect during the war's first two months because the U-boats were focused on attacking the Grand Fleet. But toward the end of September the situation in France took a different turn and the U-boats found themselves looking down the Dover Straits at Britain's cross-channel supply lines. During the next five weeks the Germans discovered that the Prize Regulations seriously hampered their ability to conduct a campaign against British cross-channel traffic.

During the last half of September the war in France produced a crisis situation for the Royal Navy. Following the Battle of the Marne both the Allies and the Germans started what became known as the "Race for the Sea" in which the German goal was to seize the Belgian ports from Zeebrugge to Calais. For the British Admiralty, the possibility of the Germans controlling the Belgian ports was a military nightmare "that would disturb the arrangements for covering the Army's lines of supply."[7] The British were so concerned with the security of their cross-channel supply lines that they had already shifted their main supply base in France from Le Havre to Saint Nazaire.

As the crisis unfolded, the German army finally asked the navy to disrupt British attempts to land troops on the Belgian coast at Ostend. On 25 September Kapitänleutnant Heinrich von Hennig left Helgoland in

U-18 to take up a position in the area of the West Hinder Lightship, near
the entrance to the Dover Straits, to "attack transports or their escorts that
were en route Ostend."[8] There were no transports to be found because at
that particular time the British were not moving troops in either direction
in that area. That activity was occurring in the English Channel. Having
no success in his assigned area, von Hennig took U-18 into the Dover
Straits—the first U-boat to enter the straits since the war started.

On the morning of 27 September, U-18 was submerged off the Dover
entrance, where von Hennig observed "many drifters and fishing boats,
but no warships."[9] His log entry illustrated the inhibiting effect the Prize
Regulations had on his ability to stem the flow of supplies across the
channel: "There were only merchant ships, none of which displayed any
outward signs of being used by the military, and I had to consider the
English reaction should I sink one of them."[10]

At 1100, still submerged, von Hennig turned away from Dover and
headed toward Calais, looking for a warship to sink. An hour later he
came upon the light cruiser, HMS *Attentive,* and fired a torpedo that
missed. The surprise of being attacked in the straits convinced the British
that the U-boats were finally going after the cross-channel supply lines.
And to some degree they were right.

The deteriorating military situation in France and reports that the German army was reinforcing its right wing caused the British to recognize
that the loss of the Belgian ports was a growing possibility. The British
were certain that once the Germans occupied the ports the U-boats would
use them as bases from which to launch raids through the Dover Straits
and into the English Channel. The U-18's attack on the *Attentive* underscored that fear. The situation was "intolerable"[11] and called for drastic
countermeasures if the cross-channel supply lines were to be kept open.
The Admiralty's solution to the crisis was to lay an enormous minefield
across the entrance to the Dover Straits, which the Royal Navy accomplished on the night of 2 October. The minefield was Britain's first use
of mines as an antisubmarine weapon, but it was a case of bark and not
much bite. The minefield actually played a larger role in turning the
U-boats to attacks on shipping than it did in deterring them from passing
through the Dover Straits.

The British were unaware that their 2 October minefield was largely
ineffective, but they were aware that since they laid it they had still not
lost any ships carrying supplies to France. On the basis of apparent

success they assumed the minefield was doing its job. In fact, it was the German Prize Regulations that were protecting the cross-channel supply lines and the troop movements on the Belgian coast.

On 8 October 1914, at the time the Belgian and British troops were withdrawing from Antwerp, U-19 under Kapitänleutnant Walter Kolbe was patrolling submerged off the mouth of the Schelde. He observed steamer traffic that included a large passenger steamer and two smaller ships that he assumed were carrying troops from Antwerp to England. But he was unable to determine that with absolute certainty and the Prize Regulations prevented him from attacking them. Later that evening, Kolbe tried to lay U-19 on the bottom, and in doing so damaged the pressure hull. He returned to Ems for repairs without having carried out any attacks.[12]

On 13 October, U-28 under Kapitänleutnant Freiherr von Forstner was off Calais when he saw a French steamer approaching the harbor entrance. Forstner maneuvered U-28 into an attack position just as the steamer made an unexpected turn around the entrance buoy and proceeded down the entrance channel at high speed. At that moment Forstner realized the strong current was setting him onto a shoal and he had to turn his attention to taking U-28 out of danger. In his log he lamented the loss of his target: "This steamer was the only one about which I felt justified in believing was a troop transport, and warranted a torpedo attack, because there were so many people on deck."[13]

In November the trench lines were established in France, and the U-boats again focused their attention on the Grand Fleet. U-boat activity in the Dover Straits and the English Channel declined markedly. Much of the decline was because Korvettenkapitän Bauer resisted sending boats into the channel to attack the cross-channel supply lines.

His reasons were twofold. First, he felt that the restrictions imposed by the Prize Regulations meant risking his U-boats unnecessarily. For Bauer it was a matter of the returns not being worth the risk. Second, he cited technical matters that increased the risks. Specifically, he cited the boats' slow diving characteristics, the unreliability of the Körting kerosene engines installed in the U-boats through U-18, and unreliable compasses that made submerged navigation very risky. At that time the three-axis, gyroscopic compasses were just coming into service and only U-8 among the original boats had been refitted with one.[14]

Bauer had a strong point. But the question of what would have happened had the U-boats been given a free hand is impossible to answer

with absolute certainty. It is safe to say that had they been allowed to effectively interdict the Allied cross-channel supply lines during August, September, and October 1914, the outcome of the war might have been different. Consider the impact on the British public had the U-boats sunk two
or three fully laden troop ships with an attendant heavy loss of life. Certainly the British public's enthusiasm to reinforce the French army would
have been dampened. Even more significant might have been several successes against ships carrying artillery ammunition. The Allies suffered a
critical artillery ammunition shortage until well into 1915, and any dis-
ruption of their supplies would have materially increased the shortage.

Writing about the results of German inactivity during the Race to the
Sea period, Korvettenkapitän Groos wrote: "The deployment of the
British Marine Infantry at Antwerp meant the Belgians held after 3 October and effectively to 10 October. Thus the British Naval Infantry bought
valuable time during which two British and three French divisions closed
the gap between Ypres and the coast before the Germans had Antwerp
and could drive down the coast."[15]

In effect, the Germans' own Prize Regulations proved to be a more
effective antisubmarine measure than all the British measures combined.

2

The German Awakening

Legal issues stemming from the 1909 Declaration of London contributed substantially to the direction in which ASW developed and to the character of the later ASW campaign. In fact, it is safe to say that until February 1917 the legal issues were as important in the antisubmarine war as were the weapons and organization, albeit their importance was unintended. The Germans started the war with no plans to wage a submarine war on shipping, and the British had no plans for protecting their seaborne trade against the U-boats. The purely military character of the submarine war during the first months limited the British need for a strong ASW response and restricted the development of effective antisubmarine weapons, devices, and systems.

By October 1914 that situation was starting to change as the British blockade became increasingly effective and the Germans began to realize that their U-boats were not accomplishing their mandate. Both sides were aware that the Declaration of London had created unrealistic rules for use in the current war, and both sides had been changing, bending, and outright ignoring the rules since the war started. But the declaration was still in force and neither side wanted to appear to be the first one to break the law. Therefore, the measures adopted by both sides had to be at least logically justified if not entirely legally justified.

Because of their geographic position, and because they possessed the world's most powerful fleet, the British had long ago adopted the blockade as a major strategy for defeating an enemy. They would allow nothing to interfere with that strategy, not even the provisions of the Declaration of London. The British had given up the close blockade concept on the basis that modern weaponry—mines, artillery, and submarines—made a close blockade so impractical as to be suicidal. Instead, they adopted what they called a distant blockade in which they closed off the northern and southern entrances to the North Sea. Despite the practicality—in fact, the operational necessity—of such a change in strategy, the distant blockade was a violation of Chapter I of the 1909 Declaration of London. The British, however, had not ratified the declaration; therefore, they were not bound to observe its provisions.[1]

The British strategy was summed up by the Jellicoe, the commander in chief of the Grand Fleet: "Our policy should be to resist temptation to activities which entail undue risk to our heavy ships, and meanwhile devote ourselves to strangling the enemy's trade and destroying his submarines by every possible device."[2]

In order to strangle the enemy's trade, the British paid lip service to the 1909 Declaration of London without actually being bound by its provisions. They accomplished that through the charade of modifying the declaration's provisions through Orders in Council, so that as early as October 1914, they were seizing foodstuffs as contraband. They did this by expanding the rule of ultimate destination "to its utmost by applying it to food and other kinds of conditional contraband."[3]

Article 33 made conditional contraband liable to capture if it was for the use of the armed forces or a department within the government. The British justified their expanded interpretation of the rule of ultimate destination by claiming that the German government had taken over the control of food distribution in Germany. In fact, the German government had not taken over the control of food supplies in Germany.

The Germans, whose military experience was primarily land warfare, had no blockade strategy when the war started. Germany's senior naval officers certainly were aware that a German naval blockade around Britain would have seriously hurt the British war effort, but the Germans lacked the ability to carry out such a strategy. The German war plan had envisioned a short war in which a war on Britain's shipping would not be necessary. But that thinking started to change in October 1914 when it became apparent that the war would last much longer than the Germans had expected.

The event that started the ball rolling occurred when the British announced on 3 October 1914 that they had laid a minefield east of the Dover-Calais line. The British justified the minefield on purely military grounds, saying it was intended to protect their cross-channel supply lines against U-boats.[4] Many, if not most, of the German U-boat officers had believed from the start of the war that an anti-shipping war was the most efficient use of a decisive weapon. Until the British laid their big minefield, their opinions had carried little weight with the Admiralstab who opposed the idea on political rather than military grounds. The arguments in favor of a submarine anti-shipping campaign grew louder and more persuasive after 3 October.

On 8 October 1914, Korvettenkapitän Bauer sent a memorandum to Adm. Friedrich von Ingenohl, commander of the High Sea Fleet, proposing an unrestricted U-boat campaign in British waters with the object of creating a shipping panic. The idea was to starve Britain before Britain starved Germany. Bauer's memorandum was the opening shot in the battle between the U-boat sailors and the civilian government over unrestricted submarine warfare. The hard knot of the debate was how the neutrals would perceive the Germans' strategy in light of the Declaration of London. The neutral whose judgment concerned the Germans the most was the United States.[5]

While the Germans were debating, Kapitänleutnant Feldkirchner in U-17 stopped the British freighter SS *Glitra* five miles off the Norwegian coast near Stavanger on 20 October 1914. This was the first instance during World War I when a U-boat attacked and sank a merchant ship of any nation, and the episode warrants close examination.

U-17 was on the surface, the sea was calm, and the visibility was excellent when the 927-ton SS *Glitra* hove into view. Feldkirchner moved toward the freighter and hoisted the "stop or I will fire" signal, followed by the "abandon ship immediately" signal. It is interesting to note that U-17 had no deck gun with which to carry out the threat to fire and was not in a position to fire a torpedo. Nevertheless, the *Glitra* complied by stopping and lowering its boats. Feldkirchner sent a watch officer and a machinist's mate over to the freighter with orders to open the ship's Kingston valves and bring back its papers and charts.

It took fifteen minutes for the watch officer and the machinist's mate to carry out their orders and return to the U-boat, and two hours for the

Glitra to sink. Throughout the operation, the U-boat lay hove to on the surface. When the freighter went under, Feldkirchner took the lifeboats in tow and started for the Norwegian coast. Two Norwegian pilot boats soon approached; Feldkirchner turned over the *Glitra*'s boats and crew to the Norwegians and left the area.

Kapitänleutnant Feldkirchner carried out the stop and the sinking according to the Prize Regulations, but it is not clear why he even bothered to stop the ship. Within the scope of his mission, attacks on merchant ships, unless they were obviously carrying war supplies or troops, were not a part of his standing orders. On the other hand, his orders did not specifically prohibit such action. In his war diary, Feldkirchner noted that the *Glitra*'s charts showed the exact routes used by merchant ships, the positions of new navigational buoys, and new British minefields. He also noted that the merchant routes in the North Sea converged off the Norwegian coast at Lister, and he laid his course for that port "to be on the lookout."[6]

Feldkirchner's success may have given von Bethmann-Hollweg and his supporters ammunition to use against the advocates of unrestricted submarine warfare because the sinking had been accomplished under the Prize Regulations. But conditions in the North Sea were completely different than the conditions in the Dover Straits and the English Channel, a fact that was not missed by the men who commanded the U-boats. More important, Feldkirchner's action had no effect in the Admiralty, which viewed the sinking as an isolated event. An event occurred in late October, however, that did have effect and turned the debate in Germany into a full-blown campaign for unrestricted submarine warfare.

On 27 October 1914 the dreadnought HMS *Audacious,* which had been completed in 1913, struck a German mine off Tory Island and sank. As a result of this incident, Admiral of the Fleet Lord John Fisher, who at that time was the First Sea Lord, announced on 3 November 1914 that from 5 November onward all of the North Sea would become a war zone:

> [A]ll ships passing a line drawn from the northern point of the Hebrides through the Faeroe Islands to Iceland do so at their own peril. Ships wishing to trade to and from Norway, the Baltic and Denmark are advised to come, if inward bound, by the English Channel and the Straits of Dover. There they will be given sailing directions which will pass them safely, so far as Britain is concerned, up the east coast of England, whence a safe

route will, if possible, be given to Lindesnaes Lighthouse. From this point they should turn north or south according to their destination, keeping as near the coast as possible. The converse applies to vessels outward bound. By strict adherence to these routes the commerce of all countries will be able to reach its destination in safety, so far as Great Britain is concerned, but any straying, even for a few miles from the course thus indicated, may be followed by fatal consequences.[7]

The British action spurred the unrestricted submarine war proponents to press for an anti-shipping campaign. They believed that the neutrals, faced by the threat of unrestricted submarine warfare, would remain in port and trade with Britain would fall so dramatically that Britain would be forced to lift the blockade. They also believed that an anti-shipping war would force Britain to negotiate a peace.

The civilian government under von Bethmann-Hollweg resisted the idea, fearing how the United States might react to an all-out war on shipping. The heart of the issue was what exactly was meant by a submarine war on shipping. If it was carried out under the Prize Regulations—a restricted campaign—there would be no serious repercussions from the United States. But if the Germans conducted an unrestricted submarine campaign, one in which the U-boats could torpedo any merchant ship without warning, that was another matter. Since the German navy's position from the start was that only unrestricted submarine warfare would realize the U-boats' maximum potential, the civilian government remained opposed to the plan.

The civilian government had a strong point in that they could point to a specific example. On 26 October 1914 Kapitänleutnant Rudolf Schneider in U-24 had torpedoed but did not sink SS *Amiral Ganteaume* in the English Channel. Schneider said that he thought the ship was a troop transport because he saw a large number of people on deck, a destroyer was escorting the ship, and the ship was headed toward a French port. If the *Amiral Ganteaume* had been a troopship, Schneider would have been fully justified torpedoing the ship without warning. The ship was carrying Belgian refugees, not British soldiers, and about forty civilians were killed.[8]

The British quickly capitalized on the propaganda opportunity that Schneider's attack created. The propaganda campaign they launched was so effective that the torpedoing of the *Amiral Ganteaume* is frequently cited as an example of German savagery. There was nothing the Germans could say that would undo the propaganda damage that Schneider's attack caused, and the world reacted with outrage.

On 21 November 1914 an American correspondent, Dr. Charles von Wiegand, interviewed Grossadmiral Alfred von Tirpitz, and the interview was published worldwide on 21 December. The interview was intended to test the water to see how the United States would react to the possibility of an all-out U-boat campaign against shipping. In the interview, von Tirpitz made three editorial points:

> America did not protest and did little or nothing about the British closing of the North Sea to neutral shipping. What will America say if Germany declares a submarine campaign against all enemy merchant ships?
>
> England wants to starve us out. We can do the same to them by torpedoing any of their ships or their Allies' ships as they approach the harbors in England and Scotland, and in that way destroy a large portion of their basic requirements. Shouldn't we be judged by the same standards as England is judged?
>
> As to the American question, does Germany have enough U-boats to carry out a blockade of England? The answer is yes. We are ahead of England in large U-boats.[9]

According to von Bethmann-Hollweg, after the interview was published the public demand for an unrestricted submarine campaign against England became too strong to ignore. He claims that he tried to rein in the press regarding its demands for an unrestricted submarine campaign, but he asked, "What good was it to try to censor something that had come from the unassailable navy authority—von Tirpitz?"[10]

Six days later von Bethmann-Hollweg agreed that the proposed war on shipping was legal, but he wanted to wait until the German military position on the Continent was secure enough to command compliance from the adjacent neutrals. Although his apparent concession to the U-boat crowd indicated a weakening position, he still had some ammunition for his defense of the Prize Regulations. On 21 and 26 November the U-21 had sunk two British steamers under the Prize Regulations in the English Channel and there had been no public outcry.

A change of command, announced late in January 1915, played a decisive role in the decision to open a war on shipping. The kaiser, Friedrich Wilhelm Viktor Albert (William II), moved Adm. Hugo von Pohl from the

Admiralstab to command of the High Sea Fleet, relieving Admiral von Ingenohl. Vizeadmiral Gustav Bachmann, a man who did not like von Tirpitz, took von Pohl's place as chief of the Admiralstab on 8 February 1915. The resulting situation alarmed von Pohl who resolved to end the debate over the anti-shipping war.

On 1 February, von Pohl, while still chief of the Admiralstab, met with von Bethmann-Hollweg. The chancellor told the admiral that he was still opposed to a war on shipping, not because of potential problems with the neutrals, but because he did not feel the navy had enough U-boats to do the job. Von Pohl assured him that there were enough U-boats to seriously damage British commerce and bring about a quick end to the war. He told the chancellor in clear terms that the U-boat captains would have no difficulty differentiating between neutral vessels and enemy vessels. In any event, he would issue specific directions to the captains.

The admiral's reassurances impressed the chancellor, especially when added to the openly expressed public opinion supporting a war on shipping, an opinion that had risen to a clamor following the publication of the Wiegand–von Tirpitz interview. And von Bethmann-Hollweg had a personal political problem that added weight to the admiral's views. The chancellor was increasingly under attack by members of the Reichstag who were accusing him of hindering the U-boat war because he was soft on England.

The following day, 2 February, von Bethmann-Hollweg phoned von Pohl and gave his agreement. It was exactly what the admiral wanted and he lost no time capitalizing on the chancellor's agreement. On 4 February, the kaiser inspected the High Sea Fleet, and von Pohl, as its new commander, accompanied the kaiser on his tour. While they were going out to the SMS *Seydlitz*, von Pohl used the opportunity to present his arguments to the kaiser, supporting them with the chancellor's approval. The kaiser agreed.[11]

The Germans had spent four months wrestling with the question of whether or not to wage an unrestricted submarine campaign. The arguments on both sides had merit, but one can only conclude that the emergence of an unrestricted submarine campaign against shipping was inevitable, and the only thing holding it back was the legacy of nineteenth-century warfare as defined by nineteenth-century technology. In 1914 a more advanced technology, expressed in modern warships, a more highly developed global economy, and the submarine, brought maritime warfare into the twentieth century.

The technological and economic advances were altering the world's morality as expressed in the 1909 Declaration of London. The suitability of the submarine for waging war against the enemy's economy in the face of ineffectual countermeasures was an advantage too valuable to waste. Nevertheless, the legacy of nineteenth-century morality remained as an effective brake on the full realization of the submarine's power until 1917. By then, however, the countermeasures were coming of age.

On 4 February, Admiral von Pohl issued the warning that all the waters around Great Britain and Ireland were to be regarded as a war zone and that after 17 February any merchant ship in the war zone would be sunk. The Germans softened the declaration with the implication that at least some consideration would be given to the safety of the crews, but not too much consideration: "nor will it always be possible to obviate the danger with which the crews and passengers are thereby threatened."[12]

The immediate British response was to lay a minefield on 4 through 16 February, across the Dover Straits from a point north of Dunkirk to Elbow Bay near Broadstairs. Beyond that the British made "no special measures to meet what looked like an empty threat. The worst they could do would have no appreciable effect on our trade."[13] In view of the British assessment of their antisubmarine capabilities that may have been the only attitude they could adopt. Writing about the existing state of British antisubmarine measures, Sir Julian Corbett said, "As yet all that had been found possible to provide against the submarine attack was far from efficient."[14] And he noted that the patrol system was also incomplete.[15]

Nevertheless, the Germans' haphazard, and unplanned, war on commerce between 20 October 1914 and 15 February 1915 gave the British a false sense of security. At the start of the war, Great Britain possessed about half the world's merchant tonnage, and the minuscule success the U-boats had in 1914 did not represent even a measurable fraction of that amount. The British success against U-15 and U-19 had made them even more complacent, so that in February 1915, the British did not view the U-boats as a major threat.

PART TWO

Early British Countermeasures in Home Waters

August 1914–September 1915

3

Channel Defenses, Mines, and Radio Intelligence

The British initiated their first submarine countermeasures on the day the war started, but they really did not know what they were up against. That realization would come with time. The Germans were in much the same boat and as a result both sides overestimated their enemy's capabilities during the early months of World War I. Kapitän-leutnant Dröscher, however, carried the practice to an extreme. On 10 October 1914, he departed Helgoland in U-20 with orders to pass through the Dover Straits and attack an inbound Canadian troop convoy in the western approaches to the English Channel. Dröscher had no diffi-culty getting through the straits, and other than sighting a few patrol boats and being illuminated by a searchlight on one occasion, he was never seri-ously threatened. Nevertheless, on 13 October when he was off Portsmouth a British destroyer fired on U-20, driving it under. On the basis of this sin-gle experience Dröscher concluded that returning through the Dover Straits was too dangerous. He explained his decision in his war log: "Fur-ther constructive activity in this area was no longer possible because the destroyer had discovered the boat, which meant that the British would hold the steamers and transports in the harbors until the danger passed. There was also the possibility that the route back through the Dover Straits would be more heavily patrolled, and the British may have laid new minefields. Added to that were the navigational problems complicated by heavy fog."[1]

Dröscher concluded that his best route would be around Ireland and Scotland, and down through the North Sea. Inasmuch as U-20 would be subjected to very heavy seas and its newly developed diesel engines had never been put under such strain—not to mention the fact that Dröscher had no charts for the west Irish and Scottish coasts—how serious were his concerns about the Channel defenses?

THE CHANNEL DEFENSES

The British fishing fleet's trawlers and drifters formed the backbone of the British antisubmarine forces. On 7 August 1914 there were eighty trawlers sweeping up mines, with a secondary duty of patrolling for German minelayers and U-boats. By 1 September the number had grown to 250 and included Herring drifters. From that time forward the Royal Navy made an organized effort to build what became the Auxiliary Patrol, which included 3,174 vessels of all descriptions.[2]

From the beginning the Admiralty made it a practice not to paint the trawlers and drifters navy gray. Instead, they left the fishing vessels in their peacetime colors, including the fishing numbers painted on their hulls. The Admiralty armed the auxiliary vessels as quickly as they could although the process was slow. Guns and peacetime colors meant that from the beginning of the war until its conclusion in 1918, a U-boat captain could never be sure if the fishing boat he was approaching was really a fishing boat or an armed auxiliary.

British and French surface patrols in the Dover Straits were very active even though they had no effective way of attacking a submerged U-boat. Nevertheless, their presence made the U-boat captains uncomfortable and forced them to spend more time submerged than they liked. Despite the absence of an antisubmarine weapon, the surface patrols fulfilled two antisubmarine missions: they kept the U-boats submerged and drove them away from their targets.

SURFACE PATROLS

The reason the British maintained such strong patrols in the Dover Straits was to force the U-boats to remain submerged until they exhausted their batteries. The idea was that when the batteries were nearly flat, the U-boat would have to surface and the patrol boats could either attack the

U-boat with gunfire or ram it. Since the U-boats at that time had no deck guns, a surfaced U-boat with dead batteries was defenseless unless it could outrun its attacker. Although the strong patrols did force the U-boats to spend more time submerged than the Germans wanted, no U-boats were destroyed during this period as a result of being forced to surface to recharge batteries.

A more serious problem that resulted from being forced to remain below periscope depth for long periods was navigation error. Shoals are extensive in the entrance to the Dover Straits and currents are an even bigger problem. Together they presented a U-boat commander with major navigational problems, and U-boats' logs are filled with examples of what can go wrong when a U-boat had to grope around in the dark. Kapitän-leutnant Heinrich von Hennig complained that U-18 could barely make 4.8 knots at full power against the current, and von Forstner broke off an attack because he kept running aground. No U-boats were lost during this period due to running aground while submerged, but there were some close calls and nearly all of them did go aground more than once.[3]

In the early months of the war the British were just beginning to develop their antisubmarine tactics and countermeasures. Although the early tactics and countermeasures were, at best, a nuisance, they worried the U-boat commanders. The most common remarks found in the logs were about strong patrols that forced the U-boats to submerge or lie on the bottom until things on the surface quieted down.

Clearly, the U-boat commanders perceived the threat posed by British antisubmarine measures as being greater than they actually were. In fact, one of the features of the war during this period is the degree to which the British and the Germans perceived the other side to be greater threats than they were. At the time, however, the dangers were real to the men who faced them.

TACTICAL REORGANIZATION

The British tinkered with their organization, trying to find the right combination. On 21 November the Channel defenses were reorganized into eight zones. Each zone was patrolled around the clock by British destroyers working in relays so that there was always one destroyer in each zone. The destroyers were supported by French submarines that were to take up positions along lines that extended from Cape Gris Nez to the Varne and from Calais to the Goodwin Sands. The British adopted this plan following U-12's attack on HMS *Niger* on 11 November 1914, but given the ineffectiveness of the existing ASW weapons the change had no effect.[4]

A more important organizational change took place on 8 December 1914 when the Admiralty eliminated the post of Captain Supervising Modified Sweeps and replaced it with the Submarine Attack Committee. The former post had been responsible for developing the explosive sweep, but the Admiralty soon recognized that the technological side of the ASW campaign needed a centralized command. The Submarine Attack Committee was responsible for investigating and developing new ideas and weapons to use against the U-boats. Among the committee's early activities were the continued development of the explosive sweep and the design and development of indicator-nets.[5]

While the Submarine Attack Committee was working on technological developments, the Admiralty reorganized the command structure and organization of the patrol system. The size of the existing organization, and its projected growth, made the early war organization unwieldy and inefficient. On 20 December the Admiralty broke down the defense organization into twenty-three patrol areas that covered the entire coastline around the British Isles. Each patrol area was a separate command under the central control of the Admiralty. Because of its geographic position, Dover soon became one of the most important commands among the twenty-three and was the first to have an admiral in command. The Dover commander was Rear Adm. Horace L. A. Hood, who had been there since 12 October 1914.

Despite numerous vessels on the surface, the British clearly had no effective means for attacking a submerged submarine. What did they have, and what were the specific antisubmarine measures that worried the Germans? The big minefield the British laid on 2 October 1914 is a good place to start.

MINES

When the Germans first confronted the British mines, they attributed to them greater effectiveness than was actually the case. Knowing nothing about the technical shortcomings of the British mines, the Germans assumed they were technically equal to German mines. The Germans' first experiences with the minefield appeared to confirm that assumption.[6]

On the night of 10 October U-28 was lying on the bottom near the North Hinder Lightship when a single screw merchant ship passed over her. A short time later the men inside the U-boat heard an explosion and correctly assumed the merchant ship had hit a British mine: "The experience served as a warning of the new danger facing the U-boats."[7]

Korvettenkapitän Bauer's first impression was that "the big British minefield was in no way a mere scare tactic, but was a serious threat."[8] He based his early assessment on reports that the British steamer SS *Ardmount* had stuck a mine and sunk on 7 October. He was also impressed by the report that British warships were patrolling fifteen to twenty nautical miles off the Hook of Holland to intercept merchant ships, warn them, and lead them through the minefield.

The Germans, however, very quickly learned that the British mines were largely ineffective due to design flaws in the mooring system and the firing device. The moorings were so weak that the mines broke loose in moderate weather, drifted away, and became a danger to British shipping.[9]

Adding to the Royal Navy's problems was the British practice of laying mines too near the surface, a result of preoccupation with surface ships. Rear Adm. Sir Reginald Bacon, who took command of the Dover Patrol in April 1915, recalled, "Our mines were designed for use against ships; their use in the antisubmarine role wasn't anticipated."[10] The Germans soon learned that at low water the British mines lay exposed on the surface and could be avoided, which explains how and why the U-boats were able to pass through the British minefields.

A mine is composed of three parts: a case, which is the mine itself; the anchor cable; and the anchor, which was essentially an iron box. The type of mine the British laid in the North Sea was known as an automatic mine because the depth at which the case—the explosive part—floated beneath the surface could be predetermined. All three parts were packaged in one piece so that the case sat atop the anchor with the cable on a reel inside.

The automatic mine was designed so that as it sank, a plummet paid out a line equal in length to the depth at which the case was to float beneath the surface. When the plummet hit the ocean floor it released the anchor cable latch and the case, the explosive part, rose toward the surface while the steel box, the anchor, settled on the bottom. The case, floating five to ten feet below the surface, was now tethered to the bottom by a steel cable that was often over one hundred feet long.

When the tide fell, the case, being buoyant, rose to the surface and became readily visible in calm to moderate seas. That meant that at low water the lookouts in the U-boat's conning tower had only to watch for

the mines as the U-boat moved slowly through the field. This sounds easier than it really was, but given close attention and careful maneuvering, the U-boats routinely crossed the British minefields on the surface.
There were even instances in which U-boats crossed the minefields at
periscope depth, the captain watching for mines on the surface through
his periscope.[11]

Most submerged passages through minefields were made at depths of
sixty feet or deeper. As the submerged U-boat passed through the minefield, the mines' anchor cables scraped down the sides of the hull, setting
up a terrific racket inside the boat. It was a nerve-racking experience and
no one got used to it. The danger was that the cable would snag on some
obstruction on the U-boat, so that the mine craned down, struck the
U-boat's hull, and exploded. Given the British mooring cable's weakness,
that was an unlikely occurrence; in virtually every instance the cable
parted. Nevertheless, the U-boat captains took precautions to reduce the
possibility that a mine might be pulled down against the hull.[12]

They fitted tubular steel guards around the diving planes and other
obstructions that extended from the hull to fend off the mine's anchor cable
as it passed down the hull. Submarines passed through the minefields at
the greatest depth possible so that if a craning effect occurred, the cable
would part before the mine touched the hull. And they tried to pass
through the field with the tidal flow, which reduced the craning effect.

The British mine's most serious deficiency was its mechanical firing
device. The Royal Navy used two types of spherical mine: the service
mine and the British Elia mine. The service mine was a British design,
but the Elia mine was a modified Italian design in which the British had
replaced the Italians' efficient electrical firing device with their own
mechanical firing arm. The Royal Navy made the change because they
distrusted electrical devices, which they felt were too prone to battery
failure and faulty contacts.[13]

Many postwar comments made by former Royal Navy officers illustrate the sad condition of British mines that were in use until late in 1917.

> German submarines could carry these ineffective engines on their bows
> and shake them or bump against them with impunity. Many German war-
> ships had as a souvenir a British mine mounted on a stand.[14]

> Our deficiency was clearly shown in trials in which one of our submarines
> was run against a number of our mines with the result that only one-third

of the mines fitted with small charges exploded. The Germans were well aware that our mines were not very effective against U-boats.[15]

Had we been in possession of a reliable mine and mooring in adequate numbers, we could have strangled the submarine menace within the first few months. The British minefields that existed in the Eastern English Channel approaches were negligible and inefficient. Our mines were unsatisfactory and the moorings were weak. The result was that practically every mine got adrift and was either sunk by our own flotillas or made its way across the North Sea. Some washed up on the Dutch coast and were turned into flowerpots.[16]

The result was that the minefield's deterrent effect exceeded its actual technical effectiveness. Nevertheless, British mines did sink U-11 on 9 December and U-5 on 18 December. While the Germans recognized that the British mines were inefficient, they never adopted a cavalier attitude toward them. The German submarine captains did, however, become proficient at passing over and under barrages that were composed of service and Elia mines. Arno Spindler summed up the German assessment of the British mines.

> The most serious threat to U-boats in the autumn of 1914 was the minefields the British laid off the coast of Belgium and in the Hoofden on the approaches to the English Channel. But even those obstacles were not insurmountable. It was soon recognized that the British mines were not technically of the highest order. And because the British planted them improperly with regard to depth, the mines were visible on the surface at low water if the sea was not too badly disturbed. A large number were also torn loose in rough weather and drifted away.[17]

RADIO INTELLIGENCE

In addition to existing antisubmarine measures, the British possessed a resource that was in its very early developmental stage—radio intelligence.[18] The British were able to read German enciphered radio traffic throughout World War I because they had broken the principal German codes by 30 November 1914. The organization charged with the responsibility of deciphering and distributing the intercepted radio messages was known as Room 40.

Room 40 could read the German codes, yet the capability itself did not automatically ensure victory. Although not always efficiently applied, the information that Room 40 provided became increasingly important as the war progressed. As early as the end of 1914, radio intercepts provided enough information for Room 40 to determine the strength and general locations of Korvettenkapitän Bauer's U-boat flotillas.

By the start of 1915 Room 40 was able to provide Winston Churchill, First Lord of the Admiralty, with a daily return on U-boat strength, general location, and last known position of boats at sea. Room 40 had a good idea about the total operational strength and the state of readiness of every individual boat in port. Room 40 routinely tracked the U-boats from the time they departed on patrol until they returned. They could not establish the immediate position of any U-boat with any degree of accuracy, but they could estimate fairly accurately a U-boat's intended operations area.

For example, Room 40 was able to report that U-35, U-36, U-39, and U-41 departed Helgoland on 29 April 1915, that they would go north around Scotland, and that they were progressing at twelve and a half knots. Room 40 added that U-20 and U-28 had departed Borkum on 30 April and also headed north. British forces along the route were alerted and deployed to intercept, but no contacts were made and all six boats returned safely.

Room 40 was not an intelligence center, however, and did not function the way the Admiralty's Submarine Tracking Room functioned during World War II. In that respect, during World War I, the British had no way of knowing if a decoded U-boat position represented an immediate threat to any British or Allied vessel because they had no way of correlating the position of the U-boat to the positions of British and Allied ships. Combined with the information that radio direction finder (RDF) stations ashore provided about the noon positions of U-boats, the British were able to determine which boats were working which areas. The British were in the process of learning. They had the beginnings of a very valuable tool, but were using it inefficiently when compared to Room 40's true potential.

4

Ramming, Gunfire, and Decoys

RAMMING

Of all the early antisubmarine measures, the threat of ramming caused the U-boat commanders more problems than any other measure. Arno Spindler described the danger: "The danger of being rammed while running submerged in a heavily patrolled area, or during a torpedo attack, was always present. This was particularly true in conditions of poor visibility. Training and experience, and improved diving gear on the newer boats reduced the danger. We also reduced the time it took to vent air from the ballast tanks until a U-boat of the U-19 type could get under in less than a minute."[1]

For German submarines of the U-type and the later UB- and UC-types, periscope depth meant the keel was at about thirty feet. The upper rim of the conning tower would be about six to eight feet below the surface and the mass of the casing and the pressure hull was about twelve feet below the surface and occupied the space down to about thirty feet. Depending on the type, a warship's draft could be from six feet to thirty feet, ample for striking some part of a submarine that was at periscope depth.[2]

The two U-boats lost to ramming during the first six months of the war were U-15 and U-18. On 9 August 1914, in a light fog, a lookout aboard the light cruiser HMS *Birmingham* spotted U-15 on the surface "immobile and hove to."[3] The captain ordered the *Birmingham* to ram, and as it drew nearer the bridge crew heard the sounds of hammering coming from U-15. Apparently it was broken down. Moments before the cruiser sliced the U-boat in two, U-15 tried to get under way, but it was too late. It sank with all hands.

The loss of U-18 to ramming illustrates the danger that attended operations in a heavily trafficked area. On 23 November 1918, Kapitänleutnant von Hennig's task was to enter Scapa Flow and attack the Grand Fleet. He reached the Hoxa entrance to the anchorage, saw that the Grand Fleet was not there, and put about to return to the Pentland Firth. While he was proceeding down the fairway, a patrol vessel spotted his periscope and raised the alarm.[4]

A short while later the destroyer HMS *Garry* rammed the after periscope, rolling U-18 to starboard, but doing no damage to the pressure hull. Moments later, U-18 experienced a complete failure of its diving controls, unrelated to the ramming, and went out of control. For the next half hour U-18 went through a series of radical diving fluctuations that carried it from the surface to its pressure hull's maximum depth rating.

At 1350 the trawler *Dorothy Gray* rammed U-18, the bow slashing through the casing over the engine room without puncturing the pressure hull. U-18 continued to sink as the trawler passed directly overhead. Twenty minutes after the *Dorothy Gray* rammed it the ballast pumps failed and U-18's fluctuations became even wilder.

Before von Hennig could get his boat under some sort of control, the destroyer HMS *Garry* rammed it again, this time for good. Von Hennig, who survived, told Arno Spindler after the war: "Suddenly there was a heavy blow forward accompanied by a loud cracking to starboard, the grinding noise of torn metal, the exploding of rivets and a noise like propellers grinding into stone. Then dead silence. The rudder jammed hard over to port, and I watched the depth gauge rapidly drop from 55 meters to 60 and finally 70. The boat was lost."[5]

Von Hennig reacted in time by shouting the order to blow the tanks and U-18 immediately started up. As soon as the hatch broke the surface, he climbed through and hoisted a white flag. As his crew was pouring out on deck through the two deck hatches, von Hennig fired a distress flare and ordered his men to put on their life vests. British patrol vessels responded to the flare and fished the crew out of the water.

Ramming was such a basic tactic that the Admiralty extended the practice to merchant ships. On 14 February 1915 the Admiralty issued instructions to merchant captains advising them that when they sighted a submarine, they were to turn their stern toward the submarine and make off at full speed—if possible into shoal water. If, however, a submarine surfaced close ahead so that by turning away the merchant vessel would only expose itself to a torpedo attack, the captain was to steer directly toward the submarine and force it to dive. The merchant vessel was directed to pass directly over the submarine and continue on at high speed. This would have the effect of presenting the merchant vessel's stern to the submarine, making a torpedo shot much more difficult.

Those instructions became known among the Germans as the ramming orders, even though there was nothing in the orders that specifically told the merchant captains to ram a U-boat. Officially, the instructions were "issued confidentially and were designed to instruct masters as to the best means of eluding submarine attack. There was no suggestion that they should attempt to destroy an assailant—nothing, indeed, which could be used by the enemy to prejudice the masters' status as non-combatants."[6]

Still, it does not take much thought to see how these orders would be put into effect.

On 28 February 1915 the collier SS *Thordis,* commanded by Capt. John W. Bell, followed the Admiralty's recommended tactic and rammed U-6 off Beachy Head. When Captain Bell saw a torpedo wake to starboard, he ordered the helm hard over and ran down the torpedo's wake toward U-6's periscope, which was still visible. As he passed over the periscope a jar and a crash told that he had hit the U-boat, and oil was seen on the water, but nothing more of the submarine.[7]

Peering through U-6's periscope, Oberleutnant zur See Reinhold Lepsius saw the collier bearing down on him and tried to go deeper. There was not enough time to even house the periscope before the collier's stem struck the conning tower and rolled U-6 sharply to starboard. Despite the violent impact, the blow did no major damage except destroy both periscopes. Blind, U-6 terminated its cruise and returned home.[8]

Throughout the period of the first anti-shipping campaign, British merchant ships intentionally or accidentally rammed or attempted to ram five U-boats. One U-boat was lost as an indirect result, and four escaped with minor damage.

The so-called ramming order had one tragic consequence that has become known as the Captain Charles A. Fryatt Affair. On 28 March 1915 the Great Eastern Railway packet SS *Brussels* was making its regular Thames to Holland run. Off the Maas Lightship, Kapitänleutnant Gansser in U-33 ordered it to stop. Captain Fryatt held his course and speed. Gansser was closing on the steamer when the *Brussels* turned and went directly at U-33. Gansser maneuvered U-33 out of the way, but it was a close call. The *Brussels* passed a few meters away and continued away on its original course at high speed.[9]

Fifteen months later, German destroyers out of Zeebrugge captured the *Brussels,* which was still operating on the Thames to Holland route. The Germans, operating under the Prize Regulations, seized the *Brussels* and took Captain Fryatt prisoner. Shortly after Fryatt arrived in Germany, the Germans were able to link him to the earlier near-ramming incident with U-33, and they charged him with being a *franc-tireur*. On 27 July 1916 a German military court in Bruges tried him, found him guilty, and executed him all in the same day.[10]

GUNFIRE

Gunfire was responsible for the loss of six U-boats and caused damage to several others in close encounters. The Germans had started to arm U-boats with deck guns, but, for the most part, the U-boats were still without them. In 1915 most of the surface encounters were one-sided because the fishing boat was the only one armed.[11] On 5 June 1915 U-14 became the first U-boat lost as a result of an encounter with an armed trawler. Because the incident illustrates so many elements that were often found in these early ASW encounters, it bears close inspection.

U-14 was a Körting kerosene engine boat that had just completed a major repair that included the addition of a 37 millimeter deck gun and the addition of an improved venting system to permit it to dive more quickly. Its crew and the captain, Oberleutnant zur See Hammerle, were so green that the half-flotilla chief, Kapitänleutnant Mühlau, was aboard to supervise.[12]

On 5 June 1915 at 0745 U-14 was off the Scottish coast between Aberdeen and Peterhead when it sighted a lone trawler, the *Oceanic II.* The gun crew manned the 37 millimeter gun and fired a warning shot while U-14 signaled the trawler to stop. To their utter surprise, the trawler returned their fire with a much heavier 12-pounder (3-inch).

Outgunned, Hammerle ordered U-14 to crash dive and ordered tanks 1, 2, 12, and 13 flooded. As the dive alarm sounded Hammerle ordered ahead full and put the rudder hard over left to bring the trawler astern. U-14 settled and then dropped 8 degrees down by the stern. Oberleutnant zur See Rupperberg hurried forward and found that the vents on tanks 12 and 13 had failed to open. Hammerle pumped water into the trim tank but the stern suddenly dropped to 20 degrees.

While U-14 hung from the surface by its bow, four more armed trawlers came up and opened fire. The U-boat was taking hits on its exposed forward section, but had suffered no damage to the pressure hull. Hammerle blew the after tanks, which brought the boat up on an even keel, and he started through the diving procedure again. At that moment a crewman stationed at the central control room periscope shouted that a trawler was going to ram them.

Hammerle ordered the tanks flooded, put the forward dive planes hard down and the after planes hard up, and went full ahead on both motors. The trawler that was bearing down on U-14 was the *Hawk*, commanded by Lt. H. J. Ferguson, RNR. The *Hawk*'s bow clipped U-14 on the edge of the deck, midway between the conning tower and the bow. As the trawler passed over, U-14's stern dropped 30 degrees, rolled 10 degrees right, and started to sink. At 250 feet Hammerle ordered the tanks blown.

When U-14 broke the surface it was down by the stern and listing 10 degrees to starboard. The trawlers immediately opened fire, scoring hits on the conning tower and forward deck, one of the hits destroying all the controls in the conning tower. Kapitänleutnant Mühlau ordered the crew to abandon ship and all were rescued except Hammerle, who apparently went down with U-14.

On 27 July 1915 U-41, commanded by Kapitänleutnant Claus Hansen, had a similar run-in with an armed trawler. The engagement took place about 0500 off Barra head, which is at the southern tip of the Hebrides, and lasted just over ten hours. The trawler *Pearl*, armed with a single 3-pounder, spotted U-41 running on the surface five thousand yards away and immediately steered to intercept the U-boat. At that time it was dawn, the skies were overcast, the sea surface was placid, and there was a light mist near the surface.

When the German lookouts in the conning tower spotted the *Pearl*, they identified it as a small steamer, and the watch officer, Leutnant zur

See Schmitt, called for the captain. Hansen and candidate captain, Kapitän-leutnant Gustav Siess, came up, and Hansen ordered the crew of the 88 millimeter gun on the foredeck to fire a warning shot across the steamer's bow. Instead of heaving to, the *Pearl* returned fire.

At that moment, U-41 suffered an unrelated steering casualty that caused it to steam in a full circle, bringing it within five hundred yards of the *Pearl*. The trawler fired six rounds in rapid succession, scoring solid hits with two of them. The first round exploded near the waterline and the second exploded against the conning tower, fatally wounding the watch officer and blowing a one-inch hole through the pressure plating. At that critical moment, the crew recovered control of the boat and Hansen ordered it to dive.

The *Pearl*, seeing the U-boat going under, turned to ram. Inside U-41 water was pouring through the hole in the conning tower, "like water from a fire hose," and Hansen ordered the crew to rush forward into the bow to speed the dive. The *Pearl* charged across U-41 just as the top of the conning tower dropped below the depth of the trawler's keel. Hansen's problems, however, were far from over.

At eighty feet the pumps could not keep up with the inflow of water. Hansen brought the boat back to fifty feet and discovered that at that depth, the pumps could hold their own. But the power required to run the pumps continuously was quickly depleting the batteries and the *Pearl* was still holding its position over the submarine. Hansen was in a very tight corner.

He tried several times to shake the trawler by changing course and running at high speed. Nothing worked. Two hours later, with the situa-tion growing worse by the minute, Hansen rose to periscope depth and extended the periscope for a look around. What he saw was the *Pearl* charging down on him to ram. Again Hansen ordered the crew into the bow and took U-41 down to the fifty-foot "floor" to avoid the blow. This time he was not quick enough to completely avoid the attack. *Pearl*'s stem smashed the periscope and U-41 rolled 30 degrees to starboard as the trawler passed over it.

Aboard the *Pearl*, the crew knew they had hit something, but they also knew the U-boat was still under way. Obviously, the blow had not been fatal. The reason the *Pearl*'s crew knew where the U-boat was and its direction of travel was the wide oil trail left on the placid surface. The *Pearl*'s first round had blown open an oil bunker, and U-41 was bleeding oil. For the men aboard the *Pearl* it was simply a matter of following the trail and waiting for the U-boat to surface. At least that is how the situation appeared at noon.

In U-41 the situation was grim. Darkness was still eight hours away and U-41's batteries would not last more than another three hours. As the batteries grew weaker, the pumps would be unable to keep up with the inflow of water. The air in the boat had become "unbearably foul," and the dying watch officer was in terrible pain. It was apparent to Hansen that he would have to surface soon and try to fight his way clear.

But the situation on top was changing too. The wind had freshened, whipping up the sea's surface, making the oil trail more difficult to see. At the same time, the *Pearl*'s engineer told the captain that the *Pearl* had a bad water pump and he would have to shut down the engine. Using the oil slick as a guide, the *Pearl*'s captain estimated the U-boat's projected track, pulled ahead five hundred yards and then detonated his explosive sweep at the place where he though the boat should be.

The explosion rattled U-41 but did no damage. Having expended his only explosive sweep, the *Pearl*'s captain pressed on for another hour, but by then the sea was much rougher, the oil was completely dispersed, and the engineer was insisting that they shut down the engine so he could repair it. At 1500 the *Pearl* broke off the chase and shut down its engine.

Shortly after 1500, U-41 rose to periscope depth and Hansen extended the auxiliary periscope. The sea was building and there was no sign of the *Pearl*. Relieved, he ordered the tanks blown and brought the damaged U-boat to the surface. He had gotten very lucky. By way of comparison, had U-41 found itself in that same situation two years later, it might have been quickly dispatched under a shattering depth charge attack. But that was two years in the future, and U-41 would not be around to see it anyway. Kapitänleutnant Hansen, his boat, and all but two of his crew would be gone in exactly two months.[13]

DECOYS

The shortest-lived decoy system was the submarine-trawler combination that operated from May to October 1915. These were U-boat traps in which an apparently innocent trawler towed a C-class submarine behind it. Communication was achieved between the two vessels by means of a telephone line run along the tow hawser. The idea was that the trawler would act as the decoy and lure the U-boat within torpedo range. As the

U-boat approached, the trawler would cast off the tow and the submarine would maneuver into position to torpedo the U-boat. The plan
depended on the U-boat's captain to operate according to the Prize Regulations and make his approach on the surface, and it worked on two occasions. The combination of the trawler *Taranaki* and the C-24 sank U-40
on 23 June. A month later the *Princess Louise* and the C-27 sank U-23.
Those were the only two successes the program enjoyed and it was shut
down in October because the Germans were aware of the trap. Although
there was no regular trawler-submarine program after that, there were
occasions in 1917 when they were paired on a catch-as-catch-can basis.[14]

In addition to the trawler-submarine combination, the British outfit-
ted the trawlers *Quickly* and the aptly named *Gunner* as true decoys and
set them to work in the North Sea. Their appearances altered to look like
tramp steamers, they regularly displayed neutral identification boards on
their hulls and flew neutral flags. They were not particularly successful,
but *Quickly* and *Gunner* did get into a fight with U-16 on 20 July 1915,
from which the U-boat escaped with moderate damage.[15]

The longest-lived decoy operation involved the Special Service Vessels,
which were more commonly called Q-ships or Mystery ships. They also
had names. The British deployed 180 decoy vessels during World War I,
conducting the operation from a separate department within the Admiralty called the Special Construction Section (SCS). The Special Service
Vessel project began in November 1914 but decoys were not used in large
numbers until 1916–17. Nevertheless, the British program operated without interruption until the spring of 1918, by which time the decoys had
played out their usefulness.

Decoy vessels were usually 200- to 4,000-ton freighters and colliers
that looked so ordinary that they appeared harmless. They were actually
armed with a variety of guns ranging from 3-pounders to 4-inch. Understandably the larger ships got the bigger guns while the 3-pounders (47
millimeter) and 6-pounders (57 millimeter) went to the smaller ships. The
SCS equipped a few of the larger ships with 14-inch and 18-inch naval
torpedo tubes.

The heavily armed ships were manned by Royal Navy crews and
changed their appearance frequently. When confronted by a surfaced
U-boat, the decoy stopped and blew off steam while a specially trained
panic crew abandoned ship. When the U-boat drew close enough, the gun
crews, who had remained hidden on board, unmasked their guns and

opened fire. The Germans soon became wary of suspicious ships, but the decoy crews were extremely clever at disguise. British decoys sank four U-boats during the period from 24 July to 24 September 1915.

The *Prince Charles* was the first Special Service Vessel to sink a U-boat, and its success occurred on 24 July 1915 against U-36. The British and German versions of this encounter vary in respect to how many rounds U-36 fired as it drew nearer and exactly when the *Prince Charles* ceased firing and started rescuing survivors. Charges, countercharges, and denials regarding inhumane behavior characterized the accounts of encounters between Q-ships and U-boats. The bare-bones facts follow.

The *Prince Charles,* a former 373-ton collier, carried one 3-pounder and one 6-pounder mounted amidships, under the command of Lt. Mark Wardlaw, RN. The *Prince Charles* was ten miles northwest-north of North Rona Island, flying no flag, and under the existing orders, rules, and guidelines the ship could have been considered a fair target for a torpedo attack. Instead, at 1900 Kapitänleutnant Ernst Graeff in U-36 signaled the *Prince Charles* to stop, and underscored the signal with a warning shot across the steamer's bow. Captain Wardlaw brought the ship into the Atlantic swell, blew three blasts, and ordered his panicked crew to abandon ship. With the ship stopped, Kapitänleutnant Ernst Graeff brought U-36 closer.[16]

A fairly new boat, U-36 had been commissioned in November 1914 and was heavily armed with two 88 millimeter guns, one on the forward deck and the other on the after deck. Still equipped with the old ballast tank venting system, however, it took the boat about three minutes just to get below the surface.[17]

When U-36 was just six hundred yards from the *Prince Charles,* Captain Wardlaw ordered his gunners to open fire. The Germans were taken completely by surprise and ran for cover behind the conning tower. Graeff tried to dive, but the old vents prevented that being accomplished quickly enough; while U-36 slowly sank, the *Prince Charles* continued to blow holes in the pressure hull and conning tower. U-36 did not return the fire and sank with a loss of half its crew.[18]

The second U-boat lost to a decoy was UB-4 on 15 August 1915. The schooner *Inverlyon,* playing the role of a fishing smack, lured the machine gun–armed UB-4 within range of its 3-pounder gun and sent the U-boat to the bottom with all hands. According to the British report, UB-4 surfaced alongside the *Inverlyon* and Oberleutnant zur See Karl Gross called across, ordering the *Inverlyon*'s crew to abandon ship. While the *Inverlyon*'s crew appeared to be carrying out the order, UB-4 moved to within thirty yards of the sailing vessel, in preparation to putting a demolition party aboard the sailing vessel. At that moment, the *Inverlyon* opened fire. The first three rounds hit the conning tower, blowing Gross overboard and blasting away the after part of the conning tower. UB-4 continued forward slowly and passed ten yards from the *Inverlyon*'s stern, taking four more solid hits in the hull aft of the conning tower. It appears UB-4 was trying to dive as the first rounds were blowing apart the conning tower; as the U-boat passed astern, it was down by the bow and sinking fast. Shortly after UB-4 went under, three bodies came to the surface.[19]

The third U-boat lost to a Q-ship was U-27, commanded by Kapitänleutnant Bernhard Wegener. In Germany this event is called the First *Baralong* Affair and is still roundly condemned as an unpunished war crime. It is one of the few instances in which the Germans are probably on solid ground, and the case illustrates the ferocity with which both sides waged the submarine and antisubmarine war from 1914 to 1918. Again, just the bare-bones facts follow.

On 19 August 1915, U-27 stopped the SS *Nicosian* and was firing into it when the *Baralong* came onto the scene. The 4,200-ton *Baralong*, under the command of Lt. Comdr. Godfrey Herbert, RN, was flying the U.S. flag and had American colors painted on boards that hung down the sides. Despite looking like an ordinary tramp steamer, the *Baralong* was armed with three 12-pounder guns.[20]

As the situation unfolded, U-27, which was moving slowly forward, moved so that the *Nicosian* lay between it and the approaching *Baralong*. Captain Herbert turned the *Baralong* to the right and positioned his ship so that it would be broadside to U-27 when the U-boat appeared from behind *Nicosian*. His position and timing were right and as the U-boat emerged into the open, the *Baralong*'s gunners opened fire. The fire was heavy, accurate, and very effective. U-27 sank almost immediately, leaving about a dozen of the U-boat's crew in the water. This is the point at which the controversy began.

According to American witnesses who were members of the *Nicosian*'s crew, the British sailors armed with rifles lined the *Baralong*'s rails and fired into the swimmers, killing several, including Kapitänleutnant Wegener. Some of the Germans managed to board the *Nicosian* and took refuge below decks where Royal Marines hunted them down and killed them. There were no survivors from U-27.[21]

The fourth U-boat was sunk on 24 September 1915 when the *Baralong,* now commanded by Lt. Comdr. A. Wilmont-Smith, came upon U-41, commanded by Kapitänleutnant Claus Hansen, firing into the SS *Urbino.* When Wilmont-Smith steamed toward the scene, U-41 dove, turned, and fired a torpedo at the approaching freighter. Smith altered course to avoid the torpedo, and when U-41 surfaced, he stopped in compliance with its signal.

Despite his earlier experience with *Pearl,* Hansen did not suspect that the new arrival was anything other than what it appeared to be—a commercial steamer. The fact that the *Baralong* deliberately steered toward the site of an attack should have made Hansen suspicious. But apparently it did not, and Hansen was now closing on the *Baralong,* intending to sink it under the Prize Regulations.

Wilmont-Smith waited until the U-boat was five hundred yards off his starboard quarter before he ordered his guns unmasked and the White Ensign run up. The *Baralong'*s gunners opened an accurate, deadly fire with its stern and quarter guns, scoring repeated hits at almost point-blank range. The *Baralong'*s gunners shot U-41 to pieces in only a few minutes and the U-boat sank like a stone, leaving only two men in the water. The *Baralong* picked up both survivors under circumstances that provoked German charges of war crimes and led to the engagement being labeled the Second *Baralong* Affair.[22]

5

Nets

As the war developed, the two most important commands were at Queenstown and Dover. In terms of area covered, the number of vessels employed, and the scope of the operational responsibility, however, the Dover command held first place throughout the war. Rear Admiral Hood was the first commander of the newly established independent command at Dover, and his policies, ideas, and practices were in force from 12 October 1914 to 12 April 1915 when Winston Churchill abruptly replaced him with Rear Admiral Bacon.

Despite Hood's limited resources, it was during his command that the Dover Patrol first netted the Dover Straits. The drift nets, or indicator-nets, will be discussed but first the futile attempt to construct a permanent barrier across the straits will be examined.

FOLKESTONE TO GRIS-NEZ HEAVY BOOM

The proposed net barrier came under Rear Admiral Hood's direction as a function of the Dover command. The plan involved laying a fixed barrier clear across the straits from Folkestone to Cape Gris Nez, with a strongly patrolled gate at each end through which commercial traffic could pass.[1] Construction started in late February 1915; by 26 March two lightships were in place, marking the gate at the Folkestone end of the barrier.

The net was a heavy harbor defense net constructed of two-inch diameter strands, each panel one hundred feet deep and two hundred feet long. Anchored mooring buoys held the connected panels in place. Between each pair of mooring buoys were twenty wooden floats, each weighing four tons and measuring nine feet by five feet. Those massive floats supported the head wire from which the net panels were suspended. Progress was slow because the enormous size of the nets, buoys, and floats and the strong tides in the straits made the task difficult. After four failed attempts to lay the barrier Bacon called off the scheme in May 1915, and the British resorted to a smaller boom across the northern entrance to the Downs.

INDICATOR-NETS

Indicator-nets could be towed or anchored in place, and with the exception of the Folkestone to Gris Nez heavy boom and the heavy nets used for harbor defense, all the net systems the British deployed in 1915 were indicator-nets. In addition to the harbors and anchorages used by the Grand Fleet, there were three main net areas: the Dover Straits, the English Channel, and the Irish Sea.[2]

The British indicator-nets were made of light steel wire, which the Germans described as not thicker than a man's finger.[3] The nets were manufactured in individual panels, one hundred yards long, and were produced in four depths: 30 feet, 60 feet, 84 feet, and 120 feet. The mesh was 10 feet by 12 feet on the 30-foot net, and 12 feet square on all the others. A net line consisted of up to ten panels joined together with steel clips designed to part under a 150- to 300-pound strain.[4]

Originally the nets were supported with a two-and-a-half-inch diameter, kapok-filled, canvas tube that was fastened to the net's head-wire. But the kapok only lasted a short time because of the rough handling, and the British lost hundreds of nets that sank when the kapok became waterlogged. They tried cork floats and even tin cans, but they still lost nets. In its final form, buoyancy was achieved with thick-walled glass balls, five inches in diameter, encased in hemp net-bags. Each one hundred yard by thirty foot panel required seventy-five to one hundred glass floats to hold it up, and the larger nets required greater numbers.

Each panel was equipped with a single indicator that was supposed to be activated when the net was fouled, but to "remain quiescent under all conditions of wind, weather and tide."[5] The indicators were boat-shaped devices that were attached to the net panel with a short painter. Inside the buoy was a hollow wire reel that was filled with calcium phosphide, and the wire that was on the reel was spliced to the inboard end of the painter. When a submarine struck the net and tore away the panel, the action of the wire paying out opened two small ports that allowed water to come into contact with the calcium phosphide. The chemical reaction created thick smoke. The buoy then rose to the surface and planed across the surface, emitting a cloud of smoke as the U-boat dragged it along. The British designed the indicator so that there was enough wire on a reel built inside the hull to prevent the indicator from being dragged down if the U-boat went deep.[6]

The idea was that the smoking indicator would move across the surface, indicating the submerged U-boat's direction of travel and location while the patrol boats attacked with explosive sweeps. Another possibility was that the net would foul the U-boat's propellers, forcing it to surface, and the patrol boats would attack the hobbled U-boat with gunfire and ramming.

TOWED INDICATOR-NETS

Indicator-nets could be deployed as anchored obstructions, or herring drifters could tow them or lay to them and drift with the net. All three methods were used during the war, but in every case, surface patrols had to be close at hand to take action if a U-boat fouled the net. The nets placed an enormous demand on the Royal Navy for manpower and vessels.

Towed nets, also called drift nets, were deployed in the Dover Straits and the Irish Sea. The vessels that tended the nets were herring drifters that had been taken into the Auxiliary Patrol along with their crews. Each drifter was equipped with enough nets to create a net line from five hundred to one thousand yards long.[7] Armed trawlers supported the drifters and their job was to attack the U-boat with gunfire, ramming, or an explosive sweep. In 1915, the net groups operated only during daylight, although for a short while they made an attempt to stay out around the clock. The nets were a good idea but they did not work very well.

There were two ways to tow the indicator-nets. One way was for one drifter to tow it as a long tail that stretched five hundred to one thousand yards astern. This method was used to patrol a general area when there was no certainty that a U-boat was there. Theoretically, this method required several drifters working together, steaming in two parallel rows so that the nets overlapped and closed the openings between the drifters. The British commonly used the single tow method.

The other method was to use two drifters with the net stretched between them. In this method, the drifters had to maintain a separation of five hundred to one thousand yards, depending on the length of the net, and had to maintain position off each other's beam. This method formed a moving wall across the U-boat's path and required a higher standard of seamanship than was required for a single tow. The double tow method was used when a U-boat's presence was either suspected or known, and several trawlers worked together in an attempt to surround the U-boat and trap it in a net.[8]

Towed nets were hard to manage because strong currents caused them to tangle, they snagged on submerged obstructions, and the floats—glass or kapok—filled with water, which caused the net to sink. Another common failing was the result of poor quality control in that the clips that joined the panels were either too weak to hold the panels or too strong to part when needed. The clips' inconsistent quality probably made little difference, however, because the U-boats simply went under the nets in most cases.

The most ambitious towed net defense was in the Irish Sea's North Channel between the Mull of Kintyre and the Antrim coast where the channel is about eleven miles across. North Channel is deep, averaging 70 fathoms (420 feet), which meant that it was fairly easy for a U-boat to pass under a net because the deepest British net was only 30 to 60 feet. To overcome that disadvantage, drifters operating out of Larne shot two parallel net lines twenty miles apart. Inside the twenty-mile wide strip drifters, supported by trawlers, deployed about thirty-six miles of nets, and the British stationed additional patrols at each end of the barrage so that they extended the barrage five miles at each end.

The British plan was to force the U-boats to dive outside the extended patrol lines and remain submerged for at least thirty miles while they passed under the barrage. When a U-boat reached the other end its batteries would be nearly exhausted, forcing it to surface to recharge. If all went according to plan, destroyers would spot the surfaced U-boat, which would be unable to dive, or if it did dive, it could not stay down very long. In either event, its destruction was essentially ensured. It was a good idea but it was heavy on resources and short on results. After making no contacts from 18 February to 24 September 1915 the British abandoned the project.[9]

ANCHORED INDICATOR-NETS

In addition to towed nets, the British laid anchored indicator-nets in areas where they suspected the U-boats would be particularly active. The British laid fixed nets in the Downs and across the mouth of the Thames. The largest and most ambitious undertaking was the first Dover barrage, a net that ran from the North Goodwin Sands to Dunkirk. The British reinforced this net line with mines, but strong currents caused the mines to drift into the nets, and the British were forced to take up the mines.

In 1915, the U-boat captains initially reported that the fixed net barriers were formidable obstacles, but they quickly found ways around them. For example, the north-south barrier from the North Goodwin Lightship to the Kentish Knock Lightship was easily passed south of the North Goodwin Lightship. By the autumn of 1915 the Flanders boats were having no difficulty going over, under, or around any of the net barriers.[10]

In part, the nets were easily avoided because the buoys were always visible on the surface. In fact, in some places they became navigational aids for the U-boats. Oberleutnant zur See Otto Steinbrinck told his fellow U-boat captains that "a large red telephone buoy" marked the south end of the barrier across the Thames mouth, and added that the midpoint was identified by "a wreck with two tall masts sticking up above the surface."[11]

The longer they were in place the easier it became to pass through the nets because they deteriorated so quickly. Strong currents, storms, and high seas tore apart the nets, and whales and floating debris that struck the nets tore huge holes in the barrier. The floats filled, the nets sank, and moorings broke. Despite the nets' failures, U-boats did run into them, and the nets were a constant nuisance to U-boat captains.

U-boats struck the fixed net across the entrance to the Dover Straits and the drift nets in the straits more often than any other net system. The heaviest U-boat traffic occurred in these waters and the British shot most of their nets there. The first success occurred on 4 March 1915.[12] Action on the surface began at about noon. A lookout in the destroyer HMS *Viking* spotted U-8 on the surface near the Varne Lightship. The *Viking* opened fire and U-8 disappeared below the surface. *Viking* alerted the rest of the 6th Destroyer Division and HMS *Ghurka* and HMS *Maori* soon joined in the hunt for the U-boat. An hour and twenty minutes later, the drifter *Roburn* reported that its indicator-net was moving in a northeasterly direction. The sea was calm but visibility was reduced by light fog.

When the three destroyers arrived they saw the indicator buoy functioning perfectly, scooting across the surface. Then on three closely spaced occasions they spotted U-8's periscope. At about 1500, the *Viking* ran across the target and exploded its sweep without any apparent effect. Moments later U-8's periscope popped up, rotated 360 degrees, and disappeared.

An hour later *Maori* again spotted the periscope and *Ghurka* maneuvered to drag its sweep across the U-boat's track. At 1700 *Ghurka* exploded its sweep with dramatic results. The U-8 rose rapidly to the surface stern first and the crew poured out through the after deck hatch while *Maori* and *Ghurka* fired into the hulk, hitting the conning tower twice. As it was obvious U-8 was surrendering, the destroyers ceased fire and put out boats to take aboard the German survivors. Four officers and twenty-five men were rescued.

German records detailed the action from below. U-8 left Ostend at 0700 on 4 March, crossed the Ruytingen Bank minefield without difficulty, and arrived at the Varne Shoal around noon where it encountered a newly laid minefield. This field was also crossed easily because the sea was calm and the mines were readily spotted and avoided. After U-8 had crossed the minefield, the fog rolled in and visibility dropped to nearly zero. At this point the captain, Kapitänleutnant Alfred Stoss, decided it would be better to rest on the bottom until the weather cleared up. A combination of a very strong current and a very rocky bottom, however, made that plan unworkable, and U-8 surfaced to continue on its way.

At 1300 a lookout in the conning tower sighted a destroyer four miles away, approaching at high speed. The destroyer opened fire and U-8 immediately dove to sixty-five feet. For the next three hours Stoss and his officers listened to the destroyers' propeller sounds and concluded that they were being followed. At 1530 they heard and felt an explosion some distance off that did no damage to the boat, but they were now certain that the British were tracking them. The question they asked one another was how did the British know where the U-boat was? The answer, or at least the probable answer, came at 1600 when Oberleutnant zur See Sauerland relieved Leutnant zur See Morganroth as the steering officer.

Sauerland immediately noticed that the men operating the diving planes were having difficulty holding U-8 at its assigned depth. The boat was normally docile and easy to trim, and Sauerland knew it well, having been aboard since June 1914. Sauerland called for Stoss and the two officers concluded that they might have fouled a net. But Stoss said he could not see any sign of a net through the periscope housed in the central control room, nor could he see anything through the ports in the conning tower. Both officers agreed that a net equipped with some sort of indicating device would explain the destroyers' constant presence above them.

At 1745 a tremendous explosion jolted the boat, knocked out all electric power, including the motors, and started a fire in the control panel. The lights went out and stayed out because the blast had also destroyed the back-up emergency lighting. Water poured in through the conning tower and through a hole in the pressure hull aft of the central control room. The steering and depth controls failed and the boat started to sink.

Stoss ordered the tanks blown but the forward ballast tanks had been damaged, causing U-8 to rise stern first. As the stern rose and the down angle on the bow increased to nearly vertical, the batteries toppled over, spilling acid. Chlorine gas quickly formed inside the boat.

Stoss ordered his crew to be ready to abandon ship as soon as it broke surface. The crew carried out that order enthusiastically and without panic, everyone going out through the after deck hatch or through the conning tower. Ten minutes after reaching the surface, U-8 was gone forever, but the crew was safe.

Radio intelligence may have played a role in the destruction of U-8. According to Sauerland, he and Stoss discussed the action with the British officers who captured them. From what the British told them, Stoss and Sauerland came to the conclusion that their departure from Ostend was known to the British. The fact that the destroyers were able to waylay them was probably no accident. The U-boats did use the radio to announce their departures, daily positions, and results. And Room 40 listened to it all.

U-8's loss was an example of the British antisubmarine measures working in textbook fashion. The U-boat fouled the net, the indicator buoys led the destroyers to the target, and the explosive sweep killed the U-boat. It was one of the very rare instances when that happened.

The U-boats continued to foul the nets but no more were lost as a result of fouling the nets during the first anti-shipping campaign. In most instances the U-boats were able to tear free in less than an hour by going ahead and back. Some boats simply sank to the bottom and let the boat's weight tear apart the net, and some waited until night to surface and clear away the net.

Besides U-8, the only other recorded net casualty occurred on 25 July 1915 when UC-3 became entangled in an indicator-net and spent the entire day trying to free itself. Surfacing at night, the crew cut away the net, but part of it had fouled a propeller, forcing UC-3 to break off its minelaying operation and return to Zeebrugge.[13]

Before the end of the first anti-shipping campaign, Kapitänleutnant Karl Bartenbach started equipping the UB and UC boats with net cutters. These steel triangles, with a serrated leading edge, were welded to the deck at the bow. The net cutters were an inexpensive, easily produced field expediency that worked surprisingly well.

Despite the fact that very few U-boats were damaged or lost as a result of a net encounter, U-boat captains treated the nets with respect and avoided them whenever possible. The most remarkable example of the nets' effectiveness in blocking the U-boats from entering the Dover Straits came about on 12 April 1915, when Korvettenkapitän Bauer barred his U-boats from using the Dover passage to reach operations areas in the English Channel and the Irish Sea. Bauer's decision illustrates, on one hand, how the Germans often provided the British with their best anti-submarine defenses and, on the other hand, how the various U-boat commands went their separate ways. In any event, his decision was based on his perception of the nets' effectiveness, and it bears closer examination.

The event that led to Bauer's decision occurred on 6 April 1915 when U-32, under the command of Kapitänleutnant Adolf Freiherr von Spiegel, left Zeebrugge and proceeded to the Ruytingen Bank. Like U-8 in March, von Spiegel had just crossed the last minefield when a British destroyer spotted him and forced U-32 under. Moments later U-32 ran aground on the east edge of the Ruytingen Bank. After a harrowing thirty minutes during which his entire conning tower was exposed, von Spiegel was able to get his boat off and back in deep water.

U-32 ran submerged across Dover Straits to the French side, arriving off Calais sometime after noon. At that point von Spiegel realized that two British destroyers were following him; despite his best efforts, he could not shake them off. At around 1800 he heard a heavy explosion that shook the boat but did no serious damage. The destroyers continued to dog him, until he finally lost them at dusk. Von Spiegel assumed U-32 was leaking oil due to its grounding, and the destroyers had been following the oil trail on the surface.

After dark, U-32 surfaced in mid-Channel, south of Dungeness, and the crew discovered a heavy steel net draped across the hull. The destroyers had been following the net's indicator. The crew cut away the net with a cutting torch, and von Spiegel carried on with his patrol. The experience convinced him to go home along the outside route.[14]

U-32's experience set Bauer to thinking about the dangers involved in using the Dover Straits for access to the English Channel and the Channel western approaches. He was overly worried by British antisubmarine measures—minefields and nets—and navigational problems caused by strong currents and numerous shoals. He ignored or overlooked the fact that the minefields and nets, while posing a threat, were not very effective. The indicator-nets obviously worried him more than the minefields, and he was concerned about the British use of explosive sweeps in conjunction with the nets.[15]

Bauer was overcautious. His U-boat captains were regularly crossing the minefields and even passing under them without serious problems. The fact that British mines had sunk only two U-boats should have confirmed to him that British mines were largely ineffective. As for the nets, with the exception of U-8, nets had played no role in a U-boat's destruction up to that point in time. The navigational hazards found in the Dover Straits were a reality and there was no way to overcome them; U-32's grounding on Ruytingen Bank served as the best example. Bauer was also concerned by the fact that the U-boats, whether surfaced or submerged, could only transit the Dover Straits with the current.

He then compared the time required to reach the operations areas by going north around Scotland and by passing through the Dover Straits. The north around route was about five hundred nautical miles longer. According to Bauer, however, the longer route was safer, easier on the crews, and more fuel efficient because the U-boats could spend most of their time on the surface. This meant that less engine time was needed to recharge batteries. As an added advantage, the U-boats could attack the ships of the 10th Cruiser Squadron and the Grand Fleet as targets of opportunity along the way.

Weighing all the pros and cons as he saw them, Bauer concluded that the rewards to be earned going through the Dover Straits did not justify the risks. He concluded that going north around Scotland offered the best of all worlds and on 12 April 1915, he ordered his boats to use the north about route exclusively. Bauer's decision gave the British a false sense of security. Interestingly, Room 40 knew about the change, but the information was either not provided to the Dover command or ignored.[16]

Bauer's decision to have his boats go north about put them in an unfavorable strategic position. The significant result of Bauer's 12 April decision was that for the next two months and a week there were no U-boats of any type in the Dover Straits, which gave the Admiralty a false sense of confidence about the effectiveness of their defenses. "[T]he apparent success . . . was the more welcome for in the last half of April three more divisions of the Territorial forces were crossing to France."[17] In view of Bauer's order barring his boats from the Dover Straits passage, the Admiralty had cause to feel confident. However, once the Flanders boats starting passing through the Dover Straits on 21 June 1915, they easily made night passages on the surface or day passages submerged and under the nets.

Churchill did not share the Admiralty's confidence in British antisubmarine measures because Room 40 was telling him that the U-boats were passing through the Dover Straits at will. On 12 April 1915 he summarily dismissed Hood from the Dover command and replaced him with Rear Admiral Bacon, who assumed command on 13 April. The change of command was both unjust and ineffective, because Bacon carried on with the programs already in place. He said of this period, "our main work consisted of drifting nets to catch submarines."[18]

From Bacon's point of view his statement is correct. But the British also used neutral flags to shield their merchant ships and explosive sweeps to hunt U-boats. One was pretty basic and very effective while the other was much more complicated and hardly worth the effort.

6

Neutral Flags, Explosive Sweeps, and Lance Bombs

When the Germans opened their first unrestricted submarine warfare campaign on 22 February 1915, the Admiralstab's orders directed the U-boat captains to attack British ships, that is, those flying the British flag. On the other hand, the U-boat captains were to spare any ship that was clearly marked as a neutral, that is, any ship flying a neutral country's flag and bearing distinctive hull markings. The Admiralstab hedged a bit, however, when it added that even clearly marked neutrals were subject to attack since it was possible that England would adopt those markings to avoid attack.[1]

NEUTRAL FLAGS

The Germans were already well aware that the British were making wholesale use of neutral flags to protect their merchant ships from the U-boats' attacks. On 31 January 1915 the Germans had intercepted a British radio transmission in which the Admiralty directed British merchant captains to fly neutral flags as a defense against U-boats. The British did not deny that the direction had been broadcast, but they did say that it was a "confidential instruction advising merchantmen to keep a sharp lookout for submarines and when near the British Isles to show either neutral colors or none at all." The British also maintained that flying neutral flags was a "well established ruse of war, which all nations had practiced as a matter of course."[2]

By 1914 the practice of using neutral flags to protect a ship from attack or to lure a victim closer was over three centuries old. On that basis the British argued that using neutral flags to hide a ship's true identity was an established ruse de guerre that was legitimized by tradition and usage. Nevertheless, the United States protested to Britain about their use of the U.S. flag. Whether the practice was or was not legal is not the issue here. The question is: Was the use of neutral flags an effective antisubmarine measure? And the answer is yes.

But the British use of neutral flags worked effectively only while the German policy was to spare neutral ships. Under the German policy neutral ships were still subject to stop and visit, and destruction, according to the Prize Regulations. The Germans did sink several vessels according to the Prize Regulations, but their efforts to do so were often thwarted by the technical and armament limitations suffered by the U-boats, especially the UB and UC types. Taken as a whole, with the restrictions under which the U-boats operated—policy, technical, and armament—the British practice of flying neutral flags was a very effective antisubmarine measure.

EXPLOSIVE SWEEP

The British had two devices that were intended to attack submerged U-boats: the explosive sweep and the lance bomb. The British had been developing explosive sweeps since 1910 and in 1915 they had two versions in service: the single sweep and the modified sweep.[3]

The single sweep, which had been in use since the start of the war, consisted of a hydroplane, an 80-pound guncotton charge, and a two-inch diameter, electric tow cable.[4] The hydroplane supported the charge, which was about forty feet below the surface. The idea was to cross the U-boat's suspected track, foul the boat with some part of the cable, and electrically detonate the charge.[5] There are no confirmed instances in which a single sweep destroyed or damaged a U-boat, but there is one documented instance in which a single sweep struck a U-boat, but failed to explode.

The U-12, commanded by Kapitänleutnant Walter Forstmann, torpedoed the British gunboat HMS *Niger* on 11 November 1914 off Deal. Forstmann set the torpedo to run five feet below the surface and fired at three hundred yards, hitting the *Niger* amidships with catastrophic results.

Forstmann did not wait to watch his victim sink; instead he took the U-12 down to sixty feet and laid a course away from the scene. He described in his log what happened an hour later.

> At South Goodwin I came up to periscope depth to fix my position, but as we came to thirty feet the boat broached. A British torpedo boat immediately turned toward U-12 at high speed, forcing us to crash dive. The torpedo boat passed over us as we crossed forty-seven feet and we heard something heavy scraping across the hull. The men in the forward part of the boat said that it sounded like heavy wires or chains being dragged across the deck. Suddenly we felt a tremendous blow that drove us down to seventy feet, and I immediately altered course 90 degrees.[6]

Other than a good scare, U-12 and its crew suffered no ill effects from having been clobbered by a 70-pound charge that failed to explode.

The other sweep was the more powerful and more complicated modified sweep of which over one thousand were manufactured and issued. They were fitted to destroyers, torpedo boats, sloops, minesweepers, and trawlers. The modified sweep offered the advantage that its charges would explode on contact or they could be electrically fired. The modified sweep was an enormous loop that trailed three hundred yards astern of the towing vessel. The loop tracked the ship in a vertical plane, the upper wire having nine large floats and the lower wire having nine 80-pound guncotton charges spaced one hundred feet apart. The floats were submerged twenty-four feet below the surface and the guncotton charges were twenty-four feet deeper. Depth was maintained with a kite and there was no way to vary the depth of the charges, which meant that any U-boat deeper than seventy feet was safe. Again, the goal was to foul the U-boat and detonate the charges or place the charges close enough to the boat to damage it when the operator fired the charges electrically. The system rarely worked and there are several examples of U-boats being struck by the sweep without the charges detonating.[7]

Nevertheless, these two weapons were the first attempts to address the need for an underwater explosive device. An explosive sweep had been used successfully in conjunction with an indicator-net against U-8 on 4 March 1915 (see Chapter 5), and an explosive sweep may have been used against U-12 on 10 March. If so, then U-12 may have been the only U-boat to have been struck by both the single sweep and the modified sweep. In any event, the destruction of U-12 provides another rare example of the primitive British antisubmarine measures working perfectly.[8]

Kapitänleutnant Kratzsch had replaced Forstmann as U-12's captain and was on his first war patrol, a fact that played a major role in U-12's destruction. On 6 March the trawler *Duster* spotted U-12 twenty-five miles off Aberdeen, but could not report the sighting because the *Duster* lacked a radio. The following morning the *Duster* passed on the report to the armed yacht, *Portia*, which was radio equipped. Upon receipt of the sighting report, Rear Adm. R. S. Lowry, commanding Patrol Area 5 at Peterhead, sent all his available patrol vessels to sea. Included were the destroyers HMS *Acheron, Attack,* and *Ariel.*

During the next four days, several patrol vessels reported sighting U-12, and on the evening of 9 March HMS *Leviathan* confirmed the boat's presence. The following morning the trawler *May Island* forced U-12 to dive twenty-five miles from Fife Ness, and broadcast the sighting report. The chase was on.

At 1010 the three British destroyers were steaming in line abreast, one mile apart, when they spotted U-12 on the surface one and a half miles ahead. HMS *Attack* opened fire and went full ahead to ram, passing over the boil without making contact. For the next two minutes the three destroyers steamed in circles, unable to locate the U-boat.

At this point a human element came into play that contributed substantially to the outcome. Kapitänleutnant Kratzsch was at that moment safe, his boat was fifty feet below the surface, and the British had lost contact with him. Kratzsch now decided to rise to periscope depth and attack the destroyers. His watch officer, Leutnant zur See Max Seeburg, warned him not to do that because it was too dangerous. But Kratzsch rejected the experienced watch officer's advice, "because he didn't want to return home without a military victory."[9] Kratzsch had previously attacked a British destroyer and a cruiser unsuccessfully and he had one torpedo left. He ordered U-12 to be brought to periscope depth and extended the periscope.

Ariel saw the periscope pop up two hundred yards off the starboard bow. Lt. Comdr. J. V. Creagh went to full speed, put the helm hard over, and drove in to ram. *Ariel*'s bow struck the conning tower at a 70 degree angle just as it came awash. There is no mention in the British report that an explosive sweep was fired at the same time, or at any other time. But to the people in U-12, there was definitely an explosion followed by the ramming blow.

Kratzsch had just rotated the periscope to starboard and was shouting the order to dive when a tremendous explosion and a nearly simultaneous blow occurred. U-12 rolled 80 degrees to port, water poured in from around the periscope, the lights went out, the batteries shorted, and the diving controls failed. U-12 sank like a stone and Kratzsch ordered the tanks blown.

The moment U-12 broke the surface, the three destroyers opened fire at point-blank range. The first round hit the conning tower, killing Kratzsch and wounding several others. As more rounds hit the hull, the crewmen were struggling out through the forward and after deck hatches even as the boat sank. The action was brief and violent; U-12 sank in less than two minutes. There were ten survivors.

While the German survivors were aboard the *Acheron,* a British crewman showed them an explosive sweep and said that the *Ariel* had used one on U-12. U-12's navigator, Rath, described the device: "There was a steel weight about four meters long and one meter high behind which were twenty-five explosive charges bound together. The charges were about three times larger than what we use. The weight and charges were towed with a steel line, three centimeters thick. According to the British, they can tow the device for only twelve nautical miles. When the device strikes the target it explodes, and as soon as the submarine surfaces, the destroyers ram it."[10] The steel weight Rath saw was probably the kite, and he obviously counted both the charges and the floats. Or it's possible he may have seen several replacement charges.

This event illustrates two occurrences that were often found in early U-boat encounters. The first was the U-boat captains' early wartime practice of returning to periscope depth for a look around too quickly after being attacked. There are several examples of boats that were damaged or sunk because they returned to periscope depth while the enemy was still in a position to attack.

The other is that ramming was often as hard on the attacker as it was on the target. In this case, *Ariel*'s bottom was ripped open clear back to the after fire room, and the ship had to be towed to port. In an instance like this, the destroyer was effectively taken out of service at a time when the British had too few destroyers.

Despite their apparent antisubmarine activity and some successes, the British were slow off the mark in addressing the U-boat problem. In part that was because, in a material sense, there really was no problem. The

U-boats had hardly put a dent in the British merchant marine, and unless seriously provoked the British had little reason to devote much effort to ASW. The other reason was that the British believed the measures they had taken were effective. In fact, the only U-boat activity that had them really concerned was minelaying. During August 1915 the minelaying UC boats became active on the east coast, and British drifters had to sweep the traffic lanes daily. Rear Admiral Bacon, whose Dover command bore the brunt of the UC boats' activities, took immediate steps to equip all drifters and many trawlers as minesweepers. Bacon clearly believed that the principal threat to shipping was from the minelayers and not from the U-boats and UB boats.[11]

The French also manufactured an explosive sweep, but they were never happy with it and rarely used it. The French sweep was similar to the British modified sweep, but was not as easily deployed nor as effective. During the last month of the war the French obtained ten examples of an Italian sweep, called the Ginocchio, that came with 40-pound charge and 66-pound charge. Throughout the war, however, the British remained the principal users of explosive sweeps.[12]

The explosive sweeps represented new technology in the war against the U-boats, but the British continued to rely on the traditional methods of deception, ramming, and gunfire to protect their seaborne commerce.

LANCE BOMBS

The lance bomb was considerably less complicated than the explosive sweep and even less effective. Despite being a dismal failure, it was nonetheless a faltering step toward the development of the depth charge. The lance bomb was a hand-thrown weapon consisting of a 7-pound charge of amatol attached to a wooden handle that was three to four-and-a-half feet long. The head, which contained the charge, looked like a stubby bullet. The lance bomb was a contact weapon designed so that it would explode only when it struck something hard, like the hull of a U-boat.[13]

The weapon went into service in April 1915, but distribution was limited to small patrol vessels, primarily the trawlers and drifters of the Auxiliary Patrol. The British withdrew the lance bomb from service in early 1917 after producing twenty thousand units and scoring not a single success.

According to an official account, "it would be dangerous to attempt to throw it over the head or swing it behind on account of the possibility of striking some object in the rear."[14] The correct method for throwing the bomb was "by hand with a swinging motion."[15] Tests showed that the average distance a man could throw the lance bomb was thirty-six feet. People who used the device described a technique that apparently ignored the dangers expressed by the Admiralty. "A strong man could whirl one of them around his head, like a two-handed sword or a battle ax, and when the momentum was sufficient, hurl it over the water for about seventy-five feet."[16] Another description described the technique as being "much as an athlete would throw a hammer."[17] Regardless of the throwing technique used, the lance bomb's effectiveness was zero.

7

The Bombardments of Zeebrugge and Ostend, 1915

The Dover Patrol under Rear Admiral Bacon bombarded Zeebrugge and Ostend in 1915 and 1916, but only two instances were specifically intended as an antisubmarine measure: 23 August 1915 at Zeebrugge and 7 September 1915 at Ostend. The bombardments carried out in January, September, and December 1916 were intended to support BEF offensives.

THE TARGETS

The Germans had developed Bruges into their main naval base on the Flanders coast. They built bombproof U-boat shelters with steel reinforced concrete roofs several feet thick, brought in floating docks, built workshops, and developed all the facilities needed to maintain, repair, and rearm small warships.

Bruges lay eight miles inland and two canals connected the main harbor to the entrance harbors at Zeebrugge and Ostend. The eight-mile-long canal between Bruges and Zeebrugge was newer, more modern, and the more important of the two canals. The Zeebrugge-Bruges canal was almost perfectly straight along its entire length and could accommodate warships from torpedo boats to light cruisers. The Ostend-Bruges canal was much older, narrower, not as straight, and shallow. Zeebrugge and Ostend had locks so that ships could pass from the canals to the sea, or the reverse, regardless of the state of the tide. The tidal range at both harbors was fifteen feet.

The Germans kept very few ships of any type in Ostend or Zeebrugge, instead preferring to use the harbors to stage torpedo boat raids against the French and English coasts. The Germans did base some small craft—minesweepers and patrol boats—at both harbors, and both harbors were used as seaplane bases. More important, the U-boats based at Bruges were using Zeebrugge and Ostend as exits to reach their operations areas in the Hoofden, the Dover Straits, and the English Channel and its approaches. Most of those areas were behind the British net defenses, but the U-boats were crossing the nets with little difficulty in 1916. If the British could close the two exits, the U-boats would be bottled up in Bruges.[1]

It appeared to Admiral Bacon that the quickest way to close both harbors was to destroy the lock gates with gunfire, since both Zeebrugge and Ostend were open to bombardment from the sea. Of the two targets, Ostend, being smaller and having a poorer canal, was a secondary harbor to Zeebrugge. For that reason, he mounted his first attack against Zeebrugge.[2]

The Zeebrugge canal lock, located a half-mile inland from the coast, was not the biggest problem the naval gunners faced. The Germans defended Zeebrugge with guns that outranged the 12-inch guns on the monitors Bacon was going to use, and the lock gate was a very small, strongly built target. Admiral Bacon calculated that "the chance of hitting the Zeebrugge gate, assuming absolute accuracy, was once in every sixty-seven rounds." He concluded his estimate with the observation that "such accuracy is impossible with guns at sea."[3] In fact, the lock gate could only be destroyed by a direct hit, and even then the Germans might be able to quickly repair the damage. Despite the obvious difficulties, Admiral Bacon proceeded with meticulous planning and preparation for the bombardment.

THE PREPARATION

Three monitors—HMS *Lord Clive, John Moore,* and *Prince Rupert*—provided the gunfire. The monitors were specially designed gun platforms over three hundred feet long, with a beam of more than eighty feet that made them "remarkably steady gun platforms."[4] They were armed with twin 12-inch guns, each twenty-five calibers long, that had been removed from the old *Majestic*-class battleships. Bacon described them as "short

12-inch guns having a maximum range of about 20,000 yards," and they represented gun technology that was twenty-two years old. The monitors had a maximum speed of seven-and-a-half to eight knots, but in a heavy sea and steaming into the wind, they were lucky to make one or two knots. Shallow draft, ten and a half feet, and waterline bulges protected them against torpedoes.[5]

Admiral Bacon addressed the problems of establishing an aiming point and positioning observers to call the fall of shot in his typically ingenious way. Because smoke ashore would obscure the aiming points, Bacon created an aiming point by stationing a cruiser to seaward with a searchlight pointed skyward. The shaft of light became the aiming point. His solution for observing the fall of shot was more complicated and reflected his great interest in engineering.

Because he needed maximum accuracy, he chose not to use the observation platforms that were mounted high atop the monitors' main masts. Instead, he designed and constructed huge tripods that were carried close inshore and set on the bottom. The base of each tripod was an equilateral triangle, twenty-three feet on each side. The builders used railroad rails to create tripods that were forty-four feet high, weighed five tons, and were surmounted by a wooden platform measuring approximately seven feet by five feet. Two officer observers and two enlisted signalmen manned each tripod. The tripods provided the same accuracy of observation that two widely spaced forward observers ashore would have provided. The difference in this case was that the tripods were positioned off the beach in shallow water.

Training for the bombardment was carried out in the entrance to the Thames. There, Bacon created a close replica of the offing and principal landmarks at Zeebrugge, which included the compass bearings and tides they would encounter. By mid-August 1915, he felt his men, ships, and tripods were ready.

THE BOMBARDMENTS

The bombardments were a major undertaking, involving nearly eighty ships, including drifters, minesweepers, destroyers, tripod ships, and the three 12-inch monitors. The monitors took up station inshore while the drifters laid sixteen miles of ordinary and explosive nets in a triangle pattern around the monitors. Destroyers patrolled to the seaward of the net defenses.

The organization, the crossing, and the prefiring deployments off the beach went like clockwork, but the actual bombardment was a complete failure. The problem lay in the old guns and their mountings, which formed the batteries of the three monitors. The problems encountered off Zeebrugge were not new and had been apparent since the three ships had been commissioned earlier that year. According to Admiral Bacon, "Every day some pipe burst or some portion of the turret mountings gave out. The cause of these troubles was a simple one; these ships had turrets taken from old battleships of the [*Majestic*] class. Taken straight from these ships and mounted in the monitors, the copper pressure pipes, having become crystalline with age, did not stand the re-erection. New stresses during the fresh coupling-up were set up and breakdowns occurred."[6]

Off Zeebrugge on 23 August 1915, the *John Moore* and the *Prince Rupert* quickly suffered mount failures that put them out of action, leaving the *Lord Clive* to carry on alone. The bombardment had been scheduled to last two hours, but the tide turned earlier than was expected and *Lord Clive* ceased firing after one hour and forty-five minutes. Like the approach and the set-up, the withdrawal went according to plan and the fleet returned safely to its bases, taking with it all its nets and both tripods.

Two weeks later Admiral Bacon took his force to Ostend. The make-up of the force was nearly the same as it had been at Zeebrugge, but a new 12-inch monitor, HMS *General Craufurd,* replaced HMS *John Moore.* A smaller 9-inch monitor, the HMS *M25* and the cruiser HMS *Attentive* were also added to the force. The bombardment of Ostend called for a diversion at Westend, which was carried out by HMS *Redoubtable* and two gunboats, the *Excellent* and the *Bustard.*

The Dover force arrived off Ostend on the morning of 7 September 1915, but found the target obscured by a heavy mist. Nevertheless, they shot their protective nets, set out the tripods, and settled down to wait for better visibility. Despite the reduced visibility, German airplanes bombed the British ships, scoring hits on *Attentive* and causing casualties. Admiral Bacon withdrew his force and waited offshore for the mist to lift. While he was away, the German shore batteries discovered the tripods and destroyed them, leaving Bacon without his forward observation platforms.

That afternoon the monitors returned to their firing positions and opened fire under excellent visual conditions. Almost immediately the German shore batteries responded with heavy, accurate fire that forced the monitors to pull back from 18,000 yards to 19,500 yards. That still was not far enough and the Germans began scoring hits on the *Lord Clive,* causing Bacon to comment that "there followed a warm quarter of an hour."[7]

The situation had become untenable for the three monitors. The German batteries outgunned and outranged them, and their fire was much more accurate. Admiral Bacon wrote, "It was quite evident that the battery was shooting far too well for the monitors to stand a chance of surviving if we remained. I therefore made the REFORM and gave up the attack."[8]

For some unexplained reason, the Germans allowed the British ships to steam away without firing another shot at them. Just how lucky the British were is expressed in the mathematics of the situation. The German battery had an effective range of thirty-two thousand yards, and the British had to go ten thousand yards before they were out of range. The monitors were steaming away at seven knots, which meant that they would remain within the range of the German guns for another seventeen minutes.

The August and September attacks on Zeebrugge and Ostend accomplished nothing. Part of the problem stemmed from the old equipment that had been used to build the monitors. The 12-inch gun mountings on the *John Moore* and the *Prince Rupert* failed early in the attack, rendering both ships useless. Only the *Lord Clive* was able to carry on, but its fire was ineffective. Bacon admitted after the war that "the fire of the guns was not sufficiently accurate for so small a target as lock gates."[9]

Admiral Bacon took his force back to the Belgian coast six more times to bombard the German-held ports. But those subsequent bombardments were made in support of the BEF rather than being for the specific purpose of destroying the locks. But the idea of bottling up the U-boats in Bruges remained an active concept that became more active in 1916.

8

German Indecision

Great Britain's wholesale use of neutral flags was an effective antisubmarine measure. The practice did not sink any U-boats, but it achieved the goal of denying the U-boats access to targets. The important point with regard to the use of neutral flags is that the measure would not have worked without the attendant German indecision about how they should conduct their submarine war. The Germans' debate over their conduct of the submarine war shows the nature of the indecision.

Simply, the German navy took the view that the anti-shipping war had to be an unrestricted campaign. Any ship, enemy or neutral, that entered the declared war zone was a fair target and the U-boats would give no warning prior to an attack. The navy recognized that they lacked the capability to sink enough ships to starve the British into submission. They believed, however, that an unrestricted campaign would scare away the neutrals who would refuse to subject their merchant ships to the obvious dangers involved in trading with Great Britain.

In 1915 the proponents of an unrestricted campaign did not intend it to be a war-winning effort. They wanted to force the British to lift their blockade and they believed that would happen when the neutrals refused to sail through the war zone, thereby reducing the tonnage of goods received by Britain. It was hoped that the tonnage reduction resulting from an unrestricted campaign would cause the British to conclude a negotiated peace.

Von Bethmann-Hollweg's civilian government viewed unrestricted submarine warfare as a diplomatic disaster. Rather than frightening away the neutrals, the civilians feared the neutrals' reaction to an unrestricted campaign. In particular they were concerned about how the United States would react. The biggest fear was that America, with its industrial might and unlimited resources, would enter the war against Germany. The civilian government favored an anti-shipping campaign conducted according to the Prize Regulations as laid down in the 1909 Declaration of London. In the civilian government's view, operating according to the Prize Regulations was a practical solution.

From the start of the 1915 unrestricted submarine warfare campaign, the government's fears appeared to be well founded. When the Admiralstab issued the general orders for the campaign on 4 February they contained a clear warning that neutral ships should

> steer clear of these waters. It is true that the German Navy had received instructions to abstain from all violence against neutral vessels recognizable as such; but in view of the hazards of war and the misuse of the neutral flag ordered by the British Government, it will not always be possible to prevent a neutral vessel from becoming the victim of an attack intended to be directed against a vessel of the enemy.[1]

Before a torpedo was even launched, the United States filed a strongly worded protest. On 10 February President Woodrow Wilson sent a note to James W. Gerard, the U.S. ambassador in Berlin, for transmittal to the German foreign minister, Gottlieb von Jagow. In part the letter stated, "The suspicion that enemy ships are using neutral flags improperly can create no just presumption that all ships traversing a prescribed area are subject to the same suspicion. It is to determine exactly such questions that this Government understands the right of visit and search to have been recognized."[2]

The president's note also carried a warning that the civilian government inferred to be a war threat.

> If such a deplorable situation should arise, the Imperial German Government can readily appreciate that the Government of the United States would be constrained to hold the Imperial German Government to a strict accountability for such acts of their naval authorities and to take any steps

it might be necessary to take to safeguard American lives and property and to secure to American citizens the full enjoyment of their acknowledged rights on the high seas.[3]

Diplomatic exchanges continued, but the president's note directly affected Germany's anti-shipping campaign. On 18 February the kaiser issued an order written in response to the American protest:

Neutral ships should be spared. The flying of a neutral flag or display of neutral shipping line funnel marking is in itself not proof that the ship is neutral. Also, the carrying of other neutral markings, such as the national colors painted in a band on the side of the hull or at night the display of a lighted board bearing the name, nationality, etc., are not absolute proof of neutrality. The commander has to take into consideration all the existing circumstances when determining if a ship is a neutral or not. The ship's design, location, course and its general appearance are to be considered.

Merchant ships under neutral flag that are in convoy lose their neutral protection. Swedish, Danish and Norwegian ships in convoy protected by warships of any of their nations retain their neutrality

Hospital ships are to be spared. They can only be attacked if they are obviously carrying troops from England to France.

Ships of the Belgian Relief Commission are to be spared in all cases. They are marked by a large white flag with red letters spelling "Commission for Relief of Belgium." The same in large red letters will be painted on the hull. Some of these ships will be flying the British flag.

If, despite all care and efforts, an error is made and a neutral is confused with an enemy ship, the U-boat captain will be covered.[4]

Korvettenkapitän Bauer called this order the black day of the U-boat war. For the first time there appeared—not in the reserved and ambiguous form of the War Zone Declaration, but as a specific direction for the conduct of the war—an order that neutrals were to be spared.[5]

Additionally, the Admiralstab directed the U-boat captains to make special efforts to spare American and Italian ships because the foreign office wanted to avoid a major encounter with the United States. The Germans were affording the Italians special consideration because Italy was showing signs of joining the war against Germany; the foreign office did not want to give the Italians any excuse to take the plunge.

Korvettenkapitän Bauer, following the kaiser's order, succinctly described the situation:

> The fundamental question throughout the anti-shipping campaign was how to recognize a neutral. Since you were not supposed to sink them, you had to recognize them, which couldn't be done with certainty because of the British misuse of flags. And if neutrals were spared, then you should at least be allowed to attack enemy shipping with unbridled effort. The British never considered the Neutrals' rights when they issued their 31 January order to fly neutral flags. The result was that you saw only neutral flags in the war zone, especially in the coastal routes where the war zone concentrated shipping. These waters were too strongly patrolled to allow the U-boats to operate according to the Prize Regulations. The British use of neutral flags could well be viewed as an effective shield against U-boat attacks.[6]

On 18 March, just four weeks after the anti-shipping campaign opened, an incident occurred that had nothing to do with neutral flags. Nevertheless, the incident added one more conflicting directive that further complicated the debate over how the campaign was to be conducted. On 18 March 1915, HMS *Dreadnought* rammed and sank U-29 moments after the U-boat had fired a torpedo at HMS *Neptune*. The incident represented more than just the loss of a U-boat, however; it had a major impact in Germany. Otto Weddigen was U-29's captain, and it was his loss rather than the loss of the boat that caused so much anguish because he had become the symbol of the U-boat's prowess. He was, in fact, a national icon.

The kaiser was so upset that he issued an order on 2 April 1915 stating that the U-boat's safety was the captain's primary responsibility and took precedence over all other considerations. The kaiser's order made it clear that if there appeared to be a threat, surfacing to inspect a ship was not required. The fact that Weddigen was not surfacing to inspect a ship when HMS *Dreadnought* rammed him was overlooked or ignored.

The kaiser's order created more confusion and difficulty for the U-boat captains when considered against the requirements for special handling for neutrals and the absolute requirement to spare American and Italian ships. Bauer asked the rhetorical question: Given the restrictions, how else was a captain to determine if a suspected ship was neutral or not other than by surfacing and examining it? In a later war, the Americans would call a situation like this one a catch-22.[7]

From the opening of the campaign, there were incidents in which neutral ships were sunk, each incident adding fuel to the fire. From the Germans' point of view, the first serious incident occurred on 14 April when
UB-10 torpedoed the 2,040-ton Dutch steamer SS *Katwijk* near the North
Hinder Lightship. Oberleutnant zur See Otto Steinbrinck said that the
ship was darkened except for navigation lights, showed no national identification, and was sending Morse lamp signals. Adding the ship's location and heading into the equation, Steinbrinck concluded the ship was
British and torpedoed it.[8] In fact, *Katwijk* was not going to a British port—
its destination was Baltimore, Maryland. The only obvious error Steinbrinck made was that the ship was reportedly in a zone that the Germans
had declared safe for all ships.[9]

The Dutch were understandably outraged and the German foreign office
had reason to be alarmed over the Dutch reaction. Germany could not
afford a break in relations with Holland, and had the Dutch decided to
enter the war, Gen. Erich von Falkenhayn would have been hard pressed
to find the troops to meet the new threat. The crisis passed, but at the
kaiser's direction, Vizeadmiral Gustav Bachmann sent an advisory order
to Admiral von Pohl on 18 April: "On political grounds it is necessary that
for the time being every effort should be made to spare neutral ships. This
applies particularly to Dutch ships in view of public opinion in Holland following the *Katwijk* incident. Please advise your U-boats of this."[10] The advisory order did not materially change things, but it did increase the pressure
on the U-boat captains and it ensured that in their efforts to spare neutrals
the U-boat captains would sink fewer British ships.

On 3 May, Vizeadmiral Ludwig von Schröder wrote to Admiral Bachmann, chief of the Admiralstab, that it was a pointless effort to conduct
the anti-shipping war under the existing restrictions. Citing the British
use of neutral flags, he wrote: "The entire commercial traffic between
Holland and England is being done under the Dutch flag. The traffic is so
heavy that if we continue to spare neutral-flag vessels, the present U-boat
campaign will have little effect. We are faced with a military necessity
to attack without warning all neutral-flag vessels in the war zone, and that
military necessity outweighs any political considerations."[11]

In the meantime, Kapitänleutnant Walter Schwieger in U-20 torpedoed
the *Lusitania*. This caused a diplomatic crisis that had far-reaching effects,
exactly the sort of thing that von Bethmann-Hollweg had said would happen. The principal trouble came from the United States through a note,

dated 15 May 1915, written by President Wilson and addressed to Ambassador James W. Gerard for transmittal to Foreign Minister Gottlieb von Jagow. The president's note agreed with the German navy's position that submarine warfare under the Prize Regulations was impossible:

> It is practically impossible for the officers of a submarine to visit a merchantman at sea and examine its papers and cargo. It is practically impossible for them to make a prize of her; and if they can not put a prize crew on board her, they can not sink her without leaving her crew and all on board of her to the mercy of the sea in her small boats. These facts it is understood, the Imperial Government frankly admit.[12]

What the U.S. government demanded was a return to the Prize Regulation; if the U-boats were unsuited for operations under those conditions, then they should not be used in an anti-shipping campaign. The American note closed, "The Imperial German Government will not expect the Government of the United States to omit any word or any act necessary to the performance of its sacred duty of maintaining the rights of the United States and its citizens and of safeguarding their free exercise and enjoyment."[13]

On 28 May, Schröder sent a second letter to Admiral Bachmann, this time enclosing statistics for 23–26 May showing that 88.5 percent of the traffic was being done under neutral flags. Schröder asked that large destroyers and cruisers be assigned to his command so that they could conduct stop-and-visit operations according to the Prize Regulations since the UB boats were incapable of doing that. Despite Schröder's practical arguments, Bachmann rejected his request for larger surface ships with the comment, "The Admiralstab will, as before, leave large U-boats, destroyers and cruisers with the High Sees Fleet."[14]

On 30 and 31 May, von Tirpitz and Bachmann met with the kaiser. During discussions the kaiser said, "I cannot reconcile my conscience to the fact that on the one hand the U-boat warfare is to continue and on the other hand that neutrals are to be spared."[15] The kaiser's comment had summed up the navy's dilemma: In order to prosecute the war, you have to sink neutrals; but if you cannot sink neutrals, you cannot prosecute the war. It was a catch-22. Following the meeting, Admiral Bachmann issued an order:

> Until further notice, neutral ships are to be spared. Additional attacks on neutral ships have the potential of causing serious political problems, and

must be avoided at all costs. His Majesty, the Kaiser, makes it the duty of all U-boat commanders not to attack any ship unless he has irrefutable evidence that the ship is an enemy. In situations where doubt exists, it is better that an enemy merchant ship be allowed to pass rather than to sink a neutral ship.[16]

On 6 June Admiral Bachmann issued another order directed at both the boats of the High Sea Fleet and the Flanders flotilla, which prohibited attacks on large passenger ships. The prohibition included enemy passenger ships.

That same day the kaiser's naval advisor and chief of the naval cabinet, Adm. Georg von Müller, received a coded telegram from von Tirpitz and Bachmann criticizing von Bethmann-Hollweg and declaring that they could not accept responsibility for the new restrictions placed on the anti-shipping campaign. Admiral von Müller showed the telegram to General von Falkenhayn who prepared a short answer, which the kaiser approved. The answer directed the navy to deal with neutral shipping under the Prize Regulations.[17]

Throughout the remainder of June, the navy and the civilian government grappled with the problem of conducting a war on shipping without running foul of the neutrals. There was no solution, and the gap between the two sides widened. Toward the end of the month there was hope that the *Lusitania* affair was dying down. The first sign was found in a note from President Wilson to Ambassador Gerard in Berlin, for transmittal to von Jagow in the foreign ministry.

In this note, President Wilson changed his view about the unsuitability of U-boats for an anti-shipping war under the Prize Regulations. He now took the opposite view of that expressed in his May note and declared that U-boats could conduct anti-shipping operations under the Prize Regulations. President Wilson probably revised his opinion because U-boat commanders had shown that U-boat operations under the Prize Regulations were possible. The president wrote, "The events of the past two months have clearly indicated that it is possible and practicable to conduct such submarine operations as have characterized the activity of the Imperial German Navy within the so-called war zone in substantial accord with the accepted practices of regulated warfare."[18]

If von Tirpitz and Bachmann hoped that Wilson's change of mind would help their cause, their hopes were dashed a few weeks later. On

16 August 1915, U-24 torpedoed the passenger ship *Arabic* and caused a second diplomatic crisis with the United States. As the revived diplomatic flap unfolded, Admiral Bachmann sent a letter to Admiral von Pohl suggesting that in view of the *Arabic* incident, the U-boat commanders should closely follow the kaiser's 6 June order to spare large passenger ships.

On 26 August the chancellor, von Tirpitz, Bachmann, General von Falkenhayn, and a representative of the foreign ministry met with the kaiser to discuss the *Arabic* incident. Admiral von Müller described the meeting: "The conflict of opinions was in full swing and the conference was in the nature of a Battle Royal. Finally we split up to think and prepare a conciliatory reply to the Americans."[19]

The infighting and the results of the meeting were wide ranging, but as regarding the anti-shipping campaign it was evident that von Bethmann-Hollweg took a page from von Pohl's book. In a private meeting with the kaiser he undercut his opponents' position. Admiral Bachmann, reacting to the chancellor's political maneuver, issued an order to Admiral von Pohl that no U-boats were to be sent out until the *Arabic* matter was settled. The order applied only to the U-boats of the High Sea Fleet.[20]

On 30 August the kaiser issued an order expanding his 6 June prohibition on sinking large passenger liners. The new order prohibited the sinking of any passenger ship, regardless of size, without warning and only after the passengers and crew had been safely taken off. He also ordered that no more U-boats were to be sent to the British west coast. This order went to the boats of the High Sea Fleet and the Flanders flotilla.

In the fall-out from the 26 August meeting, the kaiser fired Admiral Bachmann on 2 September 1915 and replaced him with Adm. Hennig von Holtzendorff, an enemy of von Tirpitz and, initially, in agreement with the chancellor. Within a week Admiral von Holtzendorff issued two new orders that added more stringent restrictions on U-boat operations. Under the new orders, the U-boats could attack only identified enemy merchant ships without warning. In every other instance, the U-boats had to operate strictly according to the Prize Regulations. On 18 September Admiral von Holtzendorff issued an even more sweeping order:

As of now neither unrestricted submarine warfare nor operations under the Prize Regulations will be conducted on the British West Coast nor in the English Channel. Anti-shipping operations under the Prize Regulations will be conducted in the North Sea. Hereafter, military operations will take first priority.[21]

With this order, the first unrestricted campaign against shipping was ended. The stand-down was far from permanent, but for the time being, the Mediterranean would become the hot spot.

Under pressure from the United States over the conduct of the U-boat offensive, the Germans had turned away from the war against shipping. By that time British countermeasures had destroyed eleven U-boats in the waters around Britain, and a mine may have accounted for one more— U-37. Given the primitive state of the existing submarine countermeasures, those numbers are impressive because they mean that the British sank about 26 percent of the available U-boats.[22]

The figures are deceptive, however, because they do not take into account the fact that the Germans were building boats faster than the British could sink them. Postwar British writers decry the ineffectiveness of their antisubmarine measures, but in autumn 1915, the Admiralty was satisfied that the countermeasures were working. In fact, it was their confidence in what they were doing that prevented them from undertaking a more energetic ASW weapons development program until well into 1917.

The other side of that coin is the question of how effective the U-boats were against the British during this period. Number crunchers would say the answer was that they were effective because the number of ships sunk outnumbered the number of U-boats sunk by about fifty-five to one. However, those figures are not a reliable measure because about half the ships the U-boats sank were fishing boats. Tonnage figures are more reliable, but even they are misleading unless the fishing boats are eliminated.[23]

Historian Paul Halpern, *A Naval History of World War I,* points out that while the British losses represented only a small fraction of their merchant fleet, their total tonnage available was diminishing. That is, it was not being replaced by new construction as fast as it was being lost.[24] In September 1915, the rate at which British tonnage was diminishing did not represent an immediate threat to the British war effort. Instead, the numbers represented both a trend and the U-boats' potential should their numbers increase substantially and should the Germans abandon the Prize Regulations. Two things were certain: the British were alarmed over their losses despite their confidence in their countermeasures, and they were relieved that the Germans had called off their U-boat offensive against shipping.

PART THREE

Continuing British Countermeasures
in Home Waters

October 1915–January 1917

9

Armed Merchant Ships, the Paravane, and the Depth Charge

ARMED MERCHANT SHIPS

Throughout the period from October 1915 to January 1917 the British continued to rely on nets, mines, ramming, and guns to counter the U-boats. The gun, however, was the best defense against U-boats because the Germans were operating according to the Prize Regulations. Three out of four U-boat attacks on shipping occurred on the surface, thereby making the U-boats vulnerable to gunfire.

British figures show that 206 surface attacks on merchant ships occurred during the last quarter of 1916; 47.5 percent of the merchant ships were sunk and 52.5 percent escaped. Of those that escaped, 74 percent were armed while 26 percent were not. The unarmed ships that escaped did so because of their superior speed.[1]

Given the numbers, the Admiralty put their greatest faith in arming merchant ships. The arming process was slow, however, during the time when guns were the most effective weapon against U-boats. By the end of 1916 about half the British merchant ships carried some kind of defensive armament. By 22 February 1917 the British had armed 2,899 merchant ships; by the end of the war a total of 5,887 ships had been armed of which 1,648 were lost to all causes.[2]

The armed merchant ships had a major effect on the way the war was waged. The U-boat captains became increasingly wary of approaching large steamers on the surface because so many of them were armed. Part of the problem stemmed from the fact that the steamers were often more heavily armed than were the U-boats. In October 1915 the U-boat captains began demanding larger caliber deck guns. In January 1916 Kapitänleutnant Lothar von Arnauld de la Periere wrote, "Commerce warfare is made much more difficult because of the increasing presence of U-boat hunters, armed fishing boats, Q-ships, and small auxiliary cruisers that are apparently equipped with explosive sweeps. Added to that is the increasing appearance of armed merchant ships, and merchant ships equipped with radios that work in concert with the antisubmarine forces to warn others."[3]

In May 1916 Kapitänleutnant Klaus Rücker wrote that the Prize Regulations cost him many opportunities because he had to avoid numerous strongly armed merchant ships. And in November 1916, Kapitänleutnant Werner Fürbringer wrote, "It is true that due to the nearly universal arming of British steamers, the war will be increasingly directed at neutrals whose ships are not armed. The practice now is to stop all ships at substantial distance and bring them under fire at extreme range."[4]

British naval opinion was entirely in favor of arming more ships with 4-inch and 6-inch guns, but by the end of January 1917 the rising losses among armed merchantmen showed that this ASW practice was rapidly losing its efficiency. During 1915 no armed merchant ships were sunk by U-boats; until August 1916 the number remained low. Twelve armed steamers were sunk in December 1916 and twenty in January 1917.[5] The reason for the rising losses was that the U-boat captains were resorting to submerged torpedo attacks whenever the captain thought the steamer might be armed.

How effective was the practice of arming merchant ships? Statistically, an armed merchant ship had a 64 to 68 percent chance of escaping if attacked on the surface under the Prize Regulations. The chances for survival dropped dramatically if the U-boat made a submerged torpedo attack. The incontestable fact is that the armed merchant ships forced the U-boats to make submerged torpedo attacks. Arming merchant ships made good sense only as long as the Germans were willing to operate under the Prize Regulations. When the Germans completely abandoned the Prize Regulations in 1917, this ASW measure was no longer effective.

THE PARAVANE

The relatively low shipping losses during most of 1916 inhibited Britain's programs for the development and production of antisubmarine devices. Progress in all fields was made, but it was slow going and production of new devices lagged, including the development of underwater exploding devices.

Lt. C. Dennis Burney designed and developed the paravane, which is more commonly called the high-speed submarine sweep. Burney was a line officer with a keen engineering mind. Before the war he was assigned to the Anti-Submarine Committee, but he left the Royal Navy in 1911 to design a seaplane with a range of over five hundred miles that was capable of carrying a three-man crew, weapons, and a radio. The war cut short his seaplane project and Burney returned to active duty to command the torpedo boat destroyer, HMS *Velox*. Following the loss of the three *Cressy*-class cruisers on 22 September 1914, the Admiralty assigned Burney to the HMS *Vernon* torpedo school to oversee the development of an efficient underwater explosive device that could be used to attack a submerged U-boat.

Burney's antisubmarine paravane and the modified sweep were both under development at the torpedo school at the same time, but the paravane was a technologically more advanced design. The less complicated modified sweep progressed more quickly and was in general use in 1915. When the high-speed sweep went into service in 1916 it quickly surpassed the modified sweep in use.[6]

As an antisubmarine weapon, the paravane came in two versions, the high-speed paravane for use by destroyers and the low-speed paravane for use by trawlers and drifters. In either form, the antisubmarine paravane carried a 400-pound TNT charge that either detonated on contact or the shipboard operator could fire it electrically.[7]

Both the high-speed and low-speed versions were designed to be towed in pairs, one to port and one to starboard, and both could be set to run at a specific depth. A feature of Burney's device was that it would remain at its preselected depth as long as the ship was under way, regardless of the ship's speed or course. The device would also keep station at a constant distance off the sides of the ship. A destroyer could tow a paravane at higher speeds than it could an explosive sweep, and the paravane could be towed at depths down to two hundred feet.

After the device was put into service in January 1916, the Royal Navy discovered that the wire unraveled and parted after just a few hours of use. The wire was designed to withstand a ten-ton strain, but the paravane's design, and the method of attaching the wire to the device, set up harmonic conditions that caused conventional wire to fail. By October 1916 Burney's technicians had solved the problem and the redesigned wire had a one hundred hour life expectancy.[8]

The Royal Navy also introduced the depth charge in January 1916 and considered the antisubmarine paravane and the depth charge to be complementary weapons. The navy's initial policy was to use depth charges when a U-boat's location was fairly well known and use the paravane to attack a submerged U-boat whose location was either in doubt or entirely unknown. Experience and an increase in depth charge production greatly diminished the paravane's role by mid-1917, but trawlers continued to use the older slow-speed version until the end of the war.[9]

How effective was the high-speed sweep? From 18 March 1916 to 4 October 1918, there were fifty-three recorded instances in which an antisubmarine paravane was exploded during an attempt to destroy a U-boat. In twenty-one instances ships reported some effectiveness ranging from "possibly slightly damaged" to "known sunk."[10] In fact, no U-boat was sunk by an explosive paravane during World War I. Nevertheless, a very effective device did result from Burney's invention and it was called the Otter.

Though Burney designed the paravane to be an ASW weapon that would destroy a submerged U-boat, the paravane played a more important role as the premier minesweeping device. The Otter was simply Burney's explosive paravane without the explosive charge; instead, it had powerful cutting jaws capable of parting a mine's anchor cable. The Otter, which looked exactly like an explosive paravane, was fitted to the bows of minesweepers, warships, and merchant ships. Like the explosive paravane version, Otters were deployed in pairs. As the ship moved forward, the Otters cruised below the surface off the bow on each side. Because the Germans used mines as an important part of their anti-shipping campaign and many mines were laid by U-boats, the Otter qualifies in a broad sense as an ASW device.

DEPTH CHARGE

The depth charge is more closely related to the bomb lance than it is to the sweeps, but it was vastly more effective. The British had been working on a depth charge since December 1914; by January 1915 they had developed four primitive models that were issued in limited numbers. The early depth charges used guncotton for the explosive and were fired by what the British called a pull-off pistol instead of a hydrostatic pistol, which had not yet been developed. The pull-off pistol was a float with a fixed length of lanyard that was attached to the firing device. The charge, float, and lanyard were packaged as a single unit. When the device hit the water the explosive charge detached from the float and descended until the lanyard was fully paid out at which time the weight of the charge caused the lanyard to pull the pin and the device exploded.[11]

The early float and lanyard types came in four versions; three of the four versions were naval models and the forth was an aerial bomb. The naval models were designated A, B, and E, while the aerial versions, which came with either a 35- or 65-pound charge, were designated C* or C, respectively. The navy's A and B models carried thirty-two and a half pounds of guncotton, and the E model carried a 100-pound charge. According to British figures, the A, B, and C models had to explode within twenty feet of the target to do serious damage, and the larger E model had to explode within seventy feet. All of the float and lanyard types were in service in 1915 in very limited numbers, and were issued to the Auxiliary Patrol. No U-boat was damaged or sunk by any of the early models, which were rarely used.

These primitive models were too small to be effective and the British soon replaced them with the larger, more sophisticated Type D. The Admiralty approved the Type D design on 13 June 1915, authorized the ordering of 1000 units in August, and started issuing them to Fleet and Auxiliary Patrol units in January 1916.

The Type D came in two versions, one with a 300-pound TNT charge and a smaller version designated the Type D* with a 120-pound charge. Both types were equipped with a hydrostatic pistol that could be preset to explode at either forty or eighty feet. The reason for the different charges was that the explosion produced by a 300-pound charge dropped off the stern of a slow-moving vessel would probably blow off the ship's stern. The smaller 120-pound charge might shake up a slow-moving ship, but it would not sink it. Therefore, destroyers and torpedo boats carried the more powerful Type D, while slower vessels—trawlers, drifters, and motor launches (MLs)—got the smaller Type D*. According to British figures, the Type D would destroy a U-boat at a range of 70 feet and would cause severe damage out to 140 feet. The maximum effective range for the D* was about 90 feet at which the U-boat would suffer some damage.

Great Britain and its allies now had an effective underwater weapon. The depth charge's effectiveness, however, was limited by the small numbers British manufacturers were able to produce. During most of 1916 production allowed only two per vessel, and not every vessel got them; by the end of 1916 the number had risen to four per vessel. But the supply remained limited until June 1917.

U-68, commanded by Kapitänleutnant Lothar Güntzel, received the credit for being the first U-boat sunk by a depth charge, but there is a question as to whether or not the depth charge was really the cause of its loss. The depth charge certainly contributed to its loss on 22 March 1916. The decoy Q-5, better known as the *Farnborough,* was working off the coast of Kerry, Ireland, when a lookout spotted a surfaced U-boat off the port quarter about five miles away at 0640. Lt. Comdr. Gordon Campbell sent his gunners to battle stations and held his course and speed. U-68 dove and twenty minutes later fired a torpedo that passed forward of the *Farnborough.* Campbell continued to hold his course and speed. A few minutes later the U-boat surfaced one thousand yards off the port quarter and fired a shot across *Farnborough*'s bow.

Campbell stopped, blew off steam, and put the panic party over the side. The gunners manning the collier's five 12-pounders waited. Güntzel brought U-68 in to eight hundred yards and fired a round that fell fifty yards short. At that point *Farnborough*'s gunners opened fire, firing twenty-one rounds and scoring several hits on the hull and the conning tower.

Apparently Güntzel and the two lookouts were killed and the U-boat began to sink slowly with no sign of life in the conning tower. Campbell got the *Farnborough* under way and turned toward the sinking U-68 just as it went under. The *Farnborough* steamed across the spot and dropped a depth charge, which brought U-68 to the surface with the bow nearly vertical and exposed clear back to the conning tower. The *Farnborough*'s gunners pumped five more rounds into the hull. The U-boat slid under stern first and the *Farnborough* recrossed the spot, dropping two more depth charges. This time a large quantity of oil and chunks of wood came to the surface; the oil spread quickly, forming a huge slick.[12]

The Germans became aware of the depth charge in April 1916 after unsuccessful attacks on U-67 and U-69.[13] Kapitänleutnant Nieland, in U-67, was working off the southern tip of Ireland when he spotted two steamers, one of which showed Dutch colors and the other showed Swedish colors. Nieland hoisted the international signal to stop but the Swedish steamer ignored him. The Swedish ship was actually the British decoy *Farnborough*. Nieland took U-67 in to three thousand yards and fired a warning shot. Nieland reported, "In that moment the steamer opened rapid fire from several hidden guns. The rounds were falling very close. We crash dived, and as we passed sixty feet there was a tremendous explosion followed by another as we passed seventy-five feet. Other than broken lights and shaken nerves there was no damage.[14]

Kapitänleutnant Wilhelms, in U-69, was shelling SS *Cairngowan* in the same area on 20 April when a British ML forced him to break off and dive. U-69 had just passed periscope depth when the depth charge exploded, shaking the boat violently but doing no damage.[15]

It is important to remember that even though the Germans were now aware that the British had a powerful underwater weapon, they actually encountered it only infrequently during 1916. The depth charge made an impression on the U-boat crews; nearly every underwater explosion was attributed to depth charges. In fact, most of the explosions the U-boats experienced were sweeps, occasionally mines, often artillery exploding on the surface, and the occasional aerial bomb.

For example, the British credited depth charges for the destruction of UB-29 and UC-19 in 1916, but it is not certain this is true. Both boats departed Zeebrugge on 27 November 1916 to attack shipping in the English Channel, and both failed to return. During the afternoon of 6 December HMS *Ariel* sighted an unidentified U-boat that was diving about a mile away. Records exist stating that the destroyer deployed its sweep at thirty feet and obtained a contact explosion near the spot where the U-boat dove. Large amounts of oil and debris came to the surface. Another record states that HMS *Lewellyn* dropped depth charges with the same result. Based on time and location, it is possible that the *Ariel* sank either the UC-19 or the UB-29; both boats were in the area and the odds are that *Ariel* used a sweep.[16]

The more likely candidate for the honor of having been destroyed by a depth charge is UB-29. On 13 December, southeast of the Goodwin Sands, HMS *Landrail* saw a U-boat dive three hundred yards dead ahead. The destroyer went ahead full and dropped two depth charges that brought large amounts of oil and debris to the surface. Some people believe it was UB-29, but again there is no certainty; the only point on which all the experts agree is that HMS *Landrail* dropped depth charges and UB-29 never returned.[17]

British ships carried so few depth charges during 1916 that destroying a U-boat was largely a matter of luck. To be effective, depth charges had to be dropped in large numbers to saturate the target area, and the British did not have that capability until after June 1917. With the exception of the Americans, Britain's allies never acquired the necessary number of depth charges to make their depth charge attacks truly effective.

THE FRENCH DEPTH CHARGE

The French began developing a depth charge in 1914, but progress was slow and the results were disappointing. The Guiraud model came in two sizes: a 90-pound charge and a 156-pound charge. Both versions used out-dated torpedo detonators as part of the pistol, and both could be set to explode at depths down to 110 feet.[18] The French never had enough depth charges to use them effectively, and those they did have were unreliable. In a postwar assessment, the French concluded that they should have copied the British Type D. In 1917 the French asked the Americans and the British to supply them with depth charges. Both countries turned down the request, giving a lack of production capacity as the reason.[19]

THE AMERICAN DEPTH CHARGE

The United States' entry in the war materially increased the number of depth charges in all the war zones, but the United States did not supply depth charges to the British or the French. The U.S. Navy had been developing a depth charge since 1916, and early in 1917 adopted the Mark I depth charge. The Mark I featured a float and lanyard firing system similar to the British type A, and carried a 50-pound charge. The American depth charge differed from the British Type A in that the American version could be set to explode at depths from twenty-five to one hundred feet without changing the length of the lanyard. The U.S. Navy had ordered ten thousand Mark I depth charges, which were almost immediately available for issue when the United States entered the war in 1917.[20]

The U.S. Navy quickly realized that a 50-pound charge was too small to be effective against the U-boats and directed the Bureau of Ordnance to develop a more powerful version. In the meantime, the British had provided the bureau with examples and drawings of the Type D, which the Navy Department suggested that the bureau simply copy. Instead, the Bureau of Ordnance chose to make several changes in the design to make the American version safer and more reliable. The American version was the Mark II depth charge and the Bureau placed an initial order for ten thousand in July 1917, followed six months later with an order for another twenty thousand. At the same time, the bureau agreed to order fifteen thousand Type D depth charges for the British.

In terms of effectiveness, the Mark II was equal to the Type D. The British Type D design, however, suffered from premature explosion when used in a projector, which the Americans attributed to the outside location of the British detonator. The British trigger protruded several inches beyond the container, whereas the Mark II's trigger was installed inside the container to reduce the chances of accident or damage during handling. Other differences included the American hydrostatic trigger that was set from the outside with a dial and allowed a choice of depth settings ranging from fifty to two hundred feet. This was a feature that the British Type D did not have until the end of 1917. The Americans used TNT, which was more powerful than the Amatol used by the British. The Mark II depth charge was eighteen inches in diameter by twenty-eight inches long with a 300-pound TNT charge, bringing the total weight to 420 pounds. The Mark II series sank at a rate of six feet per second and was safe until it reached fifteen feet.

The Americans followed up on the Mark II with the Mark III and the Mark IV. The Mark III differed little from the Mark II except that it could be set to explode at three hundred feet; the U.S. Navy ordered ten thousand in July 1918. The Mark IV was larger and more powerful than the two earlier models. It carried a 600-pound TNT charge, was twenty-five inches in diameter and twenty-eight inches long, and weighed a total of 745 pounds. One thousand were manufactured and arrived in Europe in September 1918.

The depth charge was the weapon with the greatest future potential and it became steadily more effective as it was produced in greater numbers. Depth charges sank two U-boats in 1916, six in 1917, and twenty-two in 1918.

10

Indicator-Nets and Mine-Nets

INDICATOR-NETS

The Entente Powers—Great Britain, France, and Russia—used nets throughout the war. Although after 1917 nets were used almost exclusively to defend harbor entrances, the British were still deploying nets as a primary ASW countermeasure in 1916. They were no more efficient than they had been earlier.One net defense success did occur off Le Havre, France, on 5 April 1916. Six Auxiliary Patrol drifters—*Endurance, Welcome Star, Stately, Comrades, Pleiades,* and *Pleasance*—were drifting their nets near Whistling Buoy in the Le Havre roads. Shortly after beginning work, the *Comrades* felt a blow against the hull near the keel. Almost simultaneously the watch aboard the *Endurance* saw their net buoys disappear beneath the surface, and then felt a heavy jolt near the rudder.

Capt. T. C. Wylie immediately sounded the alarm and at the same time discovered that whatever had hit the *Endurance* had disabled the rudder. Unable to maneuver, Wylie eased the net hawser, paying out line like a fisherman working his catch. It was apparent that whatever had fouled the net had not torn the panel loose, and the net and the catch were still firmly connected to the *Endurance.* The other five drifters responded to the alarm and took up positions around the net.

For the next twenty minutes Captain Wylie continued to sound the alarm while his crew struggled to control the net. The other drifters shot their nets in the area hoping to further entangle the U-boat, but this had no effect. After twenty minutes the strain on the net was seriously endangering the *Endurance*. Wylie was forced to cast off the net, but his whistle signals had brought a French torpedo boat to the scene.

The French captain immediately recognized what was happening and dropped two depth charges on the spot where the drifters indicated the net had sunk. Two large explosions resulted and a few minutes later the U-boat came to the surface. The torpedo boat and the drifters fired into it. The Germans came on deck through all three openings and dove overboard as the U-boat quickly sank. The six drifters rescued the entire crew.[1]

German records detailed the action from below. UB-26, commanded by Oberleutnant zur See Wilhelm Smiths, was a brand-new boat making its first war patrol. UB-26 had departed Zeebrugge on 30 March 1916 to attack troop transports off Le Havre and to conduct commerce war in the English Channel. Smiths made the trip to Le Havre without incident, arriving off the French port on the morning of 4 April.

During the day he made two attempts to enter the harbor but turned back twice, once because dense fog hid the targets and once because French torpedo boats ran him off. He spent the night of 4–5 April resting on the bottom. On the morning of 5 April, the weather was clear and he turned UB-26 toward Le Havre to make another attempt to enter the harbor. Smiths described the action:

> I was making an attack approach on a 4,000-ton steamer that was entering the harbor. Before I could reach an attack position four drifters and two torpedo boats came towards me in line abreast. I dove to sixty-five feet and remained there for about twenty minutes. I was rising slowly to periscope depth and extended the periscope as we passed forty-two feet. Suddenly the periscope struck the bottom of the boat, destroying the periscope. We immediately went back down to sixty-five feet.[2]

Ernst Look, in the engine room, stated that the U-boat had "fouled the net, but after maneuvering it seemed to us that we had gotten free." This would be the point at which Wylie had cast off the net. "We could hear the net sliding along the starboard side, the electric motors were running and the boat was gathering speed. All indications that we were free. But it was not so. The starboard motor abruptly stopped and a quick check showed that the starboard propeller was fouled in the net." Smiths reported:

> We went down to just above the seabed, about eighty or ninety feet, and the starboard propeller suddenly stopped. I looked through the conning tower port and could clearly see the net and that it had fouled the propeller. I laid the boat on the bottom, planning to wait for dark and then surface to clear away the net. What I did not know was that the attached buoys and carbide indicators gave away our exact position. Moments after we touched bottom there was a tremendous explosion aft. The blow knocked out all the lights, smashed the compass and short-circuited the batteries. A fire started in the battery compartment. In the engine room two oxygen bottles were torn from their mounts, the high pressure air lines broke and oil from the after starboard fuel tank spurted through a rupture in the pressure hull, drenching the starboard electric motor. All the auxiliary machinery failed.

Smiths and his crew reacted quickly. They extinguished the battery fire, got one battery back on line, and restored the lighting. But not for long. Moments later a second, much stronger explosion shook the boat and the lights went out again.

> A second explosion occurred on the port side, forward near the torpedo room hatch. The blow sprung the forward hatch, the torpedo doors and the port side battery hatch. All compressed air except that which remained in one tank was lost, the depth gauge was smashed and we were taking water through several openings. I tried to get the boat under way on the remaining motor, but the port propeller quickly became fouled and we were helpless. The boat was lost.

Smiths now ordered the tanks blown with what compressed air they had, and ordered the scuttling charges prepared. UB-26 barely made it to the surface, but it was enough and the crew quickly abandoned ship in a hail of gunfire from the drifters and torpedo boats. There were no casualties and UB-26 quickly went down.

U-8's destruction on 4 March 1915 and UB-26's loss were the only two confirmed instances in which an indicator-net contributed to a German U-boat's destruction during World War I. The only other U-boat lost was the Austrian U-6, which fouled a net in the Otranto Straits on 3 May 1916. There were dozens of claims about U-boats destroyed in the nets, however, and the most colorful was the alleged destruction of UB-3 on 24 April 1916.[3]

According to the official British account, the drifter *Gleaner of the Sea* was lying at anchor off Thornton Ridge with its nets out astern when a deckhand heard a curious grinding noise against the anchor wire. Looking over the side, he saw a U-boat fouled in the net's heavy wire hawser. The hand shouted for the skipper, R. G. Hurren, who rushed on deck. He seized a bomb lance and threw it on the fore deck of the U-boat, causing "a great explosion." The U-boat then sank bodily on the wire hawser, which parted under the strain. The bomb badly holed the U-boat and it sank to the bottom in about ten fathoms.

Captain Hurren fired a rocket and got under way, maneuvering to wrap the nets around the U-boat. He saw a large boil of water and, thinking the U-boat was about to surface, he cast off his net and turned to ram. Once over the spot where the boil was rising he saw nothing and threw another bomb lance. The drifter *E.E.S.* now arrived and dropped more bomb lances while *Gleaner of the Sea* hurried off to find a destroyer. A short time later *Gleaner of the Sea* returned with a destroyer that fired its sweep over the spot where the bubbles were rising.

While there is no doubt that the action took place, the fact is there was no U-boat and certainly no UB-3; it had disappeared in the Mediterranean in May 1915, nearly a year before Captain Hurren claimed to have sunk it. Nevertheless, the Admiralty paid Captain Hurren 389 pounds, awarded him the Distinguished Service Cross (DSC), and gave his crew 1,000 pounds to be divided among them.

The paucity of actual successes did not dampen the Royal Navy's enthusiasm for nets as an ASW device, but it did cause them to consider ways to improve the nets. The solution was to attach mines to the nets, thus creating the mine-net, which was also known as the EC (electro-contact) mine-net.

EC MINE-NETS

Credit for inventing the successful mine-net went to Admiral of the Fleet Sir A. K. Wilson. He suggested that electro-contact mines be attached to each net panel so that they would be brought in contact with the submarine's hull when the net folded around the boat. The Admiralty agreed with the concept and in February 1915 directed the Anti-Submarine Committee to develop a lightweight electro-contact mine as an antisubmarine measure.[4]

In April 1915 the British experimented with mines attached to drift nets. The initial experiments quickly showed that towing an explosive net was extremely dangerous for the drifters and their crews. As a result the Anti-Submarine Committee abandoned the idea of towing the nets; in their final form all EC mine-nets were moored nets.[5]

The Anti-Submarine Committee's electro-contact mines carried a 45-pound charge, which made them light enough to be attached to the net, but powerful enough to severely damage a U-boat. In the original design, the batteries for the mines were in a fixed position ashore, and the electrical cables were run along the net to each mine. That design did not work for a mine-net that was laid off an enemy-held shore, as in the case of the Belgian coast barrage. The solution the British used was to house the batteries in empty mine cases moored near the net line. This made it possible for maintenance crews to deactivate the net while they worked on it, and made the net safe to take aboard when necessary.

A drawback to the moored explosive nets was that they required constant attention. Technicians had to periodically visit the nets to service the batteries and test the electrical connections and insulation. This operation, carried out under fire and in a seaway, was extremely difficult.[6]

The moored mine-nets the British planted off the Belgian coast in 1916 were indicator-nets without indicators. The net panels and the breakaway clips were standard construction; the only difference was that two mines were attached to each panel instead of an indicator. When a U-boat struck the net, the clips broke away and the net was carried away with the U-boat, folding around the boat as it moved forward. The mines exploded when they contacted the hull. The direction in which a U-boat was traveling—with or against the tidal flow—played a role in diminishing or increasing the net's potential effectiveness.[7]

The net bulges or billows in the direction the tide is running, similar to a square sail before the wind. In this condition the steel clips are already under strain. A submarine that is moving with the tidal flow when it strikes the net will increase the strain on the clips, causing them to break away and the net will fold around the hull.

If, however, the U-boat is moving against the tidal flow, and strikes the net against the belly, it relieves the strain on the clips as the U-boat forces the net back against the tidal flow. As the U-boat proceeds forward, it pushes the net through the perpendicular and the clips again begin to take up the strain. The fine mesh of the net is pressed against the sharp bow of the U-boat so tightly that the strands will probably fail before the clips do, and the U-boat will tear through the net. In theory, a U-boat had a better chance of defeating a net if it was going against the current than if it was traveling with the current.[8]

The Auxiliary Patrol laid the first Belgian mine-net barrage off the Belgian coast from Ostend to the River Scheldt on the morning of 24 April 1916. The barrage, thirteen miles off the Belgian coast, consisted of a fifteen-mile-long double line of deep mines. Seaward of the mines were stretched thirteen miles of moored mine-nets marked with fourteen light buoys. Beyond the deep mines and the explosive nets, drifters shot their indicator-nets parallel to the West Hinder Shoal thirty miles from Ostend to catch U-boats returning to their base.[9]

Dutch neutrality prevented the British from completely sealing off the U-boats' access to the Hoofden and the Dover Straits. Nevertheless, even with a considerable gap at the northeast end of the barrage the British were satisfied that the U-boats' movements would be severely restricted. The British sanguinely expected the U-boats leaving Zeebrugge to run northeast as if making for the German Bight, and cross the mouth of the Schelde before reaching the end of the barrage. The British also believed that the barrage would force inbound U-boats to take the longer way around the end before proceeding to either Zeebrugge or Ostend.[10] Rear Admiral Bacon described the British viewpoint:

> This stretch of coast also contains two of the most troublesome submarine harbors from which mine-laying submarines and torpedo submarines issue to raid our trade routes on the East Coast and the English Channel. To close these harbors would necessitate an increase of 360 miles in their round trip to the English Channel, an increase not to be lightly regarded.[11]

The British were convinced that the new explosive net barrage produced immediate results, a misconception that persisted in postwar writing. For example, according to Gibson and Prendergast, "UB-10 fouled the nets, exploding several mines as she tried to free herself. After an eight-hour struggle she freed herself and entered her base."[12] In fact, there is no mention of this incident in UB-10's war diary.

What were the drifter crews dealing with in those situations? For the most part, the false contact reports were the result of heightened expectations that exaggerated normal occurrences. "The nets were frequently fouled by whales, thrasher sharks and other large fish, besides being struck by debris and drifting wreckage," which were responsible for detonated mines and false sinking reports.[13]

There is a possibility that UC-7 was lost in the net on 5 July 1916, but there is no proof of that. UC-7 left Zeebrugge on 3 July to lay mines off Elbow Buoy, and the Germans believe that UB-12 spotted it homeward bound on 5 July. It never reached Zeebrugge. On 22 July the body of one of the officers, Oberleutnant zur see Fischer, washed up on a Dutch beach, and two days later the Dutch recovered the captain's body near the same beach. The Dutch found more of the crew a few days later. Other than the fact that the bodies were found near the northeast end of the barrier there is no firm evidence that UC-7 was destroyed in the minenet, but the probability is strong.

What the British did not know was that, the day after they had laid it, the Germans discovered the net barrage. UC-5 was a hard-luck minelayer that was supposed to be laying twelve mines off Shipwash Sands. On 24 April, it had passed through the British vessels that were in the process of planting the mines and laying the net without either side knowing of the other's presence. UC-5 was close to its operations area when it encountered numerous destroyers, whose numbers kept growing. Convinced that the surface patrols were too strong, Oberleutnant zur See Mohrbutter turned around and returned to Zeebrugge, again passing through the British net layers undetected.

The next morning, 25 April, the UC-5 made another attempt to reach its operations area. Just off Zeebrugge British torpedo boats forced the U-boat to dive and remain under for four hours. At 1400 Mohrbutter came up to periscope depth, took a look around, and decided it was safe to surface. UC-5 came up right alongside the lighted buoys that marked the net line. What Mohrbutter saw was a line of buoys supporting a heavy hawser and what was obviously a net. He also saw the mine cases that the British were using to house the batteries for the electro-contact mines. Mohrbutter, however, assumed they were active mines.

He had explosive charges brought up, and his crew attempted to blow a hole in the net. They worked for fifteen minutes until a lookout spotted a British airplane and UC-5 dove. At 1430 Mohrbutter surfaced again, and proceeded along the net looking for an opening. Unable to find one, he turned back toward Zeebrugge at 1600. An hour later he was tied up to the dock and was making his report.[14]

Despite their optimism, there were realities that the British could not ignore. Most important, they were able to maintain only daylight patrols along the net line, which allowed the Germans ample opportunities to sweep up the mines and cut gates in the nets. German tugs attacked the Belgian coast barrage at night with grapples, tore holes in it, and sank the battery cases with rifle fire.

The British abandoned the line completely during the winter of 1916–17, but laid it again on 25–27 July 1917. By then the Germans had learned from the previous year's experiences and one of their first acts in 1917 was to sink the new battery cases. This forced the British to sink the battery cases to the bottom, an effective but inconvenient procedure.[15]

The most ambitious mine-net project was the laying of a continuous net line from Goodwin Sands to Dunkirk, which the British accomplished in September and October 1916. They used the same type of nets for this project as they had used off the Belgian coast, and therein lay a problem. Nets that were forty and sixty feet deep worked well in the relatively shallow waters off the Belgian coast, but in the stretch from Goodwin Sands to Dunkirk, the British needed nets that hung down to 120 feet. Experience showed that the strong tidal currents placed enormous strain on the steel clips that fastened the net panels together and held the linked sections to the buoyed head wire. Eighty-foot nets were tried, but those too were quickly carried away. The British found that 60-foot deep nets could be used in some sections of the barrier, but 40-foot deep nets were all that could be used in other sections. The result was a partial barrier that varied in depth all along its length.[16]

Admiral Bacon tried to close the gap between the net's irregular foot and the seabed with a row of mines laid a half-mile west of the net line. The mines were planted deeply enough that they rode below the depth of the net's deepest panel. The British mines, however, still suffered from weak anchors, and the strong currents dragged the mines into the nets. It was extremely dangerous for maintenance crews to work on the nets, and the British were forced to sweep up all the mines. No new mines were laid on either side of the barrier, which meant that a large gap existed between the bottom of the net and the ocean floor. The U-boats regularly used this gap to safely pass the barrier.

The Goodwin Sands to Dunkirk mine-net barrage was approximately twenty-eight nautical miles long, easily seen and very difficult to maintain. The line was easily seen because the nets were suspended from a steel jackstay that was lighted along its length at three-mile intervals. According to Admiral Bacon, the lighted buoys were needed to protect British patrols from blundering into the barrier. Regarding the fact that the Germans could see the net line as easily as could the British patrols, Admiral Bacon said, "It mattered not if enemy submarines did see the lights, provided that they dived into the nets. If the submarines passed on the surface, then an accurate knowledge of the position of the barrage was of little value to them, but the immunity of our own vessels patrolling every night was of the greatest importance to us."[17]

Maintaining the net required "incessant" work to replace sections torn away by the wind and tide, waterlogged buoys, and chafed moorings. The clips parted, the electric mine circuits shorted, and the battery boxes leaked. The Germans raided the barrier on two occasions: 27 October 1916 and 20–21 April 1917. Replacing damaged or missing sections was a daily task, and the barrier was never efficient throughout its length. There were always holes in the barrier.

The mine-net barrier was supposed to be a sort of explosive wall across the Dover Straits, but in fact it was a sieve. The U-boats passed through the gaps or crossed the barrier on the surface without difficulty. Despite its shortcomings, the British continued to place faith in the mine-net system. Theoretically the explosive net was unquestionably superior to the indicator-net, but practical experience showed that its performance was equally poor.

11

The End of German Indecision

Following the halt of the first anti-shipping campaign in September 1915, the Germans held their North Sea boats in their bases or deployed them as picket boats to protect the Helgoland Bight against an enemy surprise attack. In addition, they occasionally sent U-boats to the Scottish east coast, the Orkneys, and the Shetlands to hunt units of the Grand Fleet. Similar patrols were conducted in the Skagerrak. Eleven war patrols were carried out during the four winter months, but the U-boats rarely sighted units of the Grand Fleet. U-boats had only two opportunities to fire torpedoes at the enemy—20 December 1915 and 24 January 1916—and they missed both times.[1]

The battle between the navy and the civilian government over whether the U-boats should operate under the Prize Regulations or carry out unrestricted submarine warfare went on. The navy was anxious to reopen the unrestricted campaign and they found an opening on 3 November 1915 when U-38 sank the SS *Woodfield* after a protracted gun battle. The German boarding party discovered that the *Woodfield*'s gun crews were Royal Navy personnel, and the Germans also found secret Admiralty orders issued to all captains of armed British merchant ships, directing them to engage any U-boat on sight. In effect, the British ordered their merchant ships to behave like warships.[2] Proof that Royal Navy gunners were serving aboard armed British merchant ships was powerful ammunition for the navy lobby's position that the U-boats should torpedo without warning. More powerful forces, however, were developing that would finally end German indecision.

When Adm. Hennig von Holtzendorff issued the order on 18 September 1915 ending the first unrestricted anti-shipping campaign he did so with a clear conscience; he did not believe that there were enough U-boats to carry out a war-winning anti-shipping campaign.[3] Two developments caused him to change his mind. First, an economic analysis concluded that if the U-boats could sink 600,000 tons per month, the British would be economically ruined in eight months.[4] Second, Bulgaria entered the war on 14 October 1915 and the German/Austrian offensive against Serbia appeared successful. In Admiral von Holtzendorff's opinion, the new military-political situation warranted a reopening of the U-boat war, and General von Falkenhayn shared that opinion.[5]

By the winter of 1915–16, it was obvious that the German army lacked the military resources to win the war; both the civilian government and the military agreed that a negotiated settlement was the only practical option. But how could the Germans create the conditions under which a satisfactory negotiated peace could be achieved?

Von Bethmann-Hollweg believed the answer lay with the United States. President Wilson had been sending out peace feelers since January 1915 and did so again in January 1916. Von Bethmann-Hollweg wanted to side with the United States on the issue of "freedom of the sea," which he believed might force Britain to lift its hunger blockade. What von Bethmann-Hollweg wanted to avoid at all costs was a war with the United States, which would inevitably follow the reopening of an unrestricted U-boat campaign.[6]

At a war council held in Berlin on 30 December 1915, the two sides argued their opposing views on how to end the war in the most favorable way. Civilians presented sound arguments opposing the return to unrestricted submarine warfare. Rather than seriously threatening the British economy, unrestricted U-boat warfare put Germany on a collision course with the United States. The American public found unrestricted U-boat warfare repugnant. They pointed out that while the United States was the world's leading advocate of freedom of the seas, and the British distant blockade violated those principles, the cash value of U.S. exports to

Britain was so great that it muted the American protests against British practices. The important difference between the British blockade and unrestricted U-boat warfare was as obvious as day and night. Despite the aggravations caused by the British blockade, American citizens were in no danger of being killed by British policies. Unrestricted U-boat warfare, on the other hand, could only lead to American loss of life and the total destruction of American property.[7]

Grossadmiral von Tirpitz summed up the position taken by the unrestricted submarine war advocates. He said that the U-boats had the ability of doing so much damage to the British economy that Great Britain would have to give up. Because there was a political and financial interest in an Entente Powers victory and a Central Powers defeat, the United States was already an active enemy. He concluded his remarks, "If we have the will to defeat England, we must expect American intervention. But if we defeat England, then it won't matter what the Americans do."[8]

General von Falkenhayn agreed with von Tirpitz. He believed that 1916 would be the year of decision and now was an opportune time to reopen the U-boat war. He was no longer convinced that Germany had to avoid war with the United States at all costs because the favorable situation in the Balkans had changed that. The United States was already an active enemy as demonstrated by its open aid to the Entente Powers, so there was no measurable difference between America remaining neutral or entering the war.[9]

The admirals also noted that trying to get Britain to lift the blockade through diplomatic efforts was futile. Britain would never trade control of the sea for international freedom of the sea. The admirals argued that, in the absence of a decisive military victory, the way to force Britain to the negotiating table was by seriously hurting its economy. Once at the negotiations table, Germany could achieve its goals only if it held the upper hand; the way to that happy situation was through the application of unrestricted submarine warfare.

General von Falkenhayn's plan was to launch a limited offensive against the French at Verdun, because he knew the French would fight tenaciously to hold even though Verdun's loss would not be militarily significant. The general's goal was to bleed the French army white at Verdun, thus "sending Britain's finest blade spinning from its hand."[10] If the British got involved in the defense of Verdun, so much the better; von Falkenhayn would then have the opportunity of inflicting heavy casualties on the

British too. Von Falkenhayn wanted the U-boats committed to an unrestricted campaign while the Verdun offensive was in progress. If the U-boats could cause substantial damage to the British economy while he was grinding down the French, the dual setbacks would set the stage for an advantageous negotiated peace.

Von Falkenhayn put the question to von Holtzendorff: In the event that a renewed U-boat war caused the United States to enter the war against Germany, did the navy have the resources to defeat Britain before America's industrial strength could make a difference? The admiral answered that a U-boat war that was started immediately and sharply prosecuted would have a devastating economic effect on England. He asserted that England would be unable to carry on the war by the end of 1916. He optimistically cut two months off the Admiralstab's economic expert's figure and stated that Britain would be broken in six months at the longest.[11] The debate ended without a decision.

The advocates of an unrestricted submarine war campaign gained a powerful ally on 8 January 1916 when Admiral Reinhard von Scheer replaced Vizeadmiral von Pohl as commander of the High Sea Fleet. Von Scheer, much more aggressive than von Pohl, was a hard-line supporter of unrestricted U-boat warfare. On that same date the opponents also received a sign of support. The United States sent a note to the Germans acknowledging the legality of submarine warfare under the Prize Regulations and suggested that armed merchant ships could be treated as warships and torpedoed without warning. The civilians interpreted this note to mean that the United States was pressuring Britain to ease the hunger blockade.

The continued indecision was illustrated on 11 February 1916 when the kaiser issued orders to reopen an anti-shipping war. The orders fell far short of authorizing an unrestricted campaign, and as such they were too broad to suit von Bethmann-Hollweg and too restrictive to suit the admirals. But at least the new anti-shipping campaign would be carried out in conjunction with General Falkenhayn's Verdun offensive, which opened on 21 February 1916. The orders were to go into effect on 29 February 1916, which allowed enough time for the government to make the decision public and notify all the neutrals.[12]

Von Bethmann-Hollweg had warned the admirals that an anti-shipping campaign that went beyond the limits of the Prize Regulations would cause a confrontation with neutral countries. And he was right. On

24 March 1916 Oberleutnant zur See Pustkuchen in UB-29 torpedoed the French channel steamer SS *Sussex*, killing and injuring approximately eighty passengers, which included several Americans. The logbook recorded the action, as seen through the periscope.

1540: A ship with two tall masts in view.

1541: Dove. The vessel appears to be a channel steamer, but has only one stack and a stern characteristic of a warship. Because it was steaming outside the Admiralty designated shipping channel it was not believed to be a passenger ship. The shape of the stern caused me to believe she was a minelayer. The steamer flew no flag and was painted entirely black.

1555: Fired torpedo. After sixty-nine seconds a strong explosion at 1,300 yards. The entire forward section back to the bridge torn apart and broken. The deck is filled with people. The steamer is a troop transport. The sinking was not observed. Left the area submerged.[13]

The *Sussex* incident caused President Wilson to warn Germany, in the strongest language, that the United States would sever diplomatic relations with Germany if there was a resumption of unrestricted U-boat warfare. In other words, do it again, and the United States will go to war.

Until Pustkuchen torpedoed the *Sussex* without warning 75 percent of the sinkings had been accomplished under the Prize Regulations, but the *Sussex* incident completely overshadowed that fact. On 24 April von Holtzendorff ordered the boats to return to the Prize Regulations; on 25 April von Scheer recalled his boats and ended the campaign. Korvettenkapitän Bartenbach did the same with the Flanders boats, leaving only the Flanders UC boats and the Mediterranean boats unaffected by the order.[14]

The U-boats of the High Sea Fleet and the Flanders command spent the next five months assigned to military operations that included the Battle of Jutland on 31 May 1916. The outcome of the Battle of Jutland, however, left the German navy with no offensive weapon other than the U-boats. How would Germany use its only weapon? There were three options: operate under the Prize Regulations, launch a partially restricted campaign, or take the leap and open a wholly unrestricted campaign. Admiral von Scheer felt there was only one option. He rejected anything but an unrestricted campaign and opted for the all or nothing approach.[15]

The failure of General von Falkenhayn's Verdun offensive, which was attended by astronomical German casualties, and the staggering German losses that accompanied the British Somme offensive in July and August caused the kaiser to sack the general. On 30 August 1916 Gen. Paul von Hindenburg und Benckendorff replaced von Falkenhayn as chief of staff and the last piece fell into place that would end the Germans' indecision about unrestricted submarine warfare.

General von Hindenburg was probably the most popular man in Germany; he was the man in whom the people placed their greatest faith, confidence, and trust. Von Hindenburg was a power that no civilian government could cross and still hope to remain in power. From the moment he assumed his duties, von Hindenburg adopted the position that the decision to reopen an unrestricted submarine campaign was his alone.

On 31 August 1916, the day after he took command, von Hindenburg held a major war conference at Pless during which both sides repeated the arguments they had made eight months earlier. No decision was reached, but von Hindenburg told the group that he favored an unrestricted submarine campaign. He did not think that the moment was right. Then he dropped his bomb: The decision was not in the hands of the navy or the civilian government and he would announce the time for the campaign to start. He directed that a Prize Regulations campaign would be a useful interim measure.

Shortly after the Pless conference, von Bethmann-Hollweg secured the kaiser's tacit agreement that there would be no unrestricted campaign until the diplomatic efforts had been fully explored. The chancellor then directed Johann Heinrich von Bernstorff, the ambassador to the United States, to recontact the U.S. government, with the view of forging ahead with the Americans' plan to mediate a negotiated peace. Von Bethmann-Hollweg's instructions arrived too late for the Americans to take any action before the winter because President Wilson was too busy campaigning for reelection.

On 6 October 1916 Admiral von Holtzendorff launched a new anti-shipping campaign under the Prize Regulations and on 18 October von Hindenburg held another war conference at Pless. Again, the main topic was the navy's demand for a resumption of unrestricted submarine warfare. Although the war situation looked better, von Hindenburg put the decision on hold until von Bethmann-Hollweg had played out his peace plan. This meeting confirmed that the decision for or against an unrestricted submarine campaign was up to von Hindenburg. Two days later the kaiser ordered von Bethmann-Hollweg to propose a peace offer to the

Entente Powers. The offer was unrealistic and its announcement in the Reichstag on 12 December 1916 was badly stated. The result was that the Entente Powers rejected the German offer out of hand.

On 20 December 1916 Gen. Erich Ludendorff notified von Bethmann-Hollweg that von Hindenburg saw no possibility for a diplomatic solution, and the way was open to resume unrestricted submarine warfare. On 9 January 1917 the Germans made the decision to resume unrestricted submarine warfare with the goal of ending the war by the autumn of 1917. The goal was based on the assumption that an unrestricted anti-shipping campaign would result in twice as much enemy tonnage being sunk as was accomplished under the Prize Regulations. Much of the calculation was based on the poor 1916–17 wheat harvest worldwide, and the Germans wanted to open their new campaign by February 1917 in order to make its effects felt before the grain shortages could be made good by the 1917–18 harvest.[16]

The die was cast. The Germans had staked everything on their U-boats. The decision was announced to the world on 31 January 1917. On 3 February the United States severed diplomatic relations with Germany, and on 6 April Congress voted to declare war. The period of German indecision was over.

PART FOUR

British Response to Unrestricted Submarine Warfare

February 1917–November 1918

12

Ramming, Nets, and Decoys

When the Germans opened their unrestricted anti-shipping campaign in 1917 the British were only partially prepared. The backbone of the British, and by extension the French, ASW was still ramming, gunfire, and nets. Depth charges were still limited to two or four per vessel and the Admiralty was just starting to issue the high-speed submarine sweep to destroyers and P-boats. The British continued to increase the number of armed merchant ships and expanded their decoy program. The emphasis on armed merchant ships and decoys is indicative of Britain's lagging technological progress in the antisubmarine war up to 1917.

More advanced devices, such as the hydrophone, were in very limited use and were still being developed. The antisubmarine howitzer and the bomb thrower were still on the drawing boards. British mines were still inefficient and the superior H2 mine would not appear until the end of 1917. The Admiralty was discussing hunter-killer groups and convoys but those measures were still in the discussion stage when the Germans launched their anti-shipping campaign.

The intensity of the German anti-shipping campaign forced the British to speed up their ASW development programs and to look at existing resources in a broader sense. An immediate result was that the British assigned their submarines to an antisubmarine role and for a brief time returned to the practice of pairing a submarine with a decoy. At the same time the British and the French increased their use of heavier than air and lighter than air aircraft for antisubmarine patrols. The first convoy systems were inaugurated in the cross-channel coal trade and in the North Sea.

The 1917–18 anti-shipping campaign spurred technological and organizational innovations to fruition. They are discussed in the approximate order in which they became fully effective or when their use became widespread, although some development histories began before the war.

RAMMING

Ramming as a countermeasure continued in use until the end of the war. It was always a spur of the moment decision. In the case of warships and patrol vessels, ramming was used when the distance was so short that it was faster for the attacker to ram than to shoot. Merchant ships rammed for much the same reason. In either case, ramming was the most expedient way to deal with the situation. The fact that surface vessels were able to ram U-boats is an indication of the volume of surface traffic in the U-boats' operation areas and of the close quarters in which the antagonists operated.

There were forty-two ramming instances from 1 February 1917 to 11 November 1918. In twenty-two instances, ramming played a significant role in a U-boat's destruction. In some cases, the surface vessel was able to ram a surfaced U-boat because the U-boat's lookouts were careless and failed to spot the danger in time. In other instances some mechanical or technical malfunction prevented the already submerged U-boat from getting deep enough to avoid the blow. There were also cases in which neither side was even aware the other was there. In every case, luck—or the lack of it—played a role in the event and its outcome. Careless lookouts probably were the cause of UC-26's loss.

Commanded by Kapitänleutnant Graf von Schmettow, UC-26 was eight nautical miles northwest of Calais on the night of 8–9 May 1917 when the lookouts on HMS *Milne* saw a surfaced U-boat literally just yards away. Comdr. Victor Campbell, the *Milne*'s captain, told a reporter:

> The submarine was so close that we rammed her almost immediately, our stem striking her at the forward part of the conning tower. She sank

immediately, but to be sure, we dropped some depth charges. We remained in the area, but the depth there, twenty-five fathoms, made any thought of survivors highly unlikely. Imagine our surprise when fifteen minutes later we heard cries for help and found two swimmers in the wreck site.[1]

Leutnant zur See Petersen, who was one of the two swimmers, furnished more detail.

We were returning to Zeebrugge after using all our mines and torpedoes. It was about 0100 on 9 May when three destroyers were suddenly upon us, and before we could dive a destroyer rammed us. The UC-26 sank very quickly and landed heavily on the bottom. Moments later a depth charge exploded very close and the lights went out. There was no panic in the boat.

The men who were trapped in the mid-section tried to blow the tanks without success. The water was rising steadily and the batteries were flooded. Some of the men took refuge in the conning tower and the rest of us retreated to the engine room. We tried to open the engine room hatch, but the water pressure was too great.

It looked like we were in for a lingering death, and Captain von Schmettow told us to prepare to die for our Kaiser, and led us in three cheers. At that point, a boatswain's mate suggested we release high-pressure air from the torpedo system into the compartment to raise the inner air pressure so that we could open the hatch. This was done and shortly the water stopped rising in the engine room.

Finally the hatch was opened, but those who were standing near it were all killed when they were blown through the opening. Then things seemed to equalize, and I was able to go through the hatch without difficulty. It took a long time to reach the surface, but I had no problems with air expanding in my lungs.[2]

Accusing the lookouts of being careless sounds harsh, but war is a harsh environment that requires constant vigilance if you want to survive. The lookouts on UC-26 should have spotted the *Milne*. Two other losses may have been the result of inattentive lookouts, men who were either preoccupied with something else or very tired.

Aggressive victims were another source of trouble for the U-boats. Merchant Marine captains who had successfully maneuvered to avoid a torpedo often ran down the torpedo's track in an attempt to ram the

U-boat. Even if they failed to make contact, they drove the boat down deep enough that the freighter could make its escape.

An example of a freighter attacking a U-boat occurred off Eddystone on 9 March 1917 when the 5,234-ton *East Point* rammed U-48. Kapitän-leutnant Buss torpedoed the *East Point* and then went down to sixty feet to start an approach on another target. Unknown to Buss, the *East Point* was not sinking; it was still under way.

As U-48 came back to periscope depth, *East Point* rammed it squarely in the conning tower. The conning tower hatch popped open and water poured in. The torpedo officer and a seaman dropped down into the command central, but the captain and the navigator, Adolf Bergmann, had been knocked unconscious by the blow. They drowned in the conning tower when the men in the command central closed the lower hatch to save the boat.[3]

Most ramming incidents occurred while a U-boat was submerged, with its presence disclosed either by its periscope or by the torpedo's wake. Oberleutnant zur See von Keyserlingk in UB-36 made a submerged torpedo attack on a French coal convoy off Lands End on 21 May 1917. The first torpedo sank the 2,062-ton SS *Ferdinand.* Forty minutes later von Keyserlingk was getting ready to fire a torpedo at the SS *Moliere* when one of its lookouts spotted the periscope and the steamer turned to ram. The torpedo wake passed down the *Moliere*'s port side and sped off into the darkness. The *Moliere*'s bow caught the submerged U-boat squarely and as the ship passed over the wreck, the water on both sides of the hull boiled with escaped air from the doomed U-boat. When the *Moliere* reached port it went into dry dock; it had suffered extensive damage to the bow.[4]

Escorts were even more dangerous than the freighters, because they were fast and had better trained lookouts. As pointed out earlier, escorts rammed when they were too close to shoot and that is what P-56, one of the escorts for a seven-ship convoy passing out of the Irish Sea, did on 12 December 1917. P-56's lookout spotted a periscope 150 yards away. The escort turned, crossed the U-boat's path, and dropped two depth charges ten feet from the periscope. The dual explosions blew the U-boat to the surface; P-56 came about and rammed U-87 at twenty knots just aft of the conning tower. The blow cut the U-boat in half, the stern section sinking immediately and the forward section remaining afloat for a few seconds. The crew of P-56 could see clearly into the forward section before it went down. There were no survivors.[5]

Some of the reported ramming incidents were actually accidental collisions; they were no less terrifying. An unidentified steamer rammed UB-34 on 13 March 1918 as the U-boat was rising from one hundred feet to periscope depth. The collision destroyed both periscopes and forced UB-34 to return to Helgoland. Two accidental collisions occurred underwater. UC-62 collided with E-50 on 19 April 1917 while both boats were submerged at periscope depth, and UC-64 had the same experience with an unidentified British submarine on 8 July 1917. In both instances none of the boats was seriously damaged.[6]

Our final example deals with a situation in which one countermeasure set up conditions that were compounded by a mechanical failure and brought about the destruction of a U-boat. On 23 September 1917, UC-33 fouled a net while submerged at sixty-five feet off Waterford. Oberleutnant zur See Alfred Arnold tore through the net by flooding and then surfaced to discover that the starboard propeller was fouled. The crew was able to clear away the net from the boat but was unable to free the propeller. Despite the loss of one propeller, Arnold continued his patrol instead of limping back to Zeebrugge.

On the morning of 26 September 1917, UC-33 torpedoed the 6,430-ton SS *San Zeferino* and then surfaced to finish the job with gunfire. P-61, which was the steamer's escort, charged at the surfaced U-boat at twenty knots to ram. UC-33 tried to dive, but at that critical moment its remaining electric motor suffered a coupling failure. The U-boat was trimmed down and stopped when P-61 rammed it just behind the conning tower. Arnold's account detailed what happened.

I could see the destroyer clearly through the conning tower port, coming down on us very quickly. Then a crash and the boat rolled hard over on her side. Water poured in at a tremendous rate, instantly flooding the engine room and command central. The electrical circuits shorted, the batteries exploded and the lights went out. The boat was sinking at a terrifying speed and at a very steep angle. The depth gauge had shown twenty meters when the lights went out and I knew the bottom here was 200 meters. Water was rising quickly in the conning tower, and the navigator and I had to grope in the dark to find the hatch release handle. He found it but the hatch would not open because the water pressure was too great. No man thinks more quickly or more clearly than he does under these conditions. I knew we had to open the hatch and I felt around until I found the compressed air valve and I opened it. The inside pressure quickly rose and the hatch popped open. We must have been at forty meters when we went out because the rise to the surface seemed very long.[7]

Arnold and the navigator were in the water for over a half an hour before P-61 found them and threw life rings to the swimmers. Arnold had enough strength left to swim, but the navigator was exhausted and sank.

NETS

The British were still deploying nets, but their use was declining. EC mine-nets remained in service until the end of the war. The big EC net that ran from the Goodwin Sands to Dunkirk was allowed to fall into disrepair. There were fifteen net strikes during this period, but the nets were more a nuisance to the U-boats than a real danger. Probably the closest call a U-boat had with a net occurred on 29 June 1917 when UC-6 fouled an explosive net.

Oberleutnant zur See Werner Löwe in UC-6 was headed home on the surface when he fouled a net in the dark off the British East Coast. UC-6 was so tangled in the net that it was dead in the water while the crew cut it away with bolt cutters and chisels. Free of the net, it again got under way. At dawn lookouts realized that UC-6 was towing one hundred yards of net festooned with class buoys and EC mines. Löwe brought UC-6 to a stop and set his crew to ridding the boat of its explosive tail. Once again the job was completed and UC-6 got under way. After they docked in Bruges, the crew found an EC mine they had missed; it was attached to a chunk of net that was wrapped around a propeller guard.[8]

DECOYS (Q-SHIPS)

The convoy system that the British initiated in 1917 actually put the decoy vessels out of a job because the U-boat captains quickly became suspicious of any ship steaming alone. The Admiralty, however, was slow to recognize that the decoys' usefulness was passed and as a result 1917 saw more decoy vessels deployed than at any other time during the war. U-boats reported eleven encounters with decoys during the thirteen-month period 4 August 1914 to 31 September 1915; twenty-one encounters during the sixteen-month period 1 October 1915 to 31 January 1917; and eighty-six encounters during the eleven-month period 1 February to 31 December 1917. In 1918 the number of encounters fell to fourteen.[9]

As early as September 1917 the utility of the Q-ships was on the wane. Nevertheless, the Admiralty increased their numbers and assigned several decoys to convoy escort duty. Some even carried cargo because that function had become more important than acting in the decoy role. Decoys adapted their role in the convoy system by playing the lame duck, falling back from a convoy to become a straggler. This attracted U-boats, but by the time the U-boats were torpedoing their targets without warning, the decoys had served their purpose and became just another loss statistic.[10]

The French and the Italians also used decoys. French decoys were called *Patrouilleur Spécial,* and they operated similar to British decoys. According to contact reports found in U-boats' war diaries, the French were less likely to use the panic party ruse than were the British, and the Italians hardly used the ploy at all. The French operated decoys in both European waters and in the Mediterranean, but the Italians deployed their decoys exclusively in the Mediterranean. Neither the French nor the Italian decoys sank a U-boat.

After they entered the war the United States tried to deploy two decoys, both former Special Service Vessels, but neither saw action. The first was the SS *Pargust,* which the Admiralty turned over to the Americans in October 1917. The ship was under repair in dry dock when the Americans took it over and remained there until May 1918, by which time it was no longer needed. The second was the SS *Arvonian,* which became the USS *Santee* on 26 November 1917, under the command of Comdr. D. C. Hanrahan. Heavily armed with three 4-inch guns, three 12-pounders, and four 18-inch torpedoes, *Santee* departed Queenstown on a training cruise on 27 December 1917. Five hours later a U-boat torpedoed it. The tug *Paladin* towed it back to Queenstown. On 4 June 1918 the *Santee* was recommissioned in the Royal Navy as the SS *Bendish.* By then the large decoys' usefulness had passed and it saw no more war service.[11]

The heyday of the decoy operation was during 1915 and 1916 when the U-boats were making most of their attacks according to the Prize Regulations. Out of thirty-two encounters that took place during that period the decoys sank nine U-boats against two losses of their own. But the scales tipped heavily against the decoys after the U-boats started torpedoing without warning.

During the last quarter of 1917 the percentage of torpedo attacks rose to 88 percent and Prize Regulations sinkings dropped to 12 percent.

Despite the increase in ships sunk without warning, there were eighty-six encounters between decoys and U-boats during 1917 and 1918. In fifty-six instances the U-boat attacked the decoy on the surface with gunfire. In those fifty-six instances, the decoys sank two U-boats and the U-boats sank four decoys; fifty encounters ended in a draw with the U-boat diving to break off the engagement. In every case, the U-boat captain had assumed the lone vessel was simply a freighter that did not warrant a torpedo.[12]

The U-boats attacked thirty decoys with torpedoes, sometimes recognizing the vessel was a decoy and other times thinking it was a freighter. In seven of those instances the U-boat surfaced after firing the torpedo and engaged the decoy with gunfire. The decoys sank three of these U-boats and damaged another so badly that it fell easy prey to British patrols while en route to Germany. In three cases the U-boat broke off the engagement as soon as the decoy revealed its real identity. The U-boats sank thirteen decoys without ever showing more than a periscope and damaged five others. Some typical encounters are discussed to examine what went right and what went wrong.

Surface gunfire attacks continued until the end of the war because the U-boats carried more ammunition for their deck guns than they did torpedoes. Depending on the size of the U-boat the number of torpedoes aboard ranged from two in the UB-9 class to nineteen in the U-140 class. To do maximum damage during a patrol, a U-boat captain had to use his deck gun whenever possible. In practice he did that only when confronted by a lone target, and even then he was taking a big risk.

The safest policy for a U-boat captain would have been to simply torpedo any ship seen and not bother using the deck gun. The limited number of torpedoes aboard, however, meant that not all targets warranted a torpedo, especially when the target was a small steamer or a sailing vessel. A similar situation existed when a U-boat captain had torpedoed a lone steamer, but the ship was either not sinking or was sinking slowly. Should he fire a second torpedo or surface and finish the job with gunfire? It was in those situations that the decoy and U-boat encounters took place.

Experiences with decoys had made the Germans increasingly suspicious of any ship that was sailing alone. Before moving in close to identify a lone ship most U-boat captains opened fire at fairly long range and continued firing at long range until the target was obviously sinking. Such was the case on the evening of 20 June 1917 when Oberleutnant zur See

Werner Fürbringer in UC-17 opened fire on a British schooner southwest of Ouessant.

Suspicious, Fürbringer opened fire at five thousand yards, but was unable to observe any hits because of the fading light. The schooner was the decoy *Mitchell* and its lookouts had been watching the U-boat for some time before it opened fire. When the first six rounds fell wide, Lt. John Lawrie hove to and put out his panic party.

Fürbringer then dove, passed within fifty yards of the *Mitchell*'s port side, and examined the schooner closely through the periscope. At that moment the conning tower broached and *Mitchell*'s gunners opened fire. Fully alerted to the schooner's true identity, Fürbringer maneuvered to fire a torpedo that missed, and the *Mitchell* used its auxiliary engine to clear the area.[13]

Fürbringer had done it right, whereas *Mitchell*'s gunners did it wrong. Had the gunners held their fire, UC-17 would have surfaced to finish the job and would have been well within the killing range of the decoy's guns. Next is an example in which the decoy's gunner did it right.

On 17 February 1917 the decoy *Farnborough* was under way at seven knots off southern Ireland when a torpedo blew a huge hole in the side. Capt. Gordon Campbell sent his gun crews to their stations and sent away three boats to make it appear his ship had been abandoned. In fact, the decoy was sinking.

One thousand yards away, Kapitänleutnant Bruno Hoppe was examining the *Farnborough* through his periscope. He saw a Norwegian ship that was badly damaged and sinking slowly. He saw no sign of any armament. Satisfied that he had just torpedoed a neutral steamer, Hope maneuvered U-83 within four hundred yards of the decoy and surfaced off the port bow to finish the job with gunfire. Hoppe brought U-83 abeam the freighter and stopped, apparently to give the gunners the best conditions to sink the ship with gunfire.

While the decoy and the U-boat lay dead in the water, the *Farnborough* opened a devastatingly effective fire at point-blank range. The *Farnborough*'s gunners concentrated their fire on the conning tower and then spread it along the hull, firing forty rounds in less than three minutes. U-83 sank like a rock, leaving only two survivors in the water, one who lived and was taken to England as a POW. The tug *Flying Sportsman* towed the *Farnborough* into Mill Cove and beached it.[14]

The U-83 case illustrates the danger U-boats faced when they came close to single vessels, even sinking vessels. Kapitänleutnant Hoppe had closely examined the *Farnborough* and its disguise fooled him, so it is impossible to say that what he did was wrong. What the *Farnborough*'s gun crews did was right, and illustrates the iron discipline that existed aboard many of the British decoys. In this case, both sides operated by the book and the U-boat was unlucky. The next case, an example of either carelessness or overconfidence, is one of the most interesting encounters of the war. It happened on 30 April 1917.

The two-hundred-ton, three-masted, topsail schooner *Prize* was a recently commissioned decoy vessel under the command of an experienced officer, Lieutenant W. E. Sanders, RNR, who had formerly been in the decoy *Helgoland*. The *Prize* was a steel hull vessel armed with two 12-pounders, one concealed forward in a collapsible deckhouse and the other on a disappearing mount in the after hold.

Commanded by Kapitänleutnant Adolf Freiherr von Spiegel, U-93 had been out since 22 April. During the past eight days, von Spiegel had sunk ten vessels, four of them according to the Prize Regulations, and had taken three prisoners aboard U-93. Typically, on two occasions he torpedoed his victims and then surfaced to finish them off with gunfire. Significantly, included in his bag were three small sailing vessels about the same size as the *Prize*.[15]

On 30 April the weather was fine, visibility almost unlimited, the wind light, and the sea calm. The *Prize* was on a broad reach with the wind across the starboard quarter, under all sail, and making only about two knots. To avoid giving away its true purpose, the *Prize* rarely used its auxiliary engine during the day. At dusk the men aboard the *Prize* saw a large U-boat running parallel to their course two miles away on the port beam. Lieutenant Sanders sent his gunners to their stations, and the panic party, the only men visible on deck, prepared to play their role.

Kapitänleutnant von Spiegel examined the *Prize* through his binoculars and saw nothing suspicious about the slow-moving schooner. Following standard procedure for 1917 he approached the *Prize* from astern and fired the routine warning shot when the schooner was still four thousand yards away. The schooner ignored the warning, so von Spiegel ordered his forward gun to fire directly at the schooner while he overtook it. Despite that fact that the *Prize* flew no national flag and was therefore probably British, he decided it was safe to approach. U-93 was 150 yards off the schooner's port quarter when the U-boat's forward gun scored a hit on the schooner's waterline, causing the *Prize* to round up and present its starboard side to the U-boat. U-93 was firing into the schooner with both deck guns as the six-man panic party rowed away.

Aboard the *Prize* the gunners hugged the deck while the U-boat pumped round after round into the hull, doing serious damage. Essentially unmanned, the *Prize* fell off, presenting its stern to the U-boat. The U-boat turned to come up along the port side as the schooner's head continued to fall off so that U-93 was once again on the *Prize*'s port quarter. U-93's gunners put another round in the schooner's waterline just as Sanders gave his gunners the order to fire.[16]

The *Prize*'s fire was accurate and effective, quickly knocking out both U-93's deck guns and scoring hits on the conning tower. The explosions killed the gun crews and blew von Spiegel and his helmsman overboard. The surviving senior officer, Oberleutnant zur See Wilhelm Ziegner, described what happened next.

> The schooner's war flag went up and she opened fire with at least four guns and several machine guns. The U-93 defended herself with both deck guns while the captain ordered full speed and turned hard to port to escape the fire. Both deck guns were hit, wounding several men, and more rounds were hitting the deck and the hull. A round exploded in the conning tower that hurled the captain and the helmsman overboard and caused the U-93 to continue turning full circle back into the fire.[17]

At that point, Ziegner, recognizing that the boat was not under command, took over and headed the battered U-boat away from the equally battered schooner. Safely out of range, and protected by the gathering night, he and the chief engineer surveyed the damage. With a large hole in the pressure hull, U-93 was unable to dive. Its fuel tanks were leaking, both guns were destroyed, and the captain was missing. Unable to go back and look for von Spiegel, Ziegner laid a course for home. On 5 November he reached List with only enough fuel remaining for two and a half hours of steaming.

The panic party picked up von Spiegel, the helmsman, and a wounded sailor who had been blown off the deck. The *Prize* was in bad shape and in danger of sinking. In one of those wartime oddities, von Spiegel found himself in a situation of helping to save the vessel he had just tried to sink. The *Prize* reached Kinsale on 4 May, partly under its own power and partly under tow. Von Spiegel and the helmsman spent the rest of the war as POWs. The wounded sailor died of his wounds.

This was a case in which an experienced U-boat captain became over-confident. It is true that he had recently dispatched three sailing vessels without difficulty, but one was a Norwegian and the other two were Danish. The *Prize* flew no flag, was alone in the western approaches, and ignored the initial warning shot. Any one of those circumstances was an indication that the vessel was a decoy; taken together they were a dead giveaway. As an experienced captain, von Spiegel was aware that the British were using sailing decoys and he should have recognized the clues.

The last confirmed encounter between a U-boat and a decoy occurred on 30 July 1918 southeast of Lizard when UB-80 torpedoed the *Stockforce*. In the ensuing surface gun battle the *Stockforce* sank. UB-80 suffered moderate damage, but was able to return to Helgoland.[18]

Considering that the ratio of decoys lost to U-boats lost was five to one, the program was not very effective. Measured against the other two objectives of denying the U-boats access to their targets and protecting the targets from attack, the decoy program was totally ineffective. Similar to antisubmarine nets, the decoy program represented a tremendous effort and use of resources for very small results.

German U-boats found lone freighters even after the convoy system was inaugurated. A U-boat torpedoed this freighter in 1918 after it had reached its dispersal point and was proceeding alone through coastal waters toward a British port. The ship displays the British Dazzle System of camouflage. In 1918 the U.S. Bureau of Risk Insurance required all American flag carriers that traded to or from ports in Europe and the Mediterranean coast of Africa to be painted in one of the approved Dazzle patterns.

The German E-mine was an efficient and very dangerous mine. The Russians used a similar type that was equally efficient, but the British were plagued with defective mines until they copied the German E-mine in 1917. The German-designed and -manufactured Carbonit mine that the Turks used was equally effective.

SMS *S135* is an example of the torpedo boat type that was popular in all the navies. Despite their designation, these vessels were actually early versions of the destroyer and performed exactly the same duties. Before the introduction of the depth charge, torpedo boats had only their deck guns, ramming, or an explosive sweep for use against a submarine.

A British torpedo boat, or a destroyer, has just dropped three depth charges over the spot where a U-boat dove. Two Thornycroft depth-charge throwers fired the depth charges represented by the water columns A and B. The boil in the destroyer's wake is from a depth charge that was rolled off the stern. The order in which the depth charges were dropped is evident from the pattern and the different sizes of the boil and water column. The first depth charge was rolled off the stern, the second was fired to port, and the third to starboard.

The kite balloon was simply a tethered observation balloon that went to sea. Small freighters and trawlers carried the kite balloons and their holds were modified for the purpose. This balloon is just rising from the deck.

Despite the added range and visibility the kite balloon provided, many naval officers objected to having a kite balloon with a convoy because it provided a U-boat with a long-range visual guide that pinpointed the convoy's location. *U.S. Naval Institute*

The SS type of airship was better known as a blimp. The pilot and the observer rode in a wingless airplane fuselage suspended beneath the envelope. The airplane's engine provided the motive power. The British produced blimps in fairly large numbers because they were inexpensive to build and easy to fly. They were great observation platforms but their slow speed prevented them from making an effective attack on a U-boat.

The American version of the blimp drew heavily on the British design. The Americans used blimps exclusively on the East Coast of the United States.

The F5 was a British improvement of the Curtiss H-12 and H-16 designs. The British retained the Curtiss wings and tail but made major hull improvements. The result was the F5 that was built in Britain and the F5L that was built in the United States. The L in the American designation stood for Liberty engine.

The British captured UC-5 in April 1916 after it became stranded in the mouth of the Thames. Its fate underscores the fact that navigational problems were often a more effective ASW measure than were nets and explosive sweeps. The mine visible on deck is very similar to the E-mine and just as effective. UB and UC boats were not subject to Kommodore Bauer's 12 April 1915 order barring the High Sea Fleet boats from passing through the Dover Straits, and their excursions from Zeebrugge and Ostend were a constant problem for the British.

An EC mine-net is being shot from the deck of a drifter. The EC mine's relatively light weight and the lightweight net construction are clearly evident. EC mine-nets were very dangerous to handle and the British used them only in anchored positions. The Germans rejected them entirely because of the danger to the handling crews.

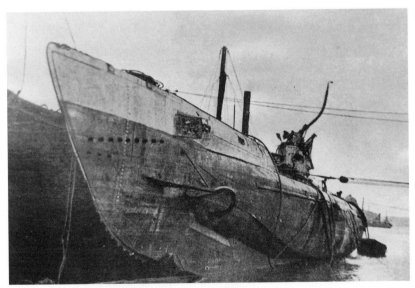

UC-44 was the victim of British radio intelligence that caused it to hit a previously laid German mine off Waterford in Saint George's Channel on the night of 4 August 1917. The British salvaged the boat and recovered documents that showed that the Dover defenses were not stopping the UB and UC boats from passing through the Dover Straits.

The bow and forward torpedo tubes of a British C-class submarine. The British deployed their submarines primarily as reconnaissance and as anti-submarine units. British submarines operating alone sank eighteen U-boats during World War I.

The British 7.5-inch howitzer came in two versions: a smooth bore called a bomb thrower, and a rifled bore (shown here) that fired an artillery-like round capable of exploding twenty feet under the water. The 7.5-inch howitzer could fire a 500-pound projectile carrying a 250-pound charge three hundred yards.

UB boats, like these tied up to the mole at Zeebrugge, were considerably smaller and had less range than the larger U-boats that were assigned to the High Sea Fleet. While the bigger U-boats took the long trip around Scotland to reach their operations areas, the UB and UC boats continued to pass through the Dover Straits until October 1918.

Kapitänleutnant Pauli took U-119 on two war patrols in October 1918. During the first patrol from Helgoland around Scotland, the British reported it sunk in the Northern mine barrage, that ran roughly from the Orkneys to Bergen, Norway. In fact, U-119 was surrendered to the French on 24 November 1918 and was renamed *Rene Audry*. The French scrapped it in 1937.

A subchaser is under construction in one of the twenty-six yards contracted to build them. The graceful hull was designed by naval architect Loring Swasey and the three engines were supplied by the Standard Motor Construction Company. Although the hull design looked more like a yacht than a warship, the SCs were in fact small warships that were fully equipped to deal with the U-boats. Despite the Americans' high expectations for the SCs, they were relatively slow and sank no U-boats. The subchasers served again during World War II.

U.S. Navy subchasers based at Queenstown, Ireland, in 1918. *U.S. Naval Institute*

U.S. Navy subchasers at Inverness, Scotland, in November 1918. After the armistice was signed, the navy used the subchasers from Queenstown to help clear the Northern mine barrage. The crews look happy here, but in fact there was much grumbling about the add-on assignment.

Most historians consider the depth charge to be the most significant antisubmarine weapon developed during World War I. When the destroyers were equipped with the Mark I rack (shown here), the true effectiveness of the depth charge was realized. With the added introduction of the Thornycroft thrower and the American Y-gun, the depth charge became a truly formidable weapon. *U.S. Naval Institute*

An American Y-gun is ready to be fired. Depending on the size of the propellant charge used, the Y-gun could simultaneously hurl two 300-pound Mark II depth charges fifty, sixty-six, or eighty yards away from the sides of the ship. *U.S. Naval Institute*

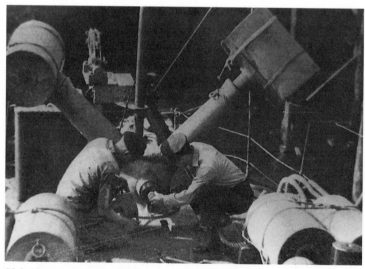

The U.S. Navy's Y-gun greatly increased the depth charge's effectiveness. The two men shown here are inserting the 3-inch blank round that provided the propellant for the depth charges mounted on the ends of the tubes. During the twelve months from 10 December 1917 to 11 November 1918 the navy installed 974 Y-guns in destroyers and subchasers.

A British aerial photograph taken on 24 April 1918, a day after the attempt to block the locks at Zeebrugge. The two funnels and upper works of the HMS *Thetis* are visible at the entrance formed by the curved piers. Inside the channel leading to the docks are HMS *Iphigenia* and HMS *Intrepid*. Despite the British claim that Zeebrugge was blocked, the Germans were using the lock again within forty-eight hours.

The USS *Fanning* captured U-58, commanded by Kapitänleutnant Gustav Amberger, on 17 November 1917. The *Fanning* and the USS *Nicholson* were escorting convoy OQ20 out of Queenstown, Ireland. The destroyers depth charged the U-boat, drove it to the surface, and shelled it. According to Amberger, the depth charging knocked out his electrical system, destroyed the diving controls, and jammed the rudder, thus forcing him to surface and surrender. All the crewmen except one man, who died of a heart attack, became POWs. *U.S. Naval Institute*

The British use of neutral flags was a sore point with the Germans, especially after the British started arming their merchant ships. This German propaganda photo, taken in Wilhelmshaven in 1917, depicts a British freighter flying the U.S. flag while the U-boat makes the stop according to the Prize Regulations.

13

Hydrophones

Hydrophones, although not a weapon, laid the foundation for a major technological innovation in ASW—sonar. Hydrophones had been under development since the 1880s and in 1905 the Submarine Signal Company laid underwater bells at the lightships off the major harbors in the United States, Canada, Great Britain, and Germany. Each bell sent a unique identifying signal that could be heard by ocean liners equipped with the Submarine Signal Company's hydrophones. When World War I started, all the big transatlantic liners were equipped with hydrophones to help them fix their positions as they approached the coastlines of Europe and the United States in reduced visibility.

The Royal Navy had no effective underwater listening equipment when the war started, and they did not have a research and development program dealing with hydrophones. It was not an oversight, it was simply a matter that prior to World War I the connection between hydrophones and submarines had not been made. Early U-boat successes made that connection and Capt. C. P. Ryan, RN, began experimenting with hydrophones at the Royal Navy's experimental station at Hawkcraig in the autumn of 1914. His early work produced shore-based hydrophone systems for controlling minefields. The fixed systems went into operation during 1916; by the end of the war eighteen shore stations were operating in Britain. The effective range of the seabed-placed phones was three miles in calm weather to about one and a half miles in rough weather when surface noise caused by wave action interfered with the phones' reception.[1]

The earliest ship-borne hydrophones for ASW appeared in 1915. They were simply hung over the side with the operator located on deck. The early devices were nondirectional, sometimes called bidirectional, which means that the device could produce a 180 degree error. In other words, the operator might think the sound was coming from the north when in fact it was coming from the south.

Another drawback was that the early models could be used only when the patrol boat was stopped and all its machinery was shut down. Otherwise the engine noise and wave action against the hull washed out the sounds the operator needed to hear. This resulted in a repetitious move, stop, and listen procedure. With each move to a new location the operator had to decide if the approach course was correct based on the change of intensity of the sound. Even with the introduction of improved hydrophones, the move, stop, and listen procedure remained a feature of hydrophone hunting throughout the war.[2]

Despite progress during 1916 the British still had no suitable hydrophones in January 1917 and the new versions that appeared in 1917 and 1918 showed little improvement over the earlier models. The first improvement that appeared in 1917 was the directional hydrophone, which eliminated the 180 degree error. In some cases the new hydrophones had a marginal ability to be used while the vessel was under way, but the need to stop and listen was never eliminated.

The hydrophone never achieved the efficiency the British had hoped for and expected. According to the Admiralty's enemy submarine losses returns, ASW units made 255 attacks on U-boats in 1918, but in only 54 instances did the hydrophones play any part. Of all the U-boats sunk during the war only UC-49 and UB-115 were definitely sunk because of hydrophone contact. In all other instances the U-boats were hunted and destroyed after some form of visual sighting.

The British produced nineteen different shipboard hydrophone models during the war. All saw service to one degree or another.

BRITISH HYDROPHONES

Portable General Service Hydrophone

The most widely used British shipboard unit was the portable general service (PGS) hydrophone, or "drifter," that entered service in late 1915.

The British produced and issued 4,534 general service hydrophones by the end of the war. The PGS hydrophone was a nondirectional device used mostly on drifters—ergo the name—and the operator simply dangled it over the side from a stationary ship. He stood or sat on deck, wearing headphones and turning the control wheel, listening. The PGS hydrophone's relatively simple construction allowed it to be produced in large numbers, and it was relatively easy to use.[3]

The operator used a specially constructed crane to lower the PGS over the side to a depth of twenty to thirty feet. He listened through headphones and rotated the hydrophone head with a wheel mounted on the crane's control panel. When he heard what he thought was the sound of a U-boat's diesel engines or electric motors, he rotated the head until he heard the sound with equal strength in each ear. That was called centering the sound. Then he read the sound's bearing off the dial attached to the wheel and plotted a line on his chart. The only problem at this point was that he could not determine from which side of the head the sound was coming, although he knew it was either from one direction or from the exact opposite direction—the 180 degree error.

Mark I and Mark II Portable Directional Hydrophone

The more sophisticated Mark I and Mark II portable directional hydrophone (PDH) entered service in the spring of 1917. As the name implies, the PDH was a directional hydrophone that eliminated the 180 degree error and could be used while the vessel was under way at low speeds. The British produced 844 Mark Is and 2,586 Mark IIs, which they installed in sloops, P-boats, and trawlers. The hunting patrols the British organized in the summer of 1917 used the Mark I and Mark II PDH devices. In an attempt to eliminate the water noise interference, the British developed several towed devices, three of which went into service in 1918.[4]

Rubber Eel

The first towed device was the eighteen inch by three inch rubber eel, so named because it had a rubber skin and the elongated, cylindrical shape of an eel. Inside the rubber skin was a tapered bronze tube with a 2-inch microphone at the front end. The tube behind the microphone was filled with a jelly-like material to dampen the sounds coming from the wrong direction. The eel was towed one hundred to two hundred yards behind the ship at a depth of twenty to thirty feet at speeds between three and eight knots. The rubber skin successfully eliminated the water noise interference, but the eel remained a nondirectional device. Despite its limitations, the eel allowed operators to listen while the vessel was under way, and the British issued 463 eels to sloops, P-boats, and trawlers during 1918.

Nash Fish

The first towed directional hydrophone was the Nash fish, named after its inventor, G. H. Nash. The Nash fish was a wooden torpedo-shaped device five feet long and a foot in diameter. It was designed to operate at a depth of twenty to thirty feet at relatively low speed. To help destroy buoyancy the body was flooded with seawater and tail fins hydro-dynamically maintained the correct depth.

Inside the water-filled body were two microphones, one stationary and one that rotated. The operator rotated the directional microphone with an electric motor mounted inside the case. The stationary microphone established the target's presence and the moveable microphone gave the operator an unambiguous bearing to the sound's source. The Admiralty accepted the Nash fish design in October 1917 and put 199 into service by the end of the war. The Nash fish was a step forward, but it did not completely solve the problem of listening for U-boats while under way.[5]

Porpoise

A more sophisticated device was the barracuda-shaped "porpoise," which went into service in September 1918. A single microphone was mounted in a wooden shell five feet long and twelve inches in diameter. A small electric motor, immersed in an oil bath to protect it from seawater, rotated the phone. A meter mounted on the operator's control panel provided bearings from 180 degrees port to 180 degrees starboard. The porpoise had good directional abilities up to six knots and was ideal for use in single ship hunts. For best results, however, the ship's engines had to be stopped. The porpoise arrived too late in the war to see much service and the British installed only thirty-one units by the end of the war.[6]

Each of the P-boats, sloops, and destroyers carried an assortment of hydrophones because there was no single type capable of performing all the tasks required. A report on an attack made in the North Sea in July

1918 illustrates typical usage. P-33 was towing its porpoise hydrophone and was stopping to use its PGS hydrophone.

1935: Hydrophone officer reported suspicious noise 14 points on port bow.

1937: Increased speed to 15 knots to close and investigate.

1943: Stopped main engines to listen.

1947: Altered course, increased to 15 knots.

1956: Stopped main engines to listen.

2020: Stopped main engines to listen, dropped explosive (paravane) sweep and veered to 150 yards.

2050: Found Porpoise hydrophone out of order. Hauled in Porpoise.

2140: Stopped engines and steamed new Porpoise.

2200: Nothing heard on Porpoise hydrophone, so streamed Eel hydrophone and again picked up sound of submarine.

2226: Hauled in Porpoise and found same foul of explosive [paravane] sweep wire. Porpoise cleared and sweep again veered to 150 yards.[7]

The submarine was not destroyed, although P-33, HMS *Narin,* and the trawler *Ida Adams* dropped a total of twenty-four depth charges. In fact, there may not have been a submarine; they may have been listening to each other's engine sounds.

U.S. HYDROPHONES

The U.S. Navy had experimented with submarine detection devices before the United States entered the war, but it had no effective unit in service when it entered the war on 6 April 1917. The navy immediately launched an energetic development program, which produced the first serviceable hydrophone within six months. The Submarine Signal Company and Western Electric Company, with a substantial contribution by General Electric Company, did most of the development work.[8]

C-Tube and SC-Tube

The U.S. Navy's first and most successful hydrophones were simple mechanical devices known as the C-tube and the SC-tube. Both were identical in design and operation; the only difference was that the C-tube was dropped over the side, and the SC-tube was mounted inside the hull. The C-tube's construction and use were so basic, and the cost so low, that both versions were being mass produced by October 1917.

The C-tube was nothing more than an inverted T made of brass tubing. The ends of the crosspiece were capped with rubber balls and inside the T were two brass tubes that conducted the sound from the rubber balls to the listener's ears. The listener used a standard doctor's stethoscope, which he attached to the ends of the copper tubes, to listen to the sounds. A wheel with an arrow pointer and a 360 degree scale were attached to the base of the T. By rotating the wheel the operator could center the sound and read the bearing from the scale.

Under normal operating conditions the C-tube had a range of about two miles and it was nondirectional. To use the tube, the vessel had to be stopped and all the machinery shut down, otherwise engine noise and wave action against the hull would drown out any other underwater sounds. Even stopped, some types of small patrol vessels rolled so badly that the water washing against the hull made it difficult to get a good center. The operator lowered the T until it was about three feet below the keel, put on his stethoscope, and rotated the wheel until the sound was centered. At that point he might assume that the source was directly in front of him, but like all nondirectional devices, the C-tube was subject to a 180 degree error.[9]

In November 1917 the Navy Department sent both C versions to the British for testing, and the trials were conducted in January 1918. The British liked the SC-tube but preferred their own Mark I PDH. Nevertheless, the SC-tube was quick to build, simple to operate, and robust; the British produced 521 units under license in 1918.

K-Tube

The K-tube was a towed, electrical device designed to eliminate all local water noises, but even with that feature the K-tube could only be used when the vessel was stopped. The advantage it enjoyed was that its design eliminated the 180 degree error and water noises did not affect it. But it was not a tube. Following the adoption of the C-tube, so named because of the bronze tube construction, the U.S. Navy designated nearly all the later hydrophone designs "tubes." In fact, they were electrical devices and not mechanical tube devices.

The K-tube was a complicated arrangement that consisted of an equilateral triangle made of brass pipe, three carbon microphones, a wooden or hollow metal float, and twelve smaller floats. A microphone, encased in a rubber ball, was located at each corner of the metal triangle, and an electrical cable connected each of the microphones to the listener's console. This cable then passed to the large float, then through each of the twelve small floats and back to a shipboard control console. The control console consisted of a tuning knob, an indicator dial, earphones, and a newly developed device called a compensator that converted the electrically produced sounds into a relative bearing that the operator read from a dial.

When sound waves struck the three microphones a signal was sent along the electrically charged cable to the compensator, which contained two telephone receivers, one left receiver and one right receiver. The sounds from the telephone receivers were transmitted to the operator's headphones. By turning the knob, or wheel, the operator was able to center the sound and read the relative bearing from a dial calibrated in degrees.

The Americans used the K-tube extensively during the war. After testing the K-tube in January 1918, the British declared it inferior to their own rubber encased eel. Another British report, however, described the K-tube as having a range of at least sixteen miles, and said the tube was very efficient at picking up the machinery sounds produced by U-boats lying on the bottom to avoid detection. The report concluded that the K-tube's sensitivity and long range made it unsuited for use in the English Channel with "its cacophony of ships' noises."[10]

MB-Tube

The MB-tube was a mechanical device that was simply a super C-tube, and looked almost exactly like it. The only real difference between the two tubes was that the MB-tube had eight rubber balls on each end of the crosspiece instead of one. The MB-tube was more accurate than the SC-tube, but it was also heavier, much more complicated, and prone to leakage where the T passed through the hull.

The MB-tube was used in conjunction with the SC-tube, and the Americans installed the MB-tube on the starboard side of their subchasers directly opposite the SC-tube. The operation of the two tubes was identical, but water noises had much less effect on the MB-tube. If there were overlapping sounds the MB-tube could eliminate all but one. With the SC-tube any sound on the horizon could be heard while the MB-tube worked more like a telescope to concentrate on one spot. Despite its advantages, the operators did not like the MB-tube and used it only occasionally.[11]

MV-Tube

The MV-tube was a major breakthrough because it was the first listening device that was contained entirely within the hull and could be used under way at speeds to twenty knots. The MV-tube consisted of 348 carbon microphones housed in a blister on each side of the ship's bow and linked to a compensator that provided a bearing to the sound's source within a few degrees. This was the first of the American or British hydrophones that was located entirely inside the hull and able to pick up identifiable sounds at long distances.

The MV-tube, including all its parts and equipment, weighed about two tons and took up thirty-eight and a half feet of space along both sides of the forward part of the keel. The device was twenty-three and a half inches wide and projected fifteen and a half inches below the keel. Because of its size and weight the MV-tube was used only in destroyers. In any event, it arrived too late in the war to play an important role, but some destroyers equipped with the MV-tube did have opportunities to try it. In one instance a destroyer running at twenty knots tracked a U-boat at periscope depth traveling at seven knots at ranges of five hundred to two thousand yards.[12]

Electric Eel

The electric eel was a towed device similar to the British eel, and the British called the American version the snake to avoid confusion with their own eel. The Americans enclosed twelve microphones in a streamlined rubber tube, and allotted six microphones to each side of the compensator to provide the target bearing. In this device, compensation was achieved electrically and not acoustically. Therefore, there was no need for the listener to center the sound; a needle gauge indicated the bearing. No distinction could be made between port and starboard—a return to the 180 degree directional error. To eliminate that problem, American vessels towed two eels, each one hundred to two hundred yards astern at a depth of one hundred feet and spaced some distance apart so that the port and starboard ambiguity could be overcome by taking two different readings, one from each eel. When two eels were used in conjunction with the MV-tube a reasonably accurate range to target could be determined by triangulation of the bearings.[13]

Both the British and the Americans experimented with equipping seaplanes and airships with hydrophones. None was successful in a practical sense and neither the Americans nor the British used the aircraft-borne devices operationally.

THE TRAILER

The "trailer," although not a hydrophone, was developed by the British to find U-boats resting on the bottom. Once a U-boat was found, patrol vessels could drop depth charges on it. The trailer was a towed, electrical detection device similar in concept to the explosive paravane. It consisted of two parts: a bronze plate that was hung over the stern in the water and phosphor wire that was weighted on its outboard end with a length of heavy chain. The wire and chain were trailed astern, the chain holding the end of the wire on the bottom. If the wire made contact with a U-boat an electrolytic action was set between the wire and the bronze plate. In some cases the towing vessel's bronze rudder quadrant served as the plate. The current rang a buzzer in the pilot house. The trailer was rarely used and did not locate any U-boats. Usually, it was used to locate wrecks.[14]

CONTROLLED MINEFIELDS

The British and the Americans used shore-based hydrophones as part of controlled minefields for harbor defense. Western Electric developed two harbor entrance detection systems used in the United States. The first used twenty microphones, each mounted on a tripod and connected in series, by a single cable. The shore-based operator could select each microphone individually by means of a selective switching system. Only one microphone operated at a time, making the system nondirectional, but the U-boat's approximate location could be determined by its nearness to the microphone.

The second system used magnetic loops similar to the Bragg loop that the British used in the Dover Straits. The loops were connected to galvanometers on shore, which indicated the passage of a U-boat over each loop. The operator determined the U-boat's exact location by the sequence of deflections indicated on his meter panel. The loops were of very short range to eliminate confusion that a large number of vessels in the area would cause. This system was in operation at the Chesapeake Bay entrance before the war ended.[15]

14

Patrols and Patrol Vessels

Throughout 1917 and 1918, the British directed the Auxiliary Patrol's activities more and more toward ASW. In the broadest sense the Auxiliary Patrol included more than three hundred destroyers, including American destroyers, P-boats, and *Flower*-class sloops, and about four thousand auxiliary vessels. The latter were mostly trawlers and drifters, but there were also 550 MLs, 24 paddle steamers, 49 yachts, and 129 American-supplied subchasers. Supporting the surface forces were 65 submarines, 550 aircraft, and 75 airships.[1]

The surface patrols and aircraft were concentrated in the coastal waters out to about fifty miles, so that the patrols were the strongest where the shipping traffic came together. The patrols around Great Britain had always been a problem to the U-boats, but in 1917 and 1918 the number of patrol vessels increased and they became better equipped. At the same time the convoy system forced the U-boats to concentrate activities in the waters relatively close to shore, which brought them into contact with the increasingly stronger antisubmarine patrols.

The patrols had three responsibilities: sink U-boats, deny the U-boats access to the inshore traffic lanes by deploying nets and laying minefields, and sweep up the mines the UC boats laid around Britain. The comments the U-boat captains made about the patrols give an indication of how the patrols' strength varied from day to day and place to place.

In February 1917, UC-64 Oberleutnant zur See Müller-Schwarz encountered weak patrols in the English Channel, but encountered exceptionally strong patrols in the Bristol Channel and the southern portion of the Irish Sea. Müller-Schwarz noted that the patrols "thickly covered" the shipping lanes, and he warned that darkened destroyers patrolled the area at night and airships were out in great numbers during the day in good weather.[2]

The strong patrols UC-64 encountered in the Irish Sea in February were gone by October when U-57, Kapitänleutnant Karl von Georg, worked in that area. He noted, "Whereas on earlier occasions in this area British patrols and American destroyers forced me to dive as often as ten times a day, on this patrol the patrols and American destroyers were hardly seen. In fact during the entire twelve days I was in my operations area, the waters off the south of Ireland and at the entrances to the St. George's Channel and the Bristol Channel, I saw only one gunboat and one American destroyer."[3]

Oberleutnant zur See Howaldt in UB-40 reported in late June 1917 that patrols in the area between the Isle of Wright and Cape Barfleur were so strong that, combined with the long summer days, the UB boats' batteries were hardly sufficient to remain submerged all day. He described an unsuccessful torpedo attack on a steamer off Lizard and said, "surfacing to complete the attack as was done frequently in the past, was impossible owing to the presence of surface and air patrols."[4] Despite the problems, Howaldt sank 39,253 tons and damaged another 17,812 tons during the five patrols he conducted from 3 June to 28 September 1917.

Oberleutnant zur See Lohs, commander of UC-75, commented in late June 1917:

The enemy destroyers give an impression of being utterly helpless. Their duty is to go to the place where the U-boats have done damage, without any hope for success, because the area has expanded so much that they always arrive too late. They have lost their enthusiasm. They content themselves with rescuing the survivors of sunken ships, but they cannot remain in the area too long or they themselves become targets. Therefore they continue along their patrol line hoping to keep the U-boat submerged longer, but more important they have to go to another place where someone is calling for help. Their attention has markedly waned. The American patrols off Fastnet are very pleasant because they are completely harmless and inattentive.[5]

By the last quarter of 1917 the British ASW patrols along the east coast were very strong and became stronger during 1918. The patrol vessels began carrying newly developed armament, more depth charges, and hydrophones. Among the newly introduced weapons were the howitzer and the bomb thrower, which were more important for the nature of the rounds they fired than for the nature of the weapons themselves. Among the patrols were four vessels—motor launches, subchasers, *Flower*-class sloops, and P-boats—that had been designed and built specifically to hunt and destroy U-boats.

MOTOR LAUNCHES

The British began using American-designed motor launches in 1916. Although most of them were built in the United States, many were built under license in Canada. A British commission came to the United States in 1915 looking for a made-to-order boat to be used by the Auxiliary Patrol. The commission visited two builders in New Jersey, the Standard Motor Construction Company in Jersey City and the Elco Works at Bayonne. The commission looked at Elco because that company had an established reputation for building large numbers of standardized boats, and the Standard Motor Construction Company was the largest builder of marine engines in the United States.[6]

On 9 April 1915 the British signed a contract with Elco and the Standard Motor Company for fifty motor launches. Those boats were seventy-five feet long, had a twelve-and-a-half-foot beam, and drew just three feet. Twin, six-cylinder, 220 horsepower Standard gasoline engines gave them a maximum speed of nineteen knots and a cruising radius of eight hundred miles on two thousand gallons of fuel. The cruising radius was lengthened to one thousand miles at fifteen knots and twenty-one hundred miles at eleven knots.

The pattern boat was in frame at the Bayonne plant on 1 May 1915 and two weeks later the Admiralty ordered 500 additional boats. The length of the add-on boats was increased to eighty feet. The French and Italians also bought motor launches, bringing the total production to 720 boats.

The motor launches were supposed to be able to keep the sea in any weather, but that was not the case. They were wet and cold. The Admiralty had intended to use the MLs to patrol the Dover Straits, but experience showed that they could "rarely stand the sea in that locality." MLs were fine weather boats only; a very moderate sea put them "hors de combat."[7]

The MLs were armed with a short 3-inch gun and two 150-pound Type D* depth charges through September 1917. In the spring of 1918 the Admiralty issued each ML four 300-pound Type D depth charges and in July 1918 upped the issue to ten per boat. The early boats also carried lance bombs, but they were later omitted.

SUBCHASERS

The 129 American subchasers (SCs) that served in European and Mediterranean waters during World War I were the prettiest, although not the most successful, patrol boats in the Entente forces' inventory. In 1916 the U.S. Navy ordered the design and contracted with forty-three builders to furnish the boats, less engines. The subchasers used the same Standard Motor Company engines that had gone into the British MLs, the only difference being that the SCs had three engines instead of two.[8]

The SCs had a thousand-mile range at twelve knots with twenty-four hundred gallons of fuel. Despite the pretty lines and the third engine, the subchasers were slower than the MLs, having a maximum, three-engine speed of sixteen to seventeen knots—not much faster than a surfaced U-boat. Another interesting point is that the third engine increased the subchasers' speed by only one-and-a-half to one-and-three-quarter knots over the maximum attainable on two engines. In at least one case the subchaser's engine room crew removed one engine entirely without any loss in top speed. A valuable feature the subchasers shared with the MLs was that the engines were compressed air started, which gave both types an almost unlimited ability to stop and quickly restart their engines while on hydrophone patrol.[9]

The subchasers' gun was a short barrel 3-inch gun that was capable of high-angle fire for anti-aircraft warfare. The gun's ammunition included anti-aircraft shrapnel and high-explosive rounds as well as a flat nose, nonricochet depth round similar to the type used with the 7.5-inch howitzer. The subchasers carried eighteen Mark II 300-pound depth charges— two loaded in a Y-gun, four in ready racks, and twelve in two Mark II launching racks on the stern.

All the subchasers were equipped with a wireless telephone, a feature found only aboard group leaders in the MLs. In addition to the wireless telephone, all the subchasers carried the standard U.S. Navy C-Tube hydrophone and either the SC-Tube, MB-Tube, or K-Tube. Toward the end of the war some of the SCs worked with the MV-Tube.

FLOWER-CLASS SLOOPS

The *Flower*-class sloops were coal-fired, single screw patrol and escort vessels capable of fifteen to sixteen knots. The Admiralty ordered the *Acacia* class in batches of twelve, the first twelve on 1 January 1915, the next twelve on 8 January, and the last twelve on 4 May. In July 1915 the Admiralty placed an order for thirty-six more of the *Acacia* class. These *Flower*-class sloops were originally designed for minesweeping, but because they were economical on coal, the Admiralty assigned them to patrol and escort duties. In fact, "with regard to convoy escort, in all except the Devonport flotillas, the word destroyers must be read as including sloops."[10]

The sloops were 267 feet long, had a 33-foot beam, drew $11\frac{1}{2}$ feet, and displaced 1,250 tons. To speed construction the sloops' design incorporated standard features found in commercial steamers, which made it possible for several private firms to build them quickly. As a result U-boat captains often mistook them for cross-channel steamers since the sloops all had twin funnels and a steamer's bow. This unexpected feature made it possible for the Admiralty to convert some of the *Flower*-class sloops to decoy operations.

The sloops were superior to trawlers in several ways. They were nearly twice as fast, carried heavier armament, and had a crew of eighty. They were good sea boats, but pitched in a seaway. Their armament consisted of two 4-inch guns, one 3-pounder, and a Thornycroft depth charge thrower. They were also equipped with hydrophones and radios. The latter may seem obvious necessity, but in 1917 and 1918 most Auxiliary Patrol vessels did not have radios.[11]

P-BOATS

The P-boats—P stood for "patrol"—were a wartime expedient. They were good sea boats, able to remain out in all weather, and men who served on them said they were very handy. Like the *Flower*-class sloops, some of the P-boats were converted to decoys, and all performed the same duties as destroyers.

These twin-screw, coal-fired, single funnel vessels' most obvious characteristic was their low-lying top hamper. At a distance, and in reduced visibility, they could easily be mistaken for a surfaced U-boat. The P-boats were 245 feet long, had a 24-foot beam, drew 8 feet, and displaced 613 tons. Their armament consisted of one 4-inch gun, one or two 12-pounders, and two 14-inch torpedo tubes. They also carried depth charge throwers as well as depth charges in racks on the stern. Additionally, they had a specially constructed, three-layer bow designed to collapse with minimum loss of the hull's watertight integrity when they rammed a U-boat. Their maximum speed was twenty knots, which made them the fastest of the specially built antisubmarine vessels. Forty-three were delivered, most of them in 1916.[12]

HUNTING PATROLS

The Admiralty viewed hunting patrols as an offensive measure, whereas the convoy system was a defensive measure. Despite the lack of measurable success, the Royal Navy enthusiastically expanded the hunting patrol program right up to the end of the war. Hunting patrols were hydrophone- and depth charge–equipped hunter-killer units that were first tried in the Aegean in February 1917. Initially destroyers and P-boats made up the hunting units, but the Admiralty quickly extended the idea to include motor launches and trawlers. Hunting patrols operated in three-vessel groups led by a destroyer, a P-boat, or a sloop. Flotillas were formed all around the coast in the spring of 1918. The Americans organized their subchasers into three-vessel units with one of the subchasers assuming the leader position.[13]

A hunting patrol operation using destroyers equipped with hydrophones was carried out in the North Sea during September 1917. It was reported that the patrol sank three U-boats, but like so many claims of U-boats destroyed, those three were unfounded. The idea of hunting patrols with destroyers and sloops was attractive, but the results were disappointing.

The first confirmed success of a hunting patrol unit operating as such occurred in the English Channel on 8 August 1918 and the success illustrates how the hunting patrols worked. The Torbay Hydrophone Unit, composed of the destroyer HMS *Opossum* and seven MLs, was hunting UC-49. Oberleutnant zur See Kükenthal had torpedoed the 5,275-ton SS *Tuscan Prince* on 5 August 1917 and the Torbay group had been hunting the U-boat for three days.

On 8 August at 1505 a lookout aboard ML-191 spotted an oil slick on the water and the ML dropped a depth charge. Fifteen minutes later, the *Opossum's* hydrophone officer picked up engine sounds on his Mark II hydrophone. His bearing was confirmed by a report from one of the MLs. Leaving three MLs over the oil slick, *Opossum* took the other three and steamed to a position about three miles away, where the hydrophone officer thought the sounds came from, identified as position 1.

The *Opossum* dropped ten depth charges on position 1, then stopped and listened. There were no more engine sounds, but that did not prove anything. Leaving the three MLs to watch position 1, *Opossum* moved to a point one and three-quarter miles away and again stopped and listened. At 1800 the hydrophone officer heard UC-49. *Opossum* signaled the three MLs stationed over position 1 to leave the area and shut down two miles away in order to fool UC-49 into believing the group had gone away.

Seventeen minutes later UC-49 surfaced seven hundred yards from the *Opossum* and two hundred yards from ML-135. The ML got off two rounds that missed before the U-boat dropped beneath the surface. But the group knew where it was and launched their second attack, the three MLs dropping five depth charges along the suspected track. The first one exploded "just astern of the submarine's wash," and the next four exploded at thirty-yard intervals in front of UC-49. After the MLs had made their runs, *Opossum* dropped its pattern around UC-49's suspected location, which brought a considerable amount of brown oil and air bubbles to the surface. The destroyer dropped a buoy to mark the spot and stopped to listen.

At 1917 ML-465 dropped one depth charge and forty-five minutes later *Opossum* dropped eight more. More brown oil and air bubbles came to the surface and the entire group settled down for the night, all engines stopped, listening.

At noon on 9 August minesweepers arrived and dragged the area looking for a wreck. They found nothing and the *Opossum* dropped thirty-six more depth charges. At 2120 there was a sudden burst of oil and air on the surface, but the hydrophone officers heard nothing. Again the groups settled in for the night.

Oil and air were still rising on the morning of 10 August when one of the sweeps fouled an obstruction. *Opossum* passed across the position and dropped four depth charges, bringing up a stronger rush of air and oil. The last attack also produced a light bulb that popped up on the surface and was retrieved by a minesweeper. The bulb bore the mark of an Austrian firm. Satisfied that they had sunk a U-boat, the group buoyed the position and returned to Dartmouth.[14]

The only other success occurred on 29 September 1918 when the British airship R-29 spotted oil on the water off the British east coast near Sunderland and called up two hunter units. HMS *Ouse* with its three hydrophone-equipped trawlers and the HMS *Star* with its three trawlers were on the scene very quickly. In this set-up, the trawlers spread out to listen and the destroyers made the depth charge runs. The attacks lasted several hours until the water was covered with a widening oil slick. Minesweepers dragged the area and found an obstruction beneath the slick. The U-boat they destroyed was UB-115, commanded by Oberleutnant zur See Reinhold Thomsen.[15]

While the hunting patrols gave the Royal Navy a sense that they were taking the offensive against the U-boats, the hunting patrols were largely a waste of resources. The routine area patrols gave the U-boats more problems and sank more U-boats than did all the hunting patrols. In 1917 and 1918 patrol vessels of all types accounted for twenty-one U-boats, damaged several others, and forced many U-boats to break off their attacks on merchant ships. In the same period the hunting patrols destroyed two U-boats. Most significant is the fact that the U-boats' war diaries are filled with comments about the area patrols, whereas almost nothing is said about the hunting patrols.

15

Aircraft

Prior to 1917 aircraft played a relatively small role in the antisubmarine war. One of the reasons was that aircraft engines during that time were too unreliable for over-water flights. Another reason was that the existing seaplanes had only a marginal ability to safely land and take off in the open sea. They lacked the power needed to lift heavy loads off the water, which meant that the size and weight of any depth charges they might carry was very limited. There was also the matter of production priority, which went to fighters and bombers for use in France. Like all other antisubmarine measures, until the U-boat problem became really serious, the British made only a minimum effort to produce a suitable aircraft for ASW.

Nonrigid airships, or blimps as the British termed them in 1915, had the largest antisubmarine role up to the beginning of 1917. Blimps protected British Expeditionary Force (BEF) troopships on their way across the channel in 1914 and continued in the ASW role until the end of the war. The blimp had its own limitations that were only partially overcome through improved design.

Despite the slow development of aircraft in the antisubmarine role, by the beginning of 1917 the British deployed aircraft of all types on antisubmarine patrols along Britain's coasts. Measured by the Germans' reactions to the air patrols, the effectiveness of aircraft in the antisubmarine role increased steadily as air crews gained experience and better aircraft and weapons became available.

Oberleutnant zur See von Dittfurth in UB-32 blamed his relative lack of success in the area south of the Scillies during 6–17 June 1917 on the constant presence of airships and aircraft. Oberleutnant zur See Wacker in UB-22 complained that strong air patrols prevented him from accomplishing anything during his patrols from 20 June to 9 August 1917, and Kapitänleutnant Walter Remy in U-90 wrote that British aircraft forced him to repeatedly dive on 17 November 1917. He added that the aircraft dropped a total of twenty depth bombs on the U-90 throughout the day.[1]

In 1918 the Germans felt the effects of increased air patrols and improved ASW weapons to an even greater degree. Kapitänleutnant Paul Hundius in UB-103 commented in June 1918 that aircraft made daylight operations impossible off the Cornwall coast. Oberleutnant zur See Hans Förste in UB-34 commented that on 24 July 1918 an enemy airplane forced him to go deep for four hours. He added that during the following days the boat's effectiveness was limited due to calm seas and the regular presence of enemy aircraft that dropped many bombs.[2]

Oberleutnant zur See Reimarus's and Oberleutnant zur See Wigankow's log entries are more dramatic. On 29 July 1917 Reimarus wrote that two British aircraft surprised UC-16 off North Hinder and dropped three bombs as the U-boat was passing twenty-five feet. The explosions sprung the torpedo doors, flooded the torpedo room, popped rivets, and damaged the batteries. UC-16 was forced to surface and engage the aircraft with rifle and machine gun fire. The damage was so serious that the boat had to return to Bruges.[3] Six weeks later, on 6 September, three British aircraft caught UB-12 on the surface. Wigankow ordered his boat to crash dive. As UB-12 passed forty-five feet several bombs exploded close by, causing moderate damage that was not serious enough to send the boat home.[4]

Compared to the French, German U-boat commanders considered the American air patrols to be more effective. On 26 October 1918, Kapitänleutnant von Glasenapp, commanding U-91, commented, "The French patrols south of Bordeaux are weak, and their air patrols are harmless since the aircraft are apparently not equipped with bombs. Off the mouth to the Gironde are regular airship patrols or kite balloons. West of La Pallice American aircraft are sharp-eyed and drop lots of bombs."[5]

Generally, land planes operated within a zone that extended twenty-miles offshore because engine failures were common. The British also found that crews in land planes became less attentive to their mission the farther out they went. The reason was stress—anxiety—caused by the hopelessness of the situation should the engine fail. The twenty-mile limit was not a hard and fast rule, however; on days when sea conditions prevented seaplanes from taking off and landing, land planes took their patrols.[6]

The twin-engine Blackburn Kangaroo was the first large land plane used for regular ASW patrols. The features that made it popular were its ability to carry a 920-pound bomb load, the bombardier's unhindered forward view, and its relatively high speed. The comparable airplanes were the DH-6 and the DH-9 that the British considered stopgap equipment. The Admiralty regarded the Kangaroo so highly that in April 1918 they converted an entire seaplane squadron to the Kangaroo. The Kangaroos operated off the east coast, and took part in twelve attacks between May and October 1918.

In general practice, seaplanes flew the longer patrols farther offshore. The British experimented with equipping seaplanes with hydrophones, but the results were poor and the effort never went beyond the experimental stage. The British recognized the land plane's superior load lifting ability, but they also accepted the fact that for over-water patrols the ability to land and take off again was critical. To cover the range of missions, the British saw a need for three types of seaplane: a large craft able to carry a heavy load and fly long distances, a medium size plane for working closer to shore, and a fighter.

The British never did get exactly the kind of airplanes they wanted, but they did get the so-called "Large America Seaplane" that was able to fly long distances and carry heavy loads. The Large America was a Curtiss design that underwent several changes and was produced in Great Britain and the United States in several variations. Despite the Large America's ability to lift heavier loads than any airplane produced in Britain, the British found fault with it. The biggest complaint was that the controls were very heavy and pilot fatigue in bad weather was a serious problem. Second, after a few weeks of service the Large America's wing coverings became slack and the airplane had a hard time getting airborne with a full load. This problem was particularly evident if the planes had been stored in the open for any length of time. Third, because of their size, the Large Americas were expensive to house, which meant that they were usually stored in the open.[7] The American version of the Large America Seaplane was the Curtiss H-12, and when equipped with Liberty engines it was designated the H-12L.

The British preferred what have become known as blimps—nonrigid airships—for protecting convoys. The blimps were slow, but their ability to remain airborne for long periods made them ideal escorts. The biggest shortcomings were their inability to operate in strong winds and the unreliability of the engines' magnetos. Initially the blimps were grounded when wind speed exceeded fifteen knots, but by 1917 they were taking off in winds up to thirty-five knots. British magnetos were faulty until the end of the war and blimp crews became expert at changing magnetos in flight.

The advantage the blimps enjoyed over airplanes was endurance. In 1915 blimps rarely patrolled longer than four hours, but by 1918 twelve-hour patrols were routine. And their slow speed was not a drawback for antisubmarine patrols. It is true that blimps were too slow to attack a U-boat before it dove, but their mere presence in the area kept the U-boats down and prevented them from using their high surface speed to reach an attack position. The blimps' efficiency is illustrated by the statistic that from 18 March 1915 to 11 November 1918 only two ships were sunk while under convoy with blimps.

The *Sea Scout*–class (SS) blimp entered service in March 1915. The SS type was an elongated, hydrogen-filled bag that used a wingless BE2's fuselage for the gondola. The BE2's 70 horsepower Renault engine provided the motive power. The SS type constituted the first purpose-built ASW airship, and the British moved quickly to deploy the SS airships. Sometime during 1915 they coined the nickname "blimp," and by the end of the year there were twenty-nine SS blimps in service. By the end of the war the British had produced bigger and more powerful blimps called the *Coastal* class, *Coastal Star* class, and *Zero* class. By 11 November 1918 the British had over one hundred blimps in service, operating from a dozen stations and sixteen substations.[8]

The kite balloon (KB) was related to the blimp. It was a manned, towed balloon that saw considerable work with convoys and inshore surface patrols. Senior British officers were divided in their opinion about the kite balloon's effectiveness with convoys. One group of officers believed that the presence of a kite balloon over a convoy acted as a deterrent to U-boats.

The opposite view held that the kite balloon revealed the convoy's presence and course to a U-boat that was still some distance away. All the U-boat had to do was follow the convoy while remaining out of sight and tracking the balloon. At night the balloon was silhouetted against the lighter sky, providing the U-boat with an excellent guide to the convoy. Finally, the Admiralty adopted the opposition's position and stopped deploying kite balloons with convoys. The KB, however, continued in use with surface patrols. And the Germans did not like it.

The first U.S. naval aviation unit arrived in France on 5 June 1917, but did not fly their first patrol until 18 November. In the meantime the French trained the American pilots at Tours while the French started building three naval air stations (NASs) at Dunkirk, Le Croisic on the Loire River, and Saint Trojan at the mouth of the Gironde. By 11 November 1918 the U.S. Navy aviators were flying from twenty-seven locations in France, England, Ireland, and Italy.[9]

During November 1917 the U.S. Navy assigned more personnel to the French airship base at Paimboeuf, where they flew the Tellier seaplane. In March 1918 the U.S. Navy assumed control of the base, renamed the field NAS Paimboeuf, and started patrolling with the French airship AT-1. The navy also acquired twelve dirigibles from the French.

AERIAL DEPTH CHARGES

During 1915 and 1916, the British produced two small aerial depth charges, designated Type C and the Type C*. Each type could be fitted with a 35-pound or a 65-pound charge. Regardless of the size of the charge, the Type C was equipped with a float and lanyard that pulled a pin to fire the charge at either forty or eighty feet. The Type C* had a hydrostatic pistol that fired the charge at fifty feet.[10]

The early aerial depth charges were too small to be really effective against a U-boat, so the British developed a 100-pound bomb and a 230-pound bomb that went into service during 1917. Both bombs were fused to explode two and a half seconds after impact, dispensing entirely with the hydrostatic fuse. The delay allowed the bomb to sink to about eighty feet before it exploded. In early 1918 the large flying boats were carrying four of the 230-pound bombs and the Kangaroo carried the 520-pound aerial depth charge, the largest aerial depth charge then in service.[11]

The French developed aerial depth charges parallel to the British and their bombs were very similar. The French produced aerial depth charges in three weights, starting with a 114-pound bomb carrying a 77-pound charge. The middleweight was a 165-pound bomb with a 110-pound charge and the largest was a 330-pounder with a 220-pound charge. All three were in use during 1917 and 1918.[12]

The U.S. Navy had been developing an aerial depth charge since 1915, but had no useful device in service when it entered the war. The problem with the American aerial depth charge was with the fuses, which did not always work or caused the bomb to explode prematurely. The Americans did produce a 163-pound bomb with a 117-pound charge, and a 276-pound bomb with a 217-pound charge. They were fused with British fuses, but were used only in the United States. The American naval aviation units overseas obtained aerial depth charges from the country in which they were operating.[13]

PATROL AND ATTACK TACTICS

ASW aircraft flew four types of missions: routine patrol, sweeps, convoy escort, and intensive patrols. Single aircraft flew routine patrols and two or more aircraft flew the sweeps and acted as convoy escorts. Although airplanes did fly convoy escort missions, that assignment fell overwhelmingly to the airships and the kite balloons. Intensive patrols were an attempt to saturate a relatively small area, but they proved difficult to maintain and were not particularly effective. In all cases the patrol planes were equipped with radios and carrier pigeons for communications with patrol headquarters. For communications with ships they used flares, message buoys, and the Aldis lamp.[14]

In 1918 the British created a plan called Operation Scarecrow in which air patrols, spaced twenty minutes apart, would cover the routes used by lone steamers sailing between ports and the convoy assembly and dispersal points. The plan called for an aircraft to pass over any given point along the routes every twenty minutes, which would mean that the U-boats would be forced to remain submerged or dive every twenty minutes. Either way, the U-boat batteries would be quickly depleted. The significance of the plan was that it did not matter if the planes were armed or not since the U-boats would dive.

The British scraped together enough DH-6s to create thirty-four two-plane flights and formed the Scarecrow units in May 1918. The operation's shoestring budget meant that it was poorly supplied and chronically short of personnel. In fact, there were many instances in which a plane went up without an observer aboard, leaving the pilot to do both tasks—fly and observe. Between 1 May and 11 November 1918, the Scarecrow planes sighted sixteen U-boats and attacked eleven. None of the attacks caused serious damage.[15]

Despite the apparent lack of success, the flights were more effective than the British realized. One of the goals of ASW is to hinder the enemy's ability to get at his targets, and Scarecrow units accomplished that. The effectiveness of the Scarecrow flights is indicated by the remarks U-boat captains entered in their war diaries. A typical example is found in Kapitänleutnant Hundius's war diary for UB-103. On 2 June 1918 he wrote that daylight operations off the Cornwall coast were impossible due to overwhelming air patrols that forced the U-boat to remain under water.[16]

RESULTS

Regardless of their nationality, airmen exaggerated their claims of having sunk or seriously damaged U-boats. British pilots claim to have sunk eleven U-boats in 1917 and 1918 and to have seriously damaged several others. One source claims that the Americans made thirty attacks and sank four U-boats; another claims twenty-five attacks that resulted in a dozen destroyed and damaged U-boats. French and Italian claims are similarly over-reported.[17]

There were four confirmed sinkings, supported by irrefutable evidence, in 1918 in which aircraft played a significant role. There is one instance in which there is a good possibility that an aircraft acting alone sank a U-boat, and one in which a kite balloon directed HMS *Patriot* in a successful attack. All the other claims are at best possible but not proven.

The problem is that there were no survivors from any of the U-boats that were reportedly sunk by aircraft, or with their assistance. And there was no identifiable wreckage to confirm the kill. The British account of UC-49's destruction on 31 May 1918 illustrates the problem. The British say that a DH-6 spotted and bombed UC-49 while the U-boat was attacking a convoy; surface vessels joined the hunt and depth charged the area thoroughly. A short time later another airplane bombed the U-boat twice, and surface vessels again followed up with heavy depth charging. The following day an FE2B dropped two 230-pound aerial depth charges on the UC-49 and the destroyer HMS *Locust* joined the attack with its depth charges, finally destroying the U-boat. The problem with the account is that on 30 and 31 May 1918, UC-49 was docked in Zeebrugge, and the

German records show no U-boat sunk off the British east coast during that period. In fact, UC-49 was sunk by HMS *Opossum* and seven MLs on 8 August 1918 in the English Channel.

A similar problem exists with the British claim that Wright seaplane 9860 sank UB-32 on 18 August 1917. UB-32's war diary shows that on 26 August—eight days after its reported demise—it torpedoed the 6,455-ton Italian steamer SS *Feltre* off Flamborough Head. The U-boat returned safely to Bruges on 30 August and remained there until 10 September when it put to sea on its last patrol. To give the British airmen their due, Large America Seaplane 8695 probably sank the UB-32 on 22 September as the U-boat was returning to Zeebrugge.[18]

Air crews claimed to have sunk several U-boats, but the truth is that most of the victories were achieved through a joint aircraft and surface vessel effort. On 5 June 1917 a British airplane led the British destroyer HMS *Ouse* to UC-70. On 2 May 1918 the British airship SSZ-29 and the French airship V-22 teamed up with three British trawlers and drove UB-31 down into the Folkestone–Gris Nez deep mine barrage. In September the British airships Z-1 and R-29 worked with surface patrols to destroy UB-103 and UB-115. In each case it is impossible to determine if the aircraft or the surface vessels were specifically responsible for the U-boat's destruction.[19]

Another example of the uncertainty that a U-boat was actually destroyed is illustrated by an American case. On 23 April 1918 two American air crews flying French seaplanes were protecting a twenty-ship convoy six miles north of Penmarch Point. Enlisted pilot R. H. Harrell, QM1c(A), and his observer H. W. Studer, QM2c(A), were in one plane and Ensign K. R. Smith and Ensign O. E. Williams were in the other. Ensigns Smith and Williams saw a suspicious wake, flew up the wake, and dropped two bombs on it. The first bomb landed on the fore part of the wake and the second ten feet ahead of it. The explosion caused a tremendous disturbance that brought air bubbles and sea growth to the surface. Harrell and Studer did not bomb, but they did drop a phosphorous buoy and circled the site while Smith and Williams flew off to fetch a destroyer. The USS *Stewart* and the French gunboat *Ardente* arrived and dropped depth charges, which brought more sea growth and oil to the surface. The French credited the officers with sinking a U-boat and awarded them the Croix de Guerre with Palm.[20]

Neither the Americans nor the French made any claim as to the U-boat's identity, and based their claim entirely on "underwater turbulence, sea growth and oil" coming to the surface. While the oil may have indicated that the bombs had broken open a U-boat's oil tank, the presence of underwater turbulence and sea growth rising to the surface was simply the result of the depth charges' explosions. The oil did not show up until after the USS *Stewart* and the *Ardente* had dropped their depth charges. It's possible that the U-boat in this incident was UB-70, which was lost ˙ en route to Cattaro sometime during April or May 1918.

The French credited the Americans with at least three other victories that were not supported by postwar evidence and there are no records supporting French claims that their aircraft sank a U-boat. There is a documented report, however, in which a French airship sank a British submarine. The British used the mistake to illustrate the fact that "there is indisputable evidence that a small bomb, properly aimed, will sink a submarine."[21]

Despite an airplane's ability to get over the target quickly, aircraft destroyed very few U-boats. Part of the problem was the lack of an efficient bombsight and the other part of the problem was the nature of the target. In most cases, the U-boat was already under by the time an airplane or blimp was in a position to bomb; usually all the air crew saw was a swirl, a diminishing wake, and maybe a trace of oil and some air bubbles. Airmen nearly always underestimated the time it took for oil and air bubbles to reach the surface, so they usually dropped their bombs well astern of a submerged U-boat.[22]

For example, two Short N2B float planes attacked UC-34 in the Otranto Straits on 17 June 1917. One pilot dropped two bombs slightly ahead of the swirl, but one bomb failed to explode. The second pilot dropped his bombs in the swirl and both exploded. Oberleutnant zur See Otto Sprenger described the encounter.

> Crash dived to avoid two enemy aircraft that were approaching rapidly from astern at about 900 feet. As we passed forty feet, 15° down angle, there was a powerful explosion close astern and two much weaker explosions farther away. The boat shook violently and we started taking water in the after torpedo room. The source of the flooding was a loosened rivet and another that had been blown completely out near the keel. Water was also entering through the hull fitting to the rudder yoke and the stern light. The bilge pump was able to handle the flooding and we plugged the empty rivet hole with a steel marlin-spike that we drove in and reinforced.

We surfaced after dark and found that the explosion had jammed the main air induction valve, ripped away the cooling water pipe to the exhaust, and had destroyed the radio mast gear and smashed the insulators. We cleared away the mast gear, repaired the air induction valve and reconnected the cooling water pipe. The damage was not serious and UC-34 was still able to dive.[23]

There was also the problem that most aerial depth charges were designed to explode at depths ranging from forty to eighty feet, which is a fairly narrow range. In those cases when the aircraft was carrying the Type C aerial depth bomb, the crews set one bomb to explode shallow and the other to explode deep, so that when they dropped them in salvo they achieved a straddling effect. The most destructive bombs, the 100-pounders and the 230-pounders, were designed to explode at about eighty feet. Most U-boat captains preferred to go deep when attacked, which meant that unless the explosions caught the U-boat as it passed seventy or eighty feet, the bombs did little or no damage.[24]

How effective were aircraft in the antisubmarine role? Based on the small number of U-boats destroyed as a result of aircraft involvement, they were not very effective. In fact, the official German view was that the losses to aircraft were so small that the few successes were essentially accidental occurrences. Too much emphasis, however, is placed on the numbers destroyed as the measure of success in ASW.[25]

The important number is how many attacks on shipping the use of aircraft prevented. Unfortunately that is an unknowable figure, much like trying to determine to what degree police patrols prevent crimes from happening. The best measure of how effective aircraft were is to look at German reactions to aircraft. The U-boats' war diaries reflect a steadily increasing concern about the presence of air patrols in the U-boats' operations areas. Complaints about being forced to remain submerged for long periods are common as are reports of being surprised by aircraft and forced to repeatedly dive. Judged by that standard, air patrols played an effective role in protecting shipping from U-boat attacks.

16

Submarines versus U-Boats

Vice Adm. William S. Sims, commander of the U.S. naval forces in Europe, suggested that setting submarines to sink U-boats may have been the most efficient use of resources. According to Sims, the Entente Powers had approximately five hundred destroyers available for ASW during the war. Thirty-three U-boats were sunk by destroyers, for a ratio of fifteen to one. Nearly three thousand auxiliary patrol vessels sank thirty-one U-boats, for a ratio of ninety-eight to one. One hundred British, French, and Italian submarines sank eighteen U-boats, for a five and a half to one ratio.[1]

During the last two years of the war, ASW was the primary mission for British submarines. In spring 1917 the Admiralty established the first submarine patrols off the north of Scotland and west of Ireland. At the same time the C-class boats, which were designed for coastal defense, were deployed in the English Channel and southern part of the North Sea (the Hoofden to the Germans). In summer 1917 the Admiralty stationed C-boats in the Fair Island Channel, and based oceangoing boats at Gibraltar to deal with the Germans' newly introduced, long-range cruiser U-boats. In March 1918 seven American L-class submarines began operations from Berehaven, Ireland. The British assigned the American boats to the English Channel and the Saint George's Channel in the southern entrance to the Irish Sea.[2]

The Admiralty divided the submarine patrol areas into squares, called billets, and assigned one submarine to each billet. As a matter of policy, a submarine was not allowed to leave its assigned area unless it was in pursuit of a U-boat. The patrolling submarines remained submerged during the day, moving at very slow speed to conserve their batteries, and surfaced at night to recharge. Patrols lasted eight days, at the end of which conditions aboard the submarines left the crews completely exhausted. Not only were the conditions aboard the British and American submarines awful, but the crews were constantly threatened by their own mines and British and American destroyers frequently depth charged them.[3]

During 1917 and 1918, British submarines in all theaters had a contact to sinking ratio of thirty to one, which meant that for every thirty sightings one successful attack was made. British submarine commanders often sighted surfaced U-boats but were unable to get close enough to attack because of their low underwater speed. Antisubmarine attack required high underwater speed, good maneuverability, and a powerful torpedo salvo. The latter was necessary because the target, a surfaced U-boat, was small, very maneuverable, and dove quickly. That meant there was rarely a chance to fire a second shot.

British submarine captains reported sighting surfaced U-boats from 364 to 390 times during 1917 and 1918. German U-boat captains reported 103 instances in which they either saw an enemy submarine or became aware of its presence when they saw the torpedo wake. German naval records list seventy torpedo attacks against U-boats that resulted in forty-three successful evasions, eight hits in which the torpedo failed to explode, and thirteen confirmed sinkings. American captains reported thirteen sightings and four unsuccessful attacks that resulted in eleven torpedoes fired and missed. American boats did not sink any U-boats, but their ratio of sightings to attacks, three to one, is nearly identical to the same calculation for British boats. What the ratio says is that American boats were as hampered by slow underwater speed as were the British.[4]

In eleven out of eighteen incidents in which a British or French submarine torpedoed a U-boat, there were at least a few survivors. In every case the survivors, usually the watch officer and two lookouts, had been outside the hull when the torpedo exploded. More men may have escaped from torpedoed U-boats, but they either died in the frigid waters or drowned when conditions prevented a rescue attempt.

British submarine G-13 torpedoed UC-43 on 10 March 1917.[5] Lt. Comdr. Bradshaw, in G-13, was patrolling on the surface twelve nautical miles north of Muckle Flugga Lighthouse. There was a gale blowing, the seas were enormous, and snow flurries reduced visibility. At 1600 Bradshaw saw an object to eastward that rose for a moment and then disappeared behind a huge wave. Bradshaw punched the dive alarm and went below, but the high seas slowed the dive. After an "intolerable wait," G-13 disappeared below the surface, but now the crew was having problems holding periscope depth.

In the meantime Bradshaw was searching for the fleeting target through his periscope when G-13 broached; in that moment he caught a glimpse of a U-boat on the surface. During the next forty minutes, Bradshaw caught only occasional glimpses of the U-boat and at 1640 heavy snow reduced visibility to zero. Five minutes later the snow stopped and Bradshaw saw that the U-boat had turned away.

The UC-43, commanded by Kapitänleutnant Sebelin, had left Helgoland on 25 February 1917 to lay mines off the south coast of Ireland and attack shipping. UC-43 passed through the Dover Straits without difficulty. Its mines accounted for two steamers, and it torpedoed two small coastal steamers and sank two sailing vessels with gunfire. His mines and torpedoes expended, Sebelin decided to take the northern route home.[6]

At 1652, UC-43 again changed course and presented its port side to G-13. Unable to get any closer, Bradshaw fired two torpedoes at three thousand yards, an extreme range under good conditions and an impossible range in heavy weather. Two and a half minutes passed without an explosion, and Bradshaw was sure he had missed. Just moments later, while he was examining the U-boat through the periscope, "there was a deafening crash and G-13 rang like a bell. The black pencil hung in the air for a long time, the top spraying away down wind. The enemy's conning tower seemed to sag aft and the bows cocked up and then disappeared."[7] There were no survivors.

Occasionally there were several survivors, as happened when E-54 torpedoed U-81 on 1 May 1917. Kapitänleutnant Raimund Weisbach, in U-81, put events in motion when he torpedoed SS *San Urbano* off Fastnet. Despite a solid hit forward of the bridge, the freighter did not sink and Kapitänleutnant Weisbach waited thirty minutes before surfacing to finish the job with gunfire. *San Urbano*'s crew had abandoned ship right after the torpedo hit, and were pulling steadily away while U-81's gun crew shelled the freighter into a sinking condition. Satisfied that *San*

Urbano was settling, Weisbach headed toward the lifeboats, which were already some distance away, to get the freighter's cargo and destination. What Weisbach did not know was that he had torpedoed *San Urbano* in E-54's patrol billet, and the British submarine was at that moment making its attack approach. Commander Raikes fired a single torpedo at a range of about nine hundred yards when he was off U-81's port quarter. His aiming point was just forward of the U-boat's bow.

Seaman Herbert Hoeck and Weisbach saw the periscope and the torpedo wake at the same time. The captain reacted immediately by ordering all ahead full in an attempt to pull ahead and let the torpedo pass astern. According to Hoeck, the captain had just shouted the command when the torpedo hit aft and exploded. Its entire stern blown away, U-81 sank in five seconds, leaving the three men on the bridge and the four gunners swimming in the water. Fifteen minutes later, G-13 surfaced and picked them up.[8]

Most often the British submarines torpedoed a U-boat that was running on the surface but not engaged in sinking a steamer. That was the case when on 3 November 1917 C-15 torpedoed UC-65 fifteen nautical miles off Beachy Head. UC-65 Kapitänleutnant Erik Lafrenz had laid mines off Le Havre and had torpedoed the British SS *North Sea* on 2 November. The freighter did not sink and patrols forced UC-65 to break off its attack. UC-65 was headed home on the afternoon of 3 November when it entered C-15's patrol billet.

The British submarine was surfaced when the lookout spotted the approaching U-boat. C-15's skipper, Lieutenant Dolphin, recorded the next events in his log.

1443: Sighted enemy submarine on the surface five points on the port bow. Dived and flooded both tubes.

1512: Sighted submarine in periscope.

1515: Fired double shot at 400 yards. One torpedo hit. Submarine sank immediately.[9]

Moments before Lieutenant Dolphin fired his torpedoes, UC-65's lookouts spotted the periscope and Kapitänleutnant Lafrenz turned hard to port and went full ahead. Kapitänleutnant Lafrenz's description of the hit is more descriptive.

The first torpedo hit us dead amidships, but did not explode, apparently because it struck us at too great an angle as we were turning, and bounced

off. The second torpedo must have hit the rudder or the propeller, because
when it exploded, it tore off the stern and the boat sank immediately.[10]

Two minutes after the explosion, Lieutenant Dolphin brought C-15 to
the surface and picked up four survivors from UC-65. In addition to
Kapitänleutnant Lafrenz, the survivors included his second in command,
Leutnant zur See Braue, and two sailors. Lafrenz was not on watch and
survived only because he had gone up on the bridge to get some air.

From 1 February 1917 to 31 October 1918, the U-boat captains recorded a total of ninety-nine British torpedoes that were fired at them and
missed. Some missed because the aim was off, but in most cases the
U-boat was able to maneuver to avoid the torpedo, or torpedoes. More
dramatic and unsettling were the eight duds that scored hits but failed
to explode.

A typical example occurred on 5 April 1917 off the Schouwen Bank
when the British submarine C-7 attacked UB-10. C-7 was trimmed down
so that only the top of its conning tower was above the surface when its
skipper, Lieutenant Forbes, spotted UB-10 approaching on the surface
from astern. Forbes wrote in his log, "5 April 1917 0332: Sighted submarine on port quarter steering north, distance 400 yards. Turned and
fired port torpedo. Hit forward with a loud explosion, sending up a column of water. Submarine turned to port and sank in a few seconds.
The night was very dark and misty, and no survivors or debris could
be seen."[11]

In fact, UB-10's lookouts saw the periscope and the twin torpedo
tracks at the same time. Oberleutnant zur See Rohrscheidt avoided the
first torpedo but the second slammed into UB-10's hull right below the
conning tower and did not detonate.[12]

British radio intelligence also played a role in the submarine versus
U-boat operations. In May 1918 Room 40 copied the radio traffic between U-153 and U-154 setting up an 11 May rendezvous 150 miles west
of Cape Saint Vincent, Portugal. Their radio traffic gave two locations
thirty miles apart, and the time was set for "any time in daylight hours
of 11 May." The Admiralty sent the submarines J-1 and E-35 to watch
both locations.[13]

Lieutenant Commander D'Oyly-Hughes, in E-35, arrived at his
assigned spot just after daylight on 11 May and began patrolling at periscope depth. There was a high sea running and E-35 had some difficulty

maintaining periscope depth; because E-35 was equipped with an extra long periscope, the difficulty did not become a real problem. At 1600 D'Oyly-Hughes spotted U-154 on the surface, moving slowly. D'Oyly-Hughes went down to sixty feet, turned toward the target, and went ahead at high speed.

He returned to periscope depth at 1616 only to find that the U-boat had changed direction and was moving away from him. Again D'Oyly-Hughes went to sixty feet and gave chase. Regular returns to periscope depth showed that E-35 was holding steady at about a mile astern of the U-boat, but was unable to close the gap. The chase continued for two hours.

At 1817 D'Oyly-Hughes took another look and saw that U-154 was coming back his way. In fact, the U-boat was a bit too close, but D'Oyly-Hughes did not want to lose his opportunity. There was no time to turn for a bow shot, so E-35 fired a single torpedo from the starboard beam tube. At the critical moment U-154 rose up on a swell and the torpedo passed under it.

The chase continued until 1822 when D'Oyly-Hughes fired two torpedoes down the trough between two waves. Both torpedoes hit, and both exploded. The first one hit directly under the forward gun and the second hit directly under the after gun, detonating U-154's magazine. The explosion obliterated the U-boat.

Four miles away, U-153's bridge watch witnessed the destruction and described the action. "U-154 was in sight four points off the port quarter about four miles away when she suddenly disappeared in a bright flash, black smoke and a high water column. Nothing more was seen of her."[14] Moments later they saw E-35 surface and remain surfaced for two to three minutes. The heavy sea prevented U-153 from making a torpedo attack on E-35, which dove and was not seen again. U-153 moved through the wreck site looking for survivors, but found only oil and debris on the surface.

Despite the success of the submarine versus U-boat operation, the high number of sightings compared to the small number of successful attacks frustrated the Admiralty. The result was the R-class design, the first true hunter-killer submarine built for the exclusive purpose of sinking U-boats. In its final form, the R-class boats had an underwater speed of fifteen knots and six 18-inch forward torpedo tubes. The British used a single hull design for minimum underwater drag, and further reduced the drag by eliminating the casing aft of the conning tower. The R-class boats had a single 240 horsepower diesel that gave it an eight-knot surface speed. For submerged power the R-class boats had two electric motors and batteries consisting of 220 cells that gave it a top underwater speed of fifteen knots for thirty minutes, and an impressive twelve and a half knots for an hour and forty-eight minutes.[15]

The British ordered twelve of the new hunter-killer R-boats in the autumn of 1917 and five were delivered before the war ended. They were small boats, 160 feet long and just 500 tons submerged displacement. The rudder and diving planes featured large surface areas that, combined with small reserve buoyancy, made the R-boats very fast divers. They were superb underwater boats, but were terrible sea boats when on the surface.

The R-class boats received the newly developed revolving directional hydrophone, designated the RD. The RD hydrophone could be used while under way and the British hoped that a submarine's crew could locate, track, and attack a target using the hydrophone supplemented with a minimum use of the periscope. British hopes far exceeded the RD hydrophone's abilities, but the concept was a radical step forward in ASW.

17

The Convoy System

During the first half of 1917 the ratio of merchant tonnage sunk to the number of U-boats destroyed remained high because the ASW measures being developed by the Anti-Submarine Division took several months to become effective. Two developments occurred at about the same time that reduced the ratio: the entry of the United States into the war and the institution of the convoy system. The effects of the convoy system began to be noticed almost immediately, but the advantages of American participation took a while longer to show effect.

Some writers credit the convoy system with defeating the U-boat, but this is an overstatement. The convoy system certainly played a deciding role in reducing shipping losses and made a major contribution to the final victory over the U-boats. Two other factors worked to ensure the success of the convoy system: the introduction of the depth charge and the increased availability of destroyers, P-boats, sloops, and subchasers.

Another important contributing factor was the Germans' failure to modify their tactics to deal with the convoy system. When that tactical failure was combined with the limited number of U-boats they were able to deploy at any one time, the result was that the convoy system simply overwhelmed Germany's resources. The latter situation was made worse by the Germans' consistent 50 percent torpedo failure.[1]

If the convoy system was so effective, why did the British wait so long to adopt it? The answer is that prior to February 1917 the situation was not serious enough to warrant adopting the convoy system. By 1916, the Royal Navy had virtually eliminated the threat of German surface raiders in the North Atlantic, and U-boats rarely operated beyond three hundred to four hundred miles from land. Thus traffic across the Atlantic was unmolested and losses in the three hundred mile danger zone were still manageable. When the Germans opened their unrestricted anti-shipping campaign in February 1917, the situation changed dramatically. As losses rose through April, the Admiralty gave increasing thought to adopting the convoy system.

Convoy sailing was the historically recognized method of trade protection since the age of sail and historical experience was a strong argument for using it again. Accurate station keeping was not particularly important in the days of sail, and the escorts' guns could deal with any threat. In those bygone days the escorts detached themselves from the convoy and sailed toward the threat to investigate and deal with it while the convoy closed up, altered course, and sailed away from the danger.

The conditions in 1917 were entirely different than had been the case in the age of sail, specifically the U-boat and the torpedo. Gunfire from escorts or armed merchant ships was a good countermeasure as long as the Germans followed the Prize Regulations, a situation that was not much different from the age of sail. The gun's value dropped to zero, however, when the U-boats took advantage of their ability to attack while submerged, a fact that caused many people to believe that the convoy concept was outdated. In fact it was not.

The British had gained modern convoy experience escorting troopships from Canada, Australia, New Zealand, and India since the first months of the war. Those convoys were politically necessary because the dominion governments would not allow their troops to sail unprotected. It is true that those early war convoys were small, the crews were of exceptional quality, and the Germans did not contest the passage. Nevertheless, the convoy concept was applied to a real situation, and it worked.[2]

Arguments against the convoy fell into two categories: administrative and tactical. Those who opposed adopting the convoy system for administrative reasons cited delays and higher costs for the shipping companies. They also argued that delays caused by the convoys' relatively slow speed would effectively reduce tonnage and anything that reduced tonnage was unacceptable.

The opponents also pointed out that convoys would result in a large number of ships arriving at any harbor at the same time and that would create instant congestion. Congestion meant delays in discharging cargoes, and there was the concern that ships anchored out, waiting for an open dock, would be easy targets for the U-boats.

Last, both merchant officers and navy officers believed that merchant officers were incapable of steaming and maneuvering in convoy. They predicted frequent collisions, especially at night and in bad weather. The merchant officers pointed out that the best watch officers had been taken into the navy and the less capable replacements were not up to the task of maintaining position in convoy.[3]

The tactical arguments against the convoy stressed the idea that a convoy grouped several targets in one place and made it easier for a U-boat to destroy large numbers in a shorter time. This argument held that when a U-boat attacked a convoy it would be like shooting fish in a barrel. Even if the torpedo missed the intended target it would simply hit another vessel in the closely packed group. There was also the mine threat. A single ship that hit a mine remained a solitary loss and revealed the location of the minefield. A convoy steaming through a minefield would result in multiple losses, including escort losses.

In fact, none of those arguments proved to be the case except that delays did occur and operating costs did go up. The fatal problems associated with collisions and grouped targets did not occur. In practice the merchant officers were fully capable of maintaining position in convoy and executing the zigzag course changes on command, and night steaming without lights was accomplished with little difficulty.

The group target problem proved to be a wholly unfounded given the fact that the U-boats did not adopt the so-called wolf pack tactic. Had they done so the convoy system would have been in serious trouble. As it was, the U-boats continued to operate alone; when one did attack a convoy its window of opportunity was limited to the time it took the convoy to pass across the U-boat's position. After that, it was a matter of chase and catch up, and the U-boats were usually not able to do that.

Despite the arguments against adopting the convoy system, it was obvious by early 1917 that something had to be done. Adopting a convoy system, however, hinged on the availability of suitable escorts. In

February 1917 the British figured they had forty destroyers and sloops plus eighteen cruisers and armed merchant auxiliaries available for ocean escort duty. That was not enough. According to their estimates they needed at least 125 destroyers and sloops plus 62 cruisers and armed merchant auxiliaries.

America's entry into the war on 6 April 1917 eased the situation but did not immediately fill the gap. The British had hoped that the U.S. Navy would furnish all its fifty-one available destroyers; instead, they got six on 4 May 1917. The situation steadily improved as U.S. destroyers arrived in six-ship groups on an almost weekly basis. Six of the new arrivals joined the American presence in Queenstown after escorting the American troopships to France, and by 15 July 1917 there were thirty-four American destroyers in Queenstown.[4]

Even before the United States declared war on Germany, the Admiralty was moving toward adopting the convoy system. The British brought the cross-Channel coal trade with France under convoy in March 1917 because the French were heavily dependent on British coal for their war industry. A coal shortage in France meant material shortages at the front. When the U-boats took a heavy toll of the cross-channel coal colliers during the last quarter of 1916 the British instituted the coal trade convoys. The British did not call them convoys, using instead the term "controlled sailing" to avoid giving the Germans legal grounds for torpedoing the colliers without warning. Despite the legal two-step, they were in fact convoys.[5]

The interesting feature of those coal convoys is that sailing ships sailed in convoy with steamers. That fact went a long way toward discounting the opponents' arguments that differences in speed would make convoys inefficient. There was also the fact that the sailing ships had to tack while staying with the convoy. The coal trade's importance to the war effort made daily convoys the rule. From March to August 1917 the British convoyed 8,825 coal vessels across the channel and lost only fourteen ships.[6]

The Scandinavian trade was brought under convoy at the end of April 1917 and losses immediately dropped. The British used trawlers to escort the Scandinavian convoys and reinforced them with airships, decoy ships, and submarines. By June the Scandinavian convoy system was so effective that the Germans were deploying their large U-boats against the convoys. The impression the Scandinavian convoys made on the U-boat captains is illustrated by Kapitänleutnant Hans Walther's 19 July log entry:

"Steamer traffic is only found in strongly escorted convoys that travel regularly, daily to and from Norway. British submarines are found everywhere along the steamer track. Airships, each with a destroyer under it, are very bothersome. As a result it is rarely possible to overtake a convoy and make a second attack on it."[7]

Even after the British organized the Scandinavian trade into convoys the U-boats still found lone ships, which they torpedoed or sank according to the Prize Regulations. UC-31 torpedoed a lone steamer off the Scottish coast on 8 September 1917 and was immediately attacked by an airship, which it had failed to spot. UC-75 torpedoed the Swedish steamer SS *Frederika* on 12 July 1917 and sank the French steamer SS *Tarapaca* according to the Prize Regulations on 1 September.[8]

Shortly after instituting the Scandinavian convoys the British did the same thing with the traffic along their east coast. They used a special route called the "war channel" to move traffic up and down the coast between the terminus of the Scandinavian convoys at Lerwick in the Shetland Islands and the Humber. In a very short time the U-boats rarely found single vessels steaming in the war channel, and the number of lone ships elsewhere steadily decreased. According to Admiral Jellicoe, between April and December 1917 the British convoyed six thousand merchant ships between the Shetlands and the Humber and lost only seventy.[9]

The French quickly followed the British example and adopted the convoy system for their coastal traffic. The Flanders boats noticed the change immediately. On 26 April 1917, Oberleutnant zur See Reinhold Saltzwedel in UC-21 wrote in his war diary:

There are no ships sailing alone on the French west coast. Every day there are many convoys along the coast with only two trawlers for escorts. For a minelayer with only four torpedoes, and whose duty is primarily minelaying, the prospects of effective anti-commerce war are small. The need for a fast boat with many torpedoes to work this area is urgent. Firing eight to ten torpedoes in two nights would be expected. In good weather it would be possible for a single boat to completely destroy a convoy in one night.[10]

On 30 April 1917 Admiral Jellicoe told Admiral Sims that a decision had been made to send an experimental convoy from Gibraltar to England. The sixteen-ship convoy left Gibraltar on 10 May 1917 and arrived safely at its dispersal site off the British coast on 20 May. On 21 May

1917 the Admiralty voted to adopt the convoy system for all merchant shipping.[11]

The North Atlantic homeward bound traffic was brought under convoy in May 1917 and homeward bound traffic from Gibraltar in July 1917. The first Atlantic convoy left New York on 14 August 1917 and its successors sailed about every sixteen days thereafter, but it took time for the British to develop a complete convoy system. At first 40 percent of the homeward bound traffic was convoyed, then gradually the numbers were increased to 60, 80, and 100 percent.[12]

The British controlled the convoys from a single location called the convoy room, which was located in the Admiralty. Every morning the heads of the departments charged with antisubmarine warfare met in the convoy room to review the current U-boat situation, which included Room 40 intercepts and radio direction finder (RDF) location reports.

A huge chart entirely covered one wall, and ladders allowed technicians to reach any part of the chart. The chart gave a comprehensive view of the North and South American coast, the Atlantic Ocean, the British Isles, and a considerable part of Europe and Africa. Seven ports were highlighted: Sydney, Halifax, New York, Hampton Roads, Gibraltar, Sierra Leone, and Dakar. Thin threads stretched from each of those ports to hand-off positions at the outer boundary of the U-boat danger zone off the British coast. Small paper boats, each one representing a convoy with its number and letter designation clearly displayed, were attached to the threads. Technicians moved the boats along the threads according to the convoy's advance.

Small circles on the chart indicated the last known position of U-boats based on radio intercepts and RDF position reports. The technicians advanced the circles each day so that the staff could determine the known track of a U-boat and make an educated guess as to its projected track. Based on a U-boat's known positions and projected track, the convoy room could reroute any convoy around the danger in its path.[13]

Ships to be escorted through the danger zone gathered at one of the seven designated gateways worldwide to form cross-ocean convoys. Convoys were usually twenty to thirty ships all sailing at the speed of the slowest vessel; whenever possible ships of about equal speed were grouped together. The Admiralty rigidly controlled the departure schedules from the seven gateways. For example, convoys from New York sailed every sixteen days and convoys bound for New York from England's west coast were also on a sixteen-day schedule. Convoys originating in Hampton Roads that were bound for Britain departed every eight days. The schedule was altered only to avoid congestion at the arrival ports.

Destroyers and patrol craft escorted each convoy from the departure gate to the outer boundary of the U-boat danger zone, which was usually three hundred miles offshore at each end of the route. There they handed off the convoy to the ocean escorts, usually cruisers or pre-Dreadnought battleships that escorted the convoy across the open sea. The open sea escort provided defense against surface raiders, not U-boats, which did not operate in the Atlantic until the introduction of the U-cruisers in September 1917.

A typical crossing from the United States to Great Britain took fifteen to twenty days, depending upon the speed of the slowest ship. The convoy was a moving antisubmarine zone covering about ten square miles with the ships spaced nine hundred to one thousand yards apart. As soon as the convoy met its destroyer escort at the outer boundary of the coastal danger zone, the ocean escort turned around and headed back to pick up another convoy. In many cases, the danger zone escorts handed off a convoy that the ocean escorts took back with them. In some cases the ocean escorts went directly into British ports to refuel and resupply.

The immediate effect the Atlantic convoy system had on the U-boats is evident in their captains' war diary entries. Kapitänleutnant Saalwächter, commanding U-94, commented on 16 August 1917:

On the West Coast only one unescorted steamer was seen, all other steam with one or more destroyers, even the fast passenger ships. Patrols on the approaches and in close to shore are much lighter than formerly. All available patrols appear to be assigned to escort duty. Given the situation, gun attacks are almost impossible and submerged attacks are much more difficult.[14]

Kapitänleutnant Heeseler, commanding U-54, was even more frustrated after a patrol that lasted from 19 November to 24 December 1917. He wrote, "The patrol produced no results. South of Ireland we encountered no traffic, fired no torpedoes and expended no ammunition."[15]

Kapitänleutnant Saalwächter, who had already experienced the convoys' effect along the British east coast, found a similar situation on his patrol that lasted from 15 September to 15 October 1917 off the northwest

Irish coast. He wrote, "During this twenty-eight day patrol we saw only one steamer and one sailing vessel. We did see two convoys that other U-boats had alerted us to by radio, but we failed to get in close enough to shoot. Part of the problem was caused by the bad weather, which limited our weapons use to three days."[16]

With the inauguration of the convoy system the Allied defenses tightened and there was an immediate drop in losses during May, June, and July. The figures started dropping dramatically in August and were down to 338,650 tons in December. Shipping was under control near the end of 1917. In 1918 the figures steadily declined from a high of 344,814 tons in March to 112,427 tons in October.[17]

The convoy system worked because it reduced the number of targets a U-boat might encounter and brought the U-boat in close contact with strong ASW forces. Under the pre-convoy sailing system, ships were strung out across the Atlantic, or the Mediterranean, separated by several hours or even days. A U-boat that was positioned along a shipping route could expect to encounter several targets during its time on station. The situation was very much like that of a sniper watching a stretch of roadway and picking off each target as it came along.

The convoys eliminated the steady stream of individual targets along any given route. Instead, a strongly escorted group showed up and moved quickly through the U-boat's station. Once the convoy passed, there would not be another for several days, sometimes not for a week or two. The convoy system created a situation similar to that of a rifle squad crossing a road. Instead of going one at a time, and giving the sniper plenty of opportunities to shoot at individual soldiers, the squad rushes across the road in one wave, giving the enemy only a fleeting opportunity to fire. For that reason, small convoys of four to five ships traveled in line abreast instead of in column.

The introduction of the convoy system had the unintended benefit that the U-boats were drawn into contact with the escorts. In a sense, a convoy was a decoy. The inauguration of the convoy system occurred at the same time that depth charges were becoming available in much greater numbers, allowing some escorts to carry as many as sixty. The methods for launching depth charges also improved so that more could be dropped over a larger area in a shorter time. Escorts working together could literally blanket an area with fearsome results. By the end of the war escorts were dropping depth charges at the rate of about twenty thousand per month in the waters around Great Britain, and individual attacks using one hundred depth charges were not uncommon.[18]

U-21, commanded by Kapitänleutnant Otto Hersing, attacked a convoy fifty miles northwest of Ireland on 17 August 1917. After Hersing fired his torpedoes the escorts carried out a ferocious attack, saturating the area with depth charges. Hersing took U-21 down to 150 feet to escape the explosions that during one two-minute period occurred every ten seconds. The destroyers remained in the area for five hours waiting for U-21 to surface. Hersing says the experience taught him to take refuge under the convoy.[19]

While it was hoped that depth charging would sink a U-boat, the depth charge's most effective accomplishment was forcing the U-boats to dive deep and turn away from the convoys. That prevented second attacks because the convoys moved away at a speed greater than the U-boats could achieve while submerged. By the time the ASW forces were finished depth charging a U-boat the convoy was too far away for the U-boat to catch up.

The Germans failed to modify their tactics to deal with the convoys. In fact, Kommodore Hermann Bauer tried to do just that, but Admiral von Holtzendorff rejected his excellent plan. Since 1915 the U-boats had used their radios to alert one another to target opportunities. There was nothing coordinated about the practice, it was just a catch as catch can thing. When the British introduced the convoy system, the practice took on a greater importance, but it was never organized into a concerted joint effort. Kommodore Bauer attempted to organize the practice into a controlled effort.

Bauer submitted a proposal in April 1917 to use the former *U-Deutschland,* now the U-155, as an offshore radio command post. Under Bauer's plan U-155 would be equipped with the latest radio equipment and stationed far offshore to intercept the inbound convoys. Radio specialists would monitor the British radio traffic between the Admiralty and the convoys at sea to determine the position and track of the convoys approaching Britain. As the situation took shape, and the convoy's route and projected track became clear, Bauer or his representative aboard U-155 would call in the prepositioned U-boats and coordinate their combined attacks on the inbound convoy. In World War II it was called the Wolf Pack. In addition to being a command post, U-155 would also carry fuel, torpedoes, and supplies for the U-boats. Bauer's idea was a forerunner of a World War II development that the Germans called the *Milchkuh* (milk cow), a seagoing supply base.[20]

U-155 was ideally suited to both roles. Built in 1915–16 to carry cargo between Germany and the United States, it was the first unit in an eight-boat, blockade breaking fleet. U-155 made two trips to the United States in 1916, the only one of the eight specially built boats to actually make the crossing. Designed as a cargo carrier, it was big and roomy, and had excellent sea-keeping qualities.[21]

In 1917 U-155 and the remaining six boats were converted to war boats, designated U-cruisers, and assigned the task of carrying the anti-shipping war to the waters off the United States and the Azores. U-155 and its sisters would have been better used in Bauer's command boat role, but the Admiralstab was in love with the U-cruiser idea so that is where U-155 went. The Germans may have had the solution to the convoy problem, but they let it slip away.

18

Howitzers, Bomb Throwers, and Depth Charge Throwers

The deck gun's inadequacy against a submerged U-boat motivated the British to develop guns that could fire underwater exploding rounds. Throughout 1915 and 1916 the British experimented with various designs that featured barrels with calibers ranging from 2-inch to 15-inch, and using CO_2, steam, gunpowder, and even a coil spring for the propellant. In the end they settled on gunpowder.[1]

Working with the basic requirement that the weapon should be capable of throwing a charge at least 250 to 300 yards, the British developed two separate howitzers: one that could throw a 100-pound projectile and the other that could throw a 200-pound projectile, each with a 1,000-yard range. The initial tests showed that the charge in the 100-pound projectile was too small, and the design was temporarily shelved while work proceeded on the 200-pound version.

Continued development resulted in the production of two distinct weapons. One was a howitzer with a rifled barrel and the other was a bomb thrower with a smooth barrel. The difference in the barrel type meant that two different rounds were developed, and the smooth bore version was essentially the predecessor to the Thornycroft bomb thrower and the American Y-gun. The rounds developed for the howitzer and the bomb thrower were closely related to the depth charge.

The British put the first service models into production in April 1917 and started issuing howitzers and bomb throwers in June 1917, giving the Auxiliary Patrol trawlers and Special Service Vessels priority for receiving the weapons. The British produced howitzers in three calibers: 5-inch, 7.5-inch, and 11-inch. They produced the bomb throwers in five calibers: 3.5-inch, 6-inch, 7.5-inch, 10-inch, and 13.5-inch. The Admiralty equipped most of the Auxiliary Patrol vessels with 7.5-inch howitzers and the rest with 3.5-inch stick bomb throwers.

HOWITZERS

The round the howitzer fired looked like a conventional artillery round but was fused to explode either on contact or at twenty feet.[2] The contact-fused shells were designed to penetrate the submarine's casing without shattering and to explode on contact with the pressure hull. A fuse designed to explode the charge two seconds after impact determined the depth. The 7.5-inch howitzer fired an improved 100-pound projectile with a 43-pound charge twenty-one hundred yards and a 500-pound projectile carrying a 250-pound charge. The latter could be lofted out three hundred yards. In June 1918 the British modified both rounds with a flat disk that broke the trajectory and caused the rounds to dive more steeply.

BOMB THROWERS

The round used with the smooth bore bomb thrower was closely related to the depth charge and its appearance was similar to an oversized German potato masher hand grenade. The can portion closely resembled a depth charge, except that the outer end of the can was rounded to give it a streamlined effect that reduced resistance. The whole assembly was called the stick bomb because it looked like a can on a stick. The stick, which was officially called the arbor or stem, went in the barrel and the stick and the can were fired as a unit. The stick bombs came with four hydrostatic fuses that offered a depth range of 40 feet, 90 feet, 140 feet, or 190 feet. The 3.5-inch stick bomb thrower fired a 200-pound bomb 1,200 yards and a 350-pound bomb 650 yards. The 200-pound bomb had a 98-pound explosive charge and the 350-pound bomb had a 200-pound charge. By 1 October 1917 the Admiralty had armed 42 Auxiliary Patrol vessels with howitzers, and the number rose steadily; a year later the number reached 174.

The British also developed a 200-pound stick bomb that was issued only to the Auxiliary Patrol for use with 12-pounders, each gun receiving four rounds. Like the other stick bombs, the 12-pounder version was equipped with four hydrostatic fuses that provided a choice of four depths: 40 feet, 90 feet, 140 feet, or 190 feet. The British turned out 3,100 12-pounder stick bombs by the end of the war.

Howitzers and bomb throwers were designed to fire dead ahead, though the howitzers had a limited traversing capability. The best place for the gun was on the forecastle head, but that was not always possible because other weapons and equipment often occupied the space. The 7.5-inch howitzers were, in almost all cases, mounted over the trawler's fish hold. The 3.5-inch stick bomb throwers, which were all issued to fish-hydrophone trawlers, were mounted on the forecastle and the 12-pounder gun was mounted on the engine room casing.

The Admiralty Historical Section did not record the instances in which these weapons were actually used, and there are no certified successes listed. But they were certainly used. Undoubtedly, many of the reports the U-boat captains entered in their war diaries about single depth charges exploding in the distance can be attributed to these weapons.

THORNYCROFT DEPTH CHARGE THROWER

Howitzers and bomb throwers fired their projectiles straight ahead and were useful aboard Auxiliary Patrol vessels, but destroyers, P-boats, and sloops needed something different. While it was true that one well-placed depth charge could sink a U-boat, the reality was that it was essentially impossible to accurately place a single depth charge. Until the introduction of the Thornycroft depth charge thrower the standard practice was to run down the U-boat's projected track and drop depth charges at ten-to-fifteen-second intervals. But that tactic did not allow for the U-boat changing direction to move out of the destroyer's path. To overcome that problem, the British developed the depth charge thrower, which allowed the destroyer to throw depth charges out from the side of the ship while dropping the pattern astern.[3] This had the effect of increasing the danger zone.

The Thornycroft single tube depth charge thrower had been under development since early in 1916 and went into general service in August 1917. Operating on the bomb thrower principle, the Thornycroft depth charge thrower could hurl a 300-pound Type D depth charge forty yards.

In its basic configuration the British fitted one on each quarter so that two could be fired to port and starboard while two more depth charges were rolled off the stern. As the throwers became available in greater numbers, the British mounted them in two- and three-gun batteries on both quarters of some destroyers, P-boats, and sloops.

The Thornycroft depth charge thrower was similar in appearance to a mortar but it functioned like an artillery piece. A standard charge was loaded into the breech at the base of the weapon and was fired with a lanyard. The Type D depth charge was fitted with an arbor or stem, in a T-shaped configuration, and the stem was set inside the smooth bore barrel. The depth charge and its attached stem were fired as a unit.

Y-GUN

The Thornycroft depth charge thrower was an efficient weapon but it was overengineered to the point that the British experienced manufacturing delays. Production was so slow that the British turned to the Americans for help. Shortly after the United States entered the war, the British supplied the U.S. Bureau of Ordnance with photographs and designs of the Thornycroft depth charge thrower. Because the Thornycroft presented manufacturing problems that bothered even the British, the Americans decided to develop a more efficient variation. Lt. Comdr. A. J. Stone, USNRF, who had worked for the General Ordnance Company in Groton, Connecticut, before the war, was put in charge of developing the American Y-gun.[4]

The Y-gun was similar in principal to the Thornycroft depth charge thrower, but it was easier to build and was able to fire two 300-pound Mark II depth charges simultaneously, one to port and one to starboard. It was more compact than the Thornycroft design, which allowed the Americans to install Y-guns on subchasers. The Y-gun, so named because it had two arms set at a 45 degree angle, was mounted over the keel line near the fantail. The depth charges were attached to plungers that fit into the bores of the gun and were discharged with the depth charges.

The propelling charge was a blank 3-inch shell that the gunner inserted in the breech at the intersection of the barrels, and he fired it by pulling a lanyard. The impulse charge—the blank round—could be varied to provide ranges of fifty, sixty-six, and eighty yards. Destroyers equipped with the Y-gun were able to saturate a wide area with depth charges, which increased the chances of achieving a kill.

Stone's old employer, General Ordnance Company, started production on 24 November 1917 and made the first deliveries on 10 December. Since the official contract was signed on 8 December the two days between contract and delivery had to have been the shortest contract to delivery period in the history of military procurement. During the twelve months from 10 December 1917 to 11 November 1918 the U.S. Navy installed 974 Y-guns in destroyers and subchasers.

MARK I DEPTH CHARGE LAUNCHING RACK

Probably the most significant contribution the Americans made was the invention of the depth charge rack that allowed timed, spaced dropping of the depth charges over the stern.[5] The depth charges could be launched from the bridge or manually from the deck. Prior to 1918 there was no standard depth charge launching rack that allowed variably timed, evenly spaced drops. In most cases two depth charges were carried singly in two slings on a destroyer's stern. The depth charges were dropped in pairs, after which two replacement charges had to be rolled into place and hooked up. Controlled timing and spacing were impossible.

The first multiple depth charge rack was the Mark I that the U.S. Navy's Bureau of Ordnance designed with help from Lieutenant Commander Isherwood, RN, in spring 1918. The Mark I launching rack held eight depth charges and could be operated from the bridge or from the deck. The Mark I was mounted in pairs on the stern, and each rack weighed about a ton, which made the rack suitable only for destroyers. The U.S. Navy issued the first production contract for two hundred on 26 March 1918. Deliveries started in June and 250 destroyers— American, British, and French—were using them by 11 November 1918.

An improved version with an extension allowed a destroyer to carry twenty-six depth charges ready to drop. The U.S. Navy placed an order for four hundred extended racks and two hundred—enough for one hundred vessels—were delivered by the end of the war. Late in the summer of 1918 a smaller rack, the Mark II, weighing 420 pounds and carrying five depth charges went into production. The Mark II was intended for subchasers that were too small to carry the Mark I, but only a few were installed before the war ended.

Increased depth charge supplies and improved equipment for dropping them gave rise to new destroyer tactics designed to saturate an area with depth charges. Standard practice in 1918 was to drop depth charges in a figure-eight pattern. To do that the destroyer immediately went to the spot where the U-boat dove or where the torpedo wake indicated the source of the firing. As the destroyer passed over the spot, it dropped a depth charge and continued to drop depth charges every ten to fifteen seconds while turning in a circle that brought it back to the original point. As it passed over the original point of contact, the destroyer continued dropping depth charges while making another circle that formed the figure-eight. The Y-guns and Thornycroft throwers greatly increased the area covered.

When working in pairs, both destroyers crossed the initial contact point and circled in opposite directions, each destroyer dropping depth charges every ten or fifteen seconds. Two destroyers working together greatly increased the chance of scoring a kill; in the case of a single destroyer the odds favored the U-boat's escape.

The problem for the destroyer was part basic math and part basic guesswork. The quicker the destroyer arrived over the point of contact, the better were the chances for destroying the U-boat, because any delay gave the U-boat more time to get away. In either case, the question was: Which way did the U-boat go, and how deep was it? Interestingly, the U-boat's depth was actually less a problem to the destroyer than its speed and direction.

In most cases the U-boat escaped, but those that did escape were usually shaken up. The depth charge served as a constant reminder to the U-boat crews that they ran a great danger when they were near destroyers or armed patrols. Nevertheless, depth charges sank or seriously damaged enough U-boats to "foreshadow the terrible shattering power which the depth charge was to have."[6]

19

The Folkestone–Gris Nez
Deep Mine Barrage

The opening of the unrestricted war on shipping in February 1917 gave the Admiralty reason for concern about the volume of U-boat traffic through the Dover Straits. The issue of whether the U-boats were or were not making maximum use of the shortest route to their operations area was argued in London and Berlin with the result that the Germans sacked Kommodore Bauer in June 1917 and the British sacked Rear Admiral Bacon in December. The politics of the debate are beyond the scope of this work, but the important outcome was that the British made a serious effort to close the Dover Straits.

Admiral Bacon had been working on a plan since February 1917 to lay a deep minefield from Folkestone to Cape Gris Nez. His plan had to wait because the British did not have an effective mine. By November, however, the British had produced the H2 mine, an excellent copy of the German Herz horn mine, in useful numbers. The Dover command began laying the Folkstone–Gris Nez barrage using the new mines on 21 November 1917, and completed the initial field on 29 December. Two mines were used: the H2 with a 300-pound charge and the H4 with a 150-pound charge. An argument now developed between Admiral Bacon and Adm. Roger Keyes, head of Plans Division, over the extent to which the barrage should be illuminated at night and how heavily the barrage should be patrolled. At the heart of the argument was how to make the barrier most effective. Should it be a passive barrier or one in which patrol vessels made an active effort to force U-boats to dive into the mines?

Bacon's plan called for a small patrol force and provided limited night-time illumination with shore-based searchlights at Cape Gris Nez and Folkestone. Keyes, on the other hand, wanted strong patrols around the clock and maximum night-time illumination across the entire barrier. Keyes was correct when he insisted that a deep mine barrage would only be effective if the patrols forced the U-boats to dive into the mines. He argued that without night-time illumination the U-boats would elude the patrols and pass across the barrier on the surface.

On 14 December Adm. Sir John Jellicoe issued a written order to Bacon to institute night patrols and illuminate the barrier. He added that the Admiralty had information that between 1 November and 9 December, thirty-five U-boats had passed through the Dover Straits and it was probable that there had been fifteen more. Room 40's estimate was very accurate. The actual number that passed through the Dover Straits from 21 November to 15 December was fifty-one.[1]

Bacon dragged his heels complying with Jellicoe's order and on 18 December Jellicoe gave him a direct verbal order to illuminate the barrier at night. Bacon complied with that order, and on the night of 19 December magnesium flares, known as Brock's flares, were used for the first time together with searchlights to illuminate the entire field. The immediate result was that UB-56, commanded by Oberleutnant zur See Hans Valentiner, was forced to dive into the minefield. At 0010 on 19 December, the destroyer HMS *Gypsy* reported a powerful explosion, and its crew reported swimmers in the water. The *Gypsy* was able to pick up only one man, maschinistenmaat Max Bleek, who died almost immediately.[2]

The barrier's first success brought about a quick change of command in which Keyes replaced Bacon at Dover. The change of command became effective on 1 January 1918 and the old "defensive" team was replaced with the new "offensive" team. The change in command did make a difference, although during the early weeks of Keyes' command things did not always go well and the barrier was not always illuminated.

Under Keyes' command, the minefield was progressively expanded and mines were replaced as the supply of new mines increased. From the beginning, the British laid the mines at different depths—usually forty, sixty, and eighty feet—to form a ladder effect. No mines were laid at

ninety feet and the deepest mines were at one hundred feet. The number
of rows in the minefield varied from two to ten. When the British completed the barrier in August 1918, they had laid ten thousand mines
across the Dover Straits.[3]

The minefield stretched twenty-two nautical miles across the Dover
Straits from Folkestone on the British side to Cape Gris Nez on the French
side. Powerful searchlights were set up at Folkestone and at Gris Nez to
illuminate the area around the gates at each end through which merchant
ships passed. Special light vessels marked the gates. There was a narrow
lane through the center of the barrier formed by the Varne Bank, a shoal
that was covered by just two to four fathoms at low water. Seventy
drifters guarded this lane.

Large anchored buoys marked the barrier from Folkestone to Gris Nez.
On each side of the barrier a line composed of patrol and flare vessels
kept station two and one half miles out. Starting at the outer ends of each
patrol line and working inward, searchlight-equipped destroyers, P-boats,
and paddle minesweepers were alternated with trawlers equipped with
Brock's magnesium flares. Unlighted drifters patrolled the five-mile strip
between the patrol and flare lines directly over the barrier. Keyes added
five armed vessels with searchlights and hydrophones to the outer lines
of patrol and light vessels.

Called Brock's flares, after their inventor, Wing Comdr. Frank Brock,
each magnesium flare produced about a million candle power illumination. Trawlers ignited flares every fifteen minutes. The drifters, which
were stationed directly over the minefield, were also equipped with flares
but had orders to light theirs only when a U-boat was heard or seen. The
flares' effectiveness was affected by the weather.[4] Fog and haze reduced
their effectiveness, but cloud cover enhanced it by reflecting the light
back down to the surface. Under cloudy skies, with good surface visibility, the flares illuminated the area for four to five miles all around the flare
vessel. An observer positioned three to four miles away from the flare,
and standing about ten feet above the water, would clearly see the surface for a distance of three-quarters of a mile to one mile on either side
of the flare. The barrier was not always well lighted or heavily patrolled
during the first quarter of 1918, but as time passed the patrols became
more effective and the lighting more brilliant.[5]

Even with increased illumination, U-boats continued to pass across the
Folkestone–Gris Nez barrier at night on the surface. Oberleutnant zur See

Stöter, in UB-35, reported that on his return trip on 1 January 1918: "The searchlights from the Varne Bank and Colbart illuminate the zone clear to the British coast, where the white cliffs are very bright. I stayed very close to the English coast, inside the traffic lanes. The boat was frequently illuminated which made things very uncomfortable when passing a patrol. However, we remained unobserved."[6]

Although some U-boats were still crossing on the surface, the overwhelming majority went through the barrier submerged. Slightly fewer than half reported that they went through at periscope depth, which meant that their keels were just a few feet above the shallowest mines. The rest went through at sixty-five feet or deeper, which meant they were right among the mines. In fact, nearly all the captains who made the deeper passage reported that they heard the sounds made by mine anchor cables scraping along their hulls. It is surprising that so many U-boats made it through the deep barrier.[7]

Despite the relatively low losses against the total number of successful passages, some U-boat captains felt the passage was too dangerous. U-110's captain, Korvettenkapitän Karl Kroll, wrote after his return to Helgoland on 15 January 1918 that in his opinion it was better to lose three days going and coming on the northern route than to face the dangers in the Dover Straits. Kapitänleutnant Walter Remy, in U-90, said on 7 February 1918, "I don't consider this route to be the safest, and it is exceptionally unpleasant."[8] On his next trip, and all subsequent trips, Remy used the northern route.

By the time Kapitänleutnant Remy voiced his opinion, the command at Flanders had decided to do something to ease the problem. On the night of 14–15 February German destroyers raided the barrier, temporarily reducing the patrols' effectiveness. Following the raid, Oberleutnant zur See Lohs, in UB-57, remarked that "since the raid the patrols are much reduced." By 31 March the patrols were back in place and up to strength, and Lohs then commented, "the watch is as active as it was prior to the destroyer raid, but strengthened with monitors and destroyers."[9]

The obvious danger involved in passing through the barrier is underscored by the losses. U-109 hit a mine off Cape Gris Nez on 26 January and there were no survivors. UB-38 was next on 8 February, followed by UB-58 on 10 March and UB-33 on 11 April. There were no survivors from any of those boats. But there were survivors from UB-55, which hit a mine on 22 April while it was outbound. When he returned to Germany after the war Kapitänleutnant Ralph Wenninger provided a written report.

> We dove at 0444 as we approached the lighted zone and went to twenty meters. At 0500 a very strong explosion on the starboard side between the after torpedo room and the engine room shook the boat severely. Both after compartments flooded very quickly and the boat fell to the bottom in thirty meters. All personnel in those compartments were lost. Attempts to blow the tanks failed due to severe damage to the starboard ballast tanks. I divided the remaining crew between the conning tower hatch and the forward torpedo room hatch, and began a controlled flooding of the boat. An hour and three-quarters after the explosion, when the internal pressure was 3 kg, the crew went out through the hatches. Fifteen to twenty men reached the surface, but those who had inflated their life vests inside the boat had their life vests burst, and the men drowned very quickly. After being in the water for about an hour and a half the British patrol boat *Mate* picked up the remaining ten survivors. One died after being brought aboard.[10]

UB-31 hit a mine on 2 May, and there were no survivors. Two days later UB-59 hit a mine at periscope depth off Gris Nez. Following a terrifying ordeal that included sinking twice UB-59 returned to Zeebrugge on the surface. Nine days later a British airplane bombed the UB-59 while it was in dry dock in Bruges. The bomb damage ended its wartime career, and on 2 October 1918 the Germans blew it up when they evacuated the Flanders coast. Although the airplane finished it off, UB-59 can be considered a victim of the Folkestone–Gris Nez deep mine barrage because it would not have been in the Bruges dry dock had it not hit the mine.[11]

The minefield claimed two more victims before the war ended: UC-64 on 20 June and UB-109 on 29 August 1918. Off all the minefield's victims, UB-109's fate is the most interesting because of the technology used to destroy it, and because there were survivors to describe what happened.

At each end of the barrier, between the gates and the shore, the British laid controlled minefields in which operators ashore could selectively detonate the mines. The heart of the system was a device called the Bragg loop, named after its inventor Professor W. H. Bragg. An electrical cable laid in loops on the seabed, it sent a signal to a galvanometer every time a steel hull vessel entered the minefield. The device worked on the principle of an interrupted magnetic field. An operator ashore could read the galvanometer, determine where the ship was in the minefield, and detonate the mine or mines nearest the indicating loop.[12]

On 29 August 1918 a Folkestone hydrophone operator reported a fast running, reciprocating engine proceeding to the eastward. About fifteen minutes later the controlled minefield operator stationed on Shakespeare Cliff saw the needle of his Bragg loop galvanometer swing, and he pressed the button. The results were dramatic and instantaneous. An enormous explosion accompanied by a powerful rumbling noise lifted the sea surface and produced a tall water column. Several minutes later nine men came to the surface and forty-five minutes later a trawler picked them up. They were the very lucky survivors of UB-109.

German records detailed the incident from below. When UB-109 arrived off Dungeness en route home, Oberleutnant zur See Ramien intended to run on the surface for as long as possible and then pass through the barrier at periscope depth. At Folkestone, about four nautical miles offshore, were the two lightships that marked the gate, and Ramien altered course to pass through the gate. He was approaching the gate on the surface when very strong surface patrols forced him to dive to periscope depth. Once under, Ramien headed toward a point about one hundred yards landwards of the northern lightship. Ramien was looking through his periscope watching the two light ships line up when there was a tremendous explosion and the lights went out. UB-109 listed heavily to port and dropped sharply by the stern. It hit bottom in one hundred feet of water. Ramien wrote in his report:

> I heard loud shouting in the boat, then everything was still. I had been thrown against the periscope tube and was momentarily knocked out. After I regained my senses, I crawled into the conning tower and tried to talk to the helmsman and another sailor. Despite shouting, we could not make ourselves heard over the roar of released high-pressure air.
>
> The boat was already fully flooded and the water was rising into the conning tower. I felt my way to the ladder, climbed it and tried to open the conning tower hatch. It immediately sprang open, and I, together with the helmsman, was blown through the hatch. We were both jammed in the hatch opening with our upper bodies outside the boat and it took about a half minute for us to free ourselves by squeezing back inside the boat.
>
> I came free and immediately started rising quickly. I had no problem with running out of air during my ascent. In fact I had to constantly expel large amounts of air because as I rose the air in my lungs constantly expanded. I

surfaced just ahead of the helmsman, the sailor, and a radioman. The radioman had no idea how he had gotten into the conning tower.

I was astounded to find five other survivors in the water around me. Immediately following the explosion, the torpedo mate had opened the forward torpedo room hatch and those five people escaped through that. One was an engine room man who said a water surge carried him through the boat and out the forward torpedo hatch.

I shed my leather clothing and my sea boots and swam with the other eight for about forty-five minutes until the trawler D-10 picked us up. One of the nine survivors sank before he was rescued, so only eight were actually saved.[13]

The deep mine barrage made the Dover Straits very dangerous, but they were still passable. Nevertheless, none of the High Sea Fleet U-boats attempted the passage after 7 February 1918 when Remy in U-90 used the straits for the last time to return to Helgoland. The Flanders UB and UC boats continued to use the route, but the losses combined with the captains' increasingly pessimistic reports finally convinced Korvettenkapitän Karl Bartenbach that the route was too dangerous. On 6 September 1918 he ordered the Flanders boats not to use the Dover Straits to reach their operations areas in the English Channel, the western approaches, and the Irish Sea. Instead they were to use the longer, but safer, northern route.[14]

In any event, by the time Bartenbach issued the order, the war was nearly over. The Entente forces were on the offensive and the Germans were losing ground all along the front. The Germans began evacuating the Flanders bases on 29 September 1918, and on 4 October the last personnel departed Ostend after blowing up the U-boats that had to be left behind.

How effective was the Folkestone to Cape Gris Nez deep mine barrier? Judged in terms of the number of U-boats it destroyed, it was somewhat effective. Measured in terms of its deterrent effect, it was very effective. Ten U-boats were destroyed in the barrage and one in the controlled minefield off Folkstone, a success that caused the British to put great faith in the Bragg loop system of controlled minefields. Had the war continued, Keyes would have carried out his plan to lay controlled minefields across the straits in two and one half mile sections, each section controlled from a huge concrete, gun-, hydrophone-, and searchlight-equipped tower.

20

Trying to Block Zeebrugge and Ostend, 1918

At the beginning of 1918 there were approximately eighteen U-boats and twenty-five destroyers at Bruges on any given day, and the British were becoming increasingly anxious to close the exits at Zeebrugge and Ostend. The key to accomplishing that was to destroy or block the locks at Zeebrugge and Ostend. The British had tried to destroy the locks with gunfire in 1915, but that task was more easily attempted than accomplished.

Since their failure to destroy the locks with gunfire the British had considered ways to capture, destroy, or block the two harbors. Various plans had been drawn up, discussed, and rejected. The best solution would have been to recapture the Flanders coast, but until October 1918 the British lacked the military strength to carry out an offensive on that scale. By mid-1917 the most attractive alternative was to sink block ships in the locks so that U-boats at sea could not get back to Bruges and the U-boats already in Bruges could not get out.

Ideas and suggestions for such an undertaking had been kicked around in the Admiralty since November 1916, but various authorities, including Admirals Bacon and Keyes, had rejected them. In November 1917 Admiral Jellicoe, then First Sea Lord, directed Admiral Keyes, director of Plans Division, to develop a plan to block the two Belgian harbors. In fact, by the time Keyes became directly involved in the planning, Admiral Bacon had already done much of the preliminary work. When Keyes took command at Dover in January 1918, the plan to block Zeebrugge and Ostend became his responsibility.[1]

Corking the bottle, as the idea came to be known, would force the UB and UC boats to operate out of Helgoland and bases on the German coast, which would result in longer, time-consuming trips to operational areas in the English Channel. The same was true with regard to German destroyers. Peripheral benefits included the added problems the Germans would face relocating fuel, ammunition, and spares stores from Bruges to other bases. There was also the morale factor: a lift in the Royal Navy's morale and a converse drop in the German navy's morale.

The outstanding physical feature at Zeebrugge is the mole, or breakwater, that curves out from the land and forms a harbor of nearly three hundred acres. The Zeebrugge mole is still one of the largest breakwaters in the world. In 1918 the total length of the mole along its curved surface was over a mile and a half. The mole was built in three sections, the first being a stone railroad pier that extended 250 yards from the shore. At that point the stone railroad pier joined an iron frame viaduct, 330 yards long, that terminated at the foot of the mole's third section. The viaduct's frame construction allowed the sea to pass through and reduced silting in the harbor. The third section was built of massive stone blocks, cement, steel, and gravel. It was 87 yards wide, paved with granite, and was over a mile long. At the far end the mole narrowed to 32 feet wide for the last 260 yards, and a lighthouse was perched on the outer end.[2]

The mole was a commercial wharf as well as a breakwater. Along the inner side were bollards, traveling cranes, passenger areas, and a large railroad passenger and freight station. There were several other buildings, including a large warehouse and a coal shed. On the inner side the mole's eighty-seven-yard-wide paved surface was nine feet above the water at high tide and twenty-three feet at low tide. On the outer side, facing the sea, the Belgians had built a high, massive wall that rose twenty feet above the granite-paved surface. This enormous wall prevented stormy seas from breaking over the mole and washing away the buildings, cranes, and the railroad. At high tide the top of the wall was twenty-nine feet above the water and at low tide the distance was forty-four feet.

The wall was twenty-five feet thick at its base on the sea bottom and ten feet thick along its top. On the inside of the wall and four feet below the top was a nine-foot-wide parapet that ran the entire length of the wall. A steel rail, three feet high, was supposed to prevent anyone from falling off the parapet to the granite surface sixteen feet below. Steel stairs spaced at wide distances along the parapet provided access to the mole.

The narrow section leading out to the lighthouse was really just an extension of the high wall. At the point the mole ended, the top of the wall widened to seventeen feet and the parapet widened to fifteen feet. This portion of the structure was hollow and inside was a tunnel that ran from the end of the mole's paved surface to the base of the lighthouse.

The channel that led from the open sea to the lock was in three legs. The distance from the end of the mole to the lock gates was about two miles. The first leg was the shortest, and passed very close to the lighthouse at the end of the mole. Just inside the harbor the channel made an 18 degree turn to the right and the second leg ran straight for about three-quarters of a mile until it made a 38 degree left turn and lined up on the lock entrance channel. This is where the navigation got tricky.

A ship approaching the lock had to pass between two curved piers, which were 270 yards long. Shoaling along the edges created a very narrow channel between the piers. Ships that drew more than twelve feet had to keep to the middle of the narrow channel or risk running aground. When a ship cleared the inner end of the piers it entered a dredged tidal channel that led to the lock gates a half mile in from the coastline.

The coast of Flanders bristled with guns. From three miles west of Ostend to six miles east of Zeebrugge, a distance of about twenty-one miles, the Germans had sited 225 guns. Most of the guns were mobile or semimobile batteries, but thirty-six were emplaced 6-inch and 15-inch guns, plus a 12-inch battery east of Zeebrugge. Some of those guns had ranges out to twenty-three miles, although in practicality they were limited to engaging only targets they could see. Nevertheless, even under direct fire conditions, those guns had formidable range and destructive power.

In addition to the coastal batteries, the Germans had fortified Zeebrugge with several batteries ranging from 4-inch to 12-inch guns, and had placed barbed wire entanglements, trenches, and machine guns along the coast from Zeebrugge to Ostend. From aerial photographs, the British knew that the Germans had mounted a six-gun battery of what they assumed were 3.5-inch guns on the lighthouse section of the mole. The same aerial photographs showed another three-gun battery on the east end of the mole's main section that the British believed were 6-inch guns. Further study of the photographs revealed buildings that appeared to be barracks, indicating that the Germans had a garrison of about one thousand men stationed on the mole itself. Near the barracks were trenches and machine gun emplacements that were surrounded with barbed wire.

Inside the harbor were torpedo boats, destroyers, and minesweepers, all of which were available to the Germans for defense. Four Rhine barges, filled with rock and chained together, were moored off the end of the mole near the lighthouse and partially obstructed the first leg of the channel. A heavy barrier consisting of steel nets suspended between buoys partially obstructed the second leg of the harbor channel.

The British recognized that any ship or ships approaching Zeebrugge would be under fire from several batteries. Depending on the weather and visibility, the approaching ships could be under accurate fire for over an hour before they actually reached the mole and the harbor entrance. As far as the British were concerned, one thousand yards constituted point-blank range at which the Germans could not miss and the attacking force would have to close within a few feet of some of the guns. They also knew that their own return fire would be much less effective given the location and construction of the German defenses.

The situation at Ostend had all the same obstacles as Zeebrugge except that there was no mole. While the absence of a mole made the attack less complicated, the Ostend harbor entrance was much more difficult to find. The harbor entrance at Ostend was similar to Zeebrugge in that there were two piers flanking the entrance channel and shore batteries commanded the entire area. There were always small craft in the harbor that could aid in the defense. The most formidable defense at Ostend was the Tirpitz Battery that effectively protected the port from sea attack. The battery mounted 11-inch guns with a range of twenty miles and was positioned just to the west of Ostend.[3]

The plan was very complicated and timing was critical. Two forces totaling 142 ships were to meet at a point north of the Goodwin Sands and proceed together to a point at the south end of the West Hinder Shoal. There they were to separate, one force of seventy-five ships heading toward Zeebrugge and the other sixty-seven ships headed toward Ostend.[4]

There were two false starts, the first on 11 April and the second on 13 April 1918. The actual assault took place on 23 April, which is Saint George's Day, allowing Keyes to fly the signal "Saint George for England," to which Captain Alfred Carpenter responded, "May we give the dragon's tail a damned good twist."[5]

ZEEBRUGGE

The execution of the plan, especially at Zeebrugge, had the appearance of a football play. While three block ships—HMS *Iphigenia,* HMS *Intrepid,* and HMS *Thetis*—were approaching the harbor, rounding the mole, and proceeding to the lock gates, seven hundred Royal Marines and two hundred sailors would storm the mole from *Vindictive.* At the same time two old C-class submarines, filled with explosives, would wedge themselves in the steel girders of the mole's second section. When the submarines' crews detonated the charges, the second section would be blown out preventing the Germans from sending reinforcements onto the mole. Timing was critical. While the storming parties were attacking the guns on the mole, HMS *Vindictive*'s guns would lend support and the three block ships would sink themselves in the entrance channel to the locks. Motor launches and coastal motorboats would speed into the harbor to pick up the crews from the three block ships and the submarines. All this had to be accomplished while facing heavy artillery and entrenched infantry.

It is surprising that the plan went as well as it did. As the *Vindictive* approached the outside of the mole, the wind changed and blew away the smoke screen that hid her. Exposed to direct fire from the batteries on the mole, the *Vindictive* suffered heavy casualties and was forced to lay alongside the wall 340 yards away from the intended place. The result was that its guns could not bear on the planned targets and the storming parties had to go over the top without artillery support. The carnage atop the wall, on the parapet below, and on the mole's paved surface equaled anything that occurred in the trenches of the Western Front.

Only one of the C-class submarines managed to reach its objective, but that was enough. The blast ripped out a large section, leaving a hole that isolated the mole from the shore. At about the same time, the three block ships rounded the end of the mole under heavy fire. Plowing through obstacles placed in their paths, the three ships steamed across the harbor and turned toward the piers marking the channel to the locks. *Thetis* took the heaviest fire, was badly holed, and sank short of its goal. *Iphigenia* and *Intrepid* managed to reach the channel leading to the gates where their crews detonated the charges that blew out the bottoms, sinking the ships.

With the scuttling of the block ships, the British withdrew under heavy fire. The MLs, acting as rescue boats, picked up the block ships' crews and the men from the C-class submarine that had destroyed the viaduct. Although the attack had not gone exactly according to plan and the casualties were heavy, the British left the area thinking that they had accomplished their mission. They had not.

OSTEND

At Ostend things went wrong from the start. The block ships HMS *Brilliant* and HMS *Sirius* reached their positions on time, only to discover that the Germans had relocated the entrance buoy. There was no diversionary action to distract the Germans who were already firing at the approaching block ships. To make matters worse, the wind failed, shifted, and began to blow offshore while the MLs were laying a smoke screen. The smoke drifted out to sea. The accompanying destroyers rushed in to lay more smoke but only managed to envelop themselves in oily, black smoke.

Comdr. A. E. Godsal in *Brilliant* and Lt. Comdr. H. N. M. Hardy in *Sirius* were not able to fix their exact positions as they steamed toward the harbor. Using their best judgment, but lacking reliable navigation aids, both ships grounded to the east of the harbor entrance. Unable to proceed, the crews blew out the ship bottoms and abandoned ship. They were all picked up by the rescue boats and returned to Dover.[6]

A second attempt was made on the night of 9–10 May 1918 using HMS *Sappho* and HMS *Vindictive* as the block ships. Again the Germans had removed the navigation buoys and to complicate matters the *Sappho* suffered boiler damage and dropped out before it had even gotten under way. The *Vindictive* managed to penetrate the harbor under heavy fire, but as it was about to turn toward the locks, it became temporarily enveloped in heavy fog.

As the *Vindictive* continued to turn, the Germans concentrated their fire on it. The *Vindictive* was absorbing an enormous amount of punishment as it turned toward the lock, but was still under way when Commander Godsal stepped out on the wing for a better look at his goal. At that moment a German round exploded on the bridge, killing Godsal. No longer under command, the *Vindictive* continued turning and grounded on the east side of the channel. Despite the executive officer's best efforts, the *Vindictive* was firmly aground, and he ordered it scuttled. The *Vindictive* was laid across the channel on an angle that did not block the lock.[7]

British losses at Zeebrugge and Ostend were typical of casualty rates during World War I. The casualties for the entire group were 35 percent and among the storming parties it was 60 percent. What was achieved?

The blocking attempt at Zeebrugge was not complete and the attempt at Ostend had failed entirely. At Zeebrugge the *Iphigenia* and *Intrepid* were inside the piers, but were lying diagonally to the channel axis. The *Intrepid* lay on the west side with its bow thirty yards from the east bank. The *Iphigenia* lay more across the channel, but there were nineteen yards of open space between its ends and both banks. The Germans moved quickly to widen the remaining passages, removing some sections of the piers and dredging around the block ships.

Forty-eight hours after the raid, UB and UC boats were again using the locks at Zeebrugge. Before the raid two U-boats a day entered or left the Flanders bases, and that number remained constant for about five weeks following the raid. The number of arrivals and departures began to fall off following a 9 June bombardment that damaged the gate at Zeebrugge, putting it out of service for five days. The flow of UB and UC boats out of Bruges continued to slow through the summer, but it was not due to the raids on Zeebrugge and Ostend. The most likely causes of the decline were increased air raids on the harbors and the effectiveness of the Folkestone–Gris Nez deep mine barrage.[8]

21

Radio Intelligence
and UC-44

By August 1917 Room 40 was providing daily situation reports to Vice Adm. Sir Lewis Bayly, commanding at Queenstown, and Vice Adm. Sir David Beatty, commander of the Home Fleet. The situation reports were based on intercepted radio traffic between the U-boats and their headquarters. The reports were not specific, but they did provide accurate information on the number of U-boats in a specific area and reasonably accurate projections of future movements.

Closely related to Room 40's operations was the British program for recovering documents and code books from sunken U-boats. Divers were standing by around the clock and the Admiralty had a standing one hundred pound reward for every diver who was successful. It was with that purpose in mind that Room 40 developed a clever plan to ambush a UC boat.

Room 40 had discovered that the German radio intelligence service had broken the code the British used to broadcast information regarding German minefields the Auxiliary Patrol had discovered and cleared. As soon as the British announced that they had cleared a minefield, the Germans sent a UC boat to replace it. Room 40 decided to use that information to their advantage.[1]

On 14 June 1917 UC-42 laid nine mines off the entrance to Waterford. The next day Admiral Bayly's minesweepers found them but did not sweep them up.[2] Admiral Bayly secretly closed the port and issued a fake clearance signal, which the Germans intercepted and decoded. The Germans immediately sent another UC boat to replace them. If the replacement were accomplished quickly enough, the British would not know the mines were back until it was too late. The Germans were clever, but they did not know that the British were reading their mail.

Kapitänleutnant Kurt Tebbenjohanns in UC-44 departed Helgoland on 31 July. He had the coordinates for the mines that UC-42 had laid, which were now presumably gone, and his orders were to lay his nine mines in exactly the same locations off Waterford. It was the sort of assignment that Tebbenjohanns had carried out on many earlier occasions.

UC-44 arrived off the Waterford entrance on the night of 4 August 1917, but the tide was not right for laying mines. Tebbenjohanns put UC-44 on the bottom to wait for the turn of the tide. Shortly after midnight he surfaced, took his bearings, and dove to thirty-five feet. At 0030 he dropped the first four mines, marked their positions on his chart, and moved forward to drop the next five. While Tebbenjohanns was fixing his exact position through the periscope the fifth mine dropped from its chute. Tebbenjohanns had just opened his mouth to tell his enlisted navigator to mark the position when a tremendous explosion shook the boat. Tebbenjohanns recounted the events after the war:

> The explosion threw me against the periscope, cut my eyelid and momentarily stunned me. I never lost consciousness. From beneath me in the command central I could hear water rushing in and I could feel the boat sinking. It hit bottom hard, but there was no sound from the crew. Not a sound. I closed the hatch into the command central.
>
> It was absolutely black in the conning tower, but I tried to contact the crew through the speaking tube. I got no answer. In the conning tower with me were two enlisted men, the navigator and a machinist's mate named Fahnster.
>
> The water was entering the conning tower slowly. We could not see it, but we could feel it rising around our feet.[3]

Tebbenjohanns knew exactly where UC-44 was in relation to the land, and the knowledge did little to reassure him. The boat was on the bottom at about one hundred feet and about three miles off shore. Tebbenjohanns estimated that even with a glassy calm sea there was little chance they could make the swim to safety. He discussed the situation with the two enlisted men and both said they wanted to try.

> I loosened the dogs on the lower hatch so that water was admitted from the command central. Then we took our positions on the ladder leading to the conning tower hatch. I carefully loosened the upper hatch to release air slowly and allow the water to rise more quickly inside the conning tower. We were soon chest-deep in water and I opened the hatch entirely.

The hatch popped open and all three men were blown out of the conning tower. Tebbenjohanns said that he had no difficulty releasing air on the way up. It simply expelled from his lungs automatically. All three men surfaced in a tight group, and Tebbenjohanns pointed toward the light tower at the Waterford entrance and told them that was their goal. But they now discovered they had another problem.

The current was setting them away from the lighthouse, and after several minutes of fruitless swimming, Tebbenjohanns told them to swim with the current toward the darkened shore. That was the last he saw of his crewmen. They became separated and lost contact in the dark. Tebbenjohanns heard one of them calling for help and then the calling ceased. There was no sound from the other man. At this point Tebbenjohanns had a more immediate problem. He was developing cramps and his sodden clothing was dragging him down.

> I was a good swimmer but my clothes were getting too heavy. I now realized what fools we had been to have not shed our clothes while we were still inside the U-boat. It would have been so easy. But now I had to struggle out of my sea boots, my heavy watch coat, and my sweater. Finally I was down to my undershirt, trousers, and socks. I remembered to unhook my iron Cross First Class from my coat and shoved it into my trousers pocket.

An hour and a half later two men in a rowboat fished Tebbenjohanns out of the water and took him to Waterford. At the time they believed he was a neutral seaman or an Auxiliary Patrol member whose ship had hit a mine. They had rowed out looking for survivors after hearing the explosion just after midnight.

If Tebbenjohanns entertained any thoughts of escaping disguised as a neutral seaman his hopes were dashed in the morning. He was lying in bed when a man entered the room with two constables. The man had Tebbenjohanns' iron cross in his hand.

"Are you a German?" he asked.

Tebbenjohanns nodded yes.

"Then you are a prisoner of war."

UC-44 had hit one of the mines that UC-42 had laid on 14 June, which is exactly what Admiral Bayly and Room 40 had anticipated. Their secret was safe with Tebbenjohanns because he believed that UC-44's ninth mine exploded when it left the chute. Several UC boats were lost when their own mines exploded, so Tebbenjohanns' assumption was logical.[4]

Room 40 deserves enormous credit for scoring an important intelligence victory. They had lured a UC boat into relatively shallow water in order to sink it and recover secret documents from the wreck. And they succeeded. British divers went down to UC-44 on 6 August and recovered the war log, code book, and several secret documents. Among the documents they recovered were specific instructions on how to pass through the German defensive minefields in the Helgoland Bight. The documents also provided specific instructions on how to pass through Admiral Bacon's mine-net barrier and how to avoid the Dover patrols. Admiral Keyes used the latter document four months later to unseat Bacon and assume command at Dover. Most important, the ambushing of the UC-44 demonstrated the level of sophistication that British radio intelligence had achieved.[5]

22

The Northern Mine Barrage

———————————————

With the introduction of the H2 mine in November 1917, the British launched a major offensive mining campaign against the U-boats. The British laid mines across the routes the U-boats took to reach their operations areas, off the Flanders coast, and in the Helgoland Bight. British mining activities were so extensive that by September 1918 the only route they had not blocked was the northern route around Scotland. To accomplish that, the British would have to lay a minefield clear across the North Sea, a distance of some 250 miles.

One of the largest difficulties with laying so large a minefield was that the British lacked the production capacity to produce enough H2 mines to do the job and at the same time continue their offensive mining campaign. America's entry into the war, however, brought with it the added industrial capacity that made it possible to produce the thousands of mines needed to create the barrage. In addition, the Americans were developing a new type of mine that covered an area two to three times greater than the H2 mine; the increased area per mine meant that fewer mines would be needed.

THE MARK VI MINE

When the United States declared war on Germany on 6 April 1917, the U.S. Navy was equipped with the naval defense mine no. 3, a model that was very similar to the unreliable British service mine. The U.S. Navy had only a few thousand of these mines on hand and was producing only 140 per month. In April 1917 the Bureau of Ordnance, acting on a civilian engineer's suggestion, undertook to develop a mine that used galvanic current to detonate it.[1]

The idea was that the ocean's salt water acts the same as the electrolyte of a voltaic battery. A weak electrical current would be created if a steel ship touched a copper wire that was attached to an electrically activated detonator. The U.S. Navy authorized development of a firing device based on this galvanic current concept. On 17 October 1917 the Bureau of Ordnance ordered 100,000 new Mark VI mines equipped with the K-1 firing device.

The Mark VI mine was a spherical case, thirty-four inches in diameter, that was filled with three hundred pounds of TNT. Assembled and ready to launch, the spherical mine rested on an iron box that was the anchor. Inside the box were the mooring cable, the mooring cable reel, and the locking gear that controlled the automatic depth setting device. On the side of the iron box was the plummet that determined how far below the surface the mine would float. A copper antenna emerged from the top of the case and was attached to a steel float. The antenna was one hundred feet long, but the depth of the mine was preset so that the antenna was submerged a few feet below the surface. The antenna was insulated from the steel float and the steel mine case.

Initially the design called for an antenna above and below the case, each seventy-five to one hundred feet long, but problems with premature explosions forced the Americans to remove the lower antenna in June 1918. Even with just one antenna, the Mark VI's danger area was more than twice that of the British H2 mine. In July 1918 the British and Americans agreed that the antenna for Mark VI mines laid near the surface should be reduced to thirty-five feet, which would put the top of the antenna ten feet below the surface and allow the mine to ride at forty-five feet. The modified mine would take care of a U-boat on the surface or at periscope depth.

THE NORTH SEA MINE BARRAGE

Both the Americans and the British like to take credit for the idea of a northern mine barrage that would pen up the U-boats in the North Sea. The truth is that the British had considered the idea early in the war, but dropped it as impractical for sound technical reasons. The Americans' entry into the war, combined with improved British mines, reopened the debate. The U.S. Navy first proposed a northern barrage to the British on 9 May 1917, but the British rejected the proposal based on their own "bitter and extensive experience." The Americans had great faith in their Mark VI mine, but the British were not convinced that the Mark VI was all the Americans claimed. Nevertheless, in July 1917 the Admiralty began reexamining proposals for a northern barrage.

The first proposal was for a line across the Helgoland Bight to the Danish coast. The Admiralty rejected that idea because both ends of the line would be footed in neutral waters, which would leave gaps through which the U-boats could easily pass. The second proposal was for a line running from the French or Belgium coast up through the North Sea and then eastward to Jutland. The Admiralty rejected that idea because it would be too long and would restrict the Grand Fleet's movements in the North Sea. The third proposal was for a line running northeast of Scotland to the Shetlands and then eastward toward the Norwegian coast. But the Admiralty ruled that idea as impractical because of strong tides and poor holding ground in the vicinity of the Fair Island Channel. Additionally, the combination of water depth and the H2 mine would create a forty-mile gap off the Norwegian coast.

The British and Americans held discussions on a northern barrage in August and September 1917. The American proposed a barrage in three sections that ran coast to coast from Aberdeen, Scotland, to Egersund, Norway, but the British were only lukewarm to the idea. The talks dragged on with both sides rejecting bits and pieces of the other side's proposals until the Americans produced what appeared to be a workable compromise in October.

The British provisionally agreed to the American plan, but continued to study options. The principal British objection to the American plan was that it inhibited the Grand Fleet's movements. In November the British proposed a dramatic revision that was less restrictive to the Grand Fleet and offered the advantage of a slightly shorter line. In December 1917 the Americans reluctantly accepted the British proposal for a line in three sections that ran roughly from the Orkneys to Bergen, Norway.

The areas were designated A, B, and C, but they were not in alphabetical order. Starting from the British side, the first was Area B, a twenty-mile-wide section extending fifty miles eastward of the Orkney Islands.

The British were responsible for laying their H2 mines in this area, fifty-six to one hundred feet deep. The center area was Area A, a fifty-mile-wide section extending 134 miles northeast from the outer end of Area B. This was the American area in which they laid their Mark VI mines, down to three hundred feet. The area off the Norwegian coast was Area C, a fifty-mile wide section extending southeast for sixty miles from the eastern end of Area A. The British were responsible for this area and they laid their H2 mines sixty-five to two hundred feet deep. Although they agreed to the revised British plan, the Americans noted:

> The original line extended from mainland to mainland, while the new [British] line extends from island to island and has in it passages completely navigable to submarines. The condition is, in our opinion, undesirable. The proposed character of the barrage does not provide for the full accomplishment of the mission. The proposed barrage will not close the northern exit from the North Sea because the barrage is not complete in a vertical plane in areas B and C. The barrage is not deep enough and the Pentland Firth is open, as are waters east of the Orkney Islands for a distance of ten miles. Patrol vessels on the surface are not sufficiently effective in barring passages to submarines. In conclusion, the barrage is of great effort, and it is our opinion that nothing short of a sound design will justify the effort. The requirements of a sound design are the extension of the barrage complete in the vertical plane from coast to coast.[2]

The Americans were also unhappy that the new Area A was deeper than the originally proposed Area A, which meant they had to reassemble the Mark VI mines with longer mooring cables.

American naval officers were open in their criticism of the changes that the British plan involved. The Americans correctly believed that the British had little faith in the Mark VI mine. The Americans were particularly irked that the British H2 mine, which the Americans felt was inferior to the Mark VI, was being used at both ends of the barrage, and the British decision not to patrol Area A galled them. One American planner said that faith in the effectiveness of the barrage was no longer justified.

The Americans continued to argue for a more complete barrage, but the British were adamant that certain areas of the barrage had to be kept absolutely safe for surface vessels. The British distrusted the Mark VI mine, which they believed was basically unsafe. As a result, the British preferred to reduce the field's effectiveness against U-boats in order to ensure more safety to their own surface vessels.

The British distrust of the Mark VI mine was well founded. The Americans had produced the mine in enormous numbers without adequate development and testing; the result was that the Mark VI was not entirely dependable. All the complaints that the British made about the Mark VI mine were applicable to their own H2 mines, but it was a matter of degree. The Mark VI mine's biggest defect was one that reduced its effectiveness considerably.

The K-1 firing devices were prone to premature firing, which frequently produced a chain reaction. One mine would explode and the blast would set off several other mines, producing a spontaneous countermining effect that created large holes in the field. U-boat captains who transited the northern barrage often reported unexplained explosions. During U-107's passage through the barrage on 8 June 1918, Kapitänleutnant Kurt Slevogt reported that he and his crew counted 167 explosions, none of them close to the boat. Oberleutnant zur See Plum in UB-120 reported that on 8 October 1918 he and his crew counted eight hundred explosions. The unexplained explosions were such a common occurrence that most of the U-boat captains believed they were intentional and intended to terrorize the U-boat crews.[3]

The British H2 mine suffered from the same problem, but to a lesser degree. Nevertheless, the problem was severe enough that the British were forced to space their four-mine clusters 150 feet apart instead of the standard 120 feet. The British mines also broke away from their moorings and washed up on beaches, while others leaked and sank.

Despite their dissatisfaction with the final plan for the barrage, the Americans turned enthusiastically to the task of laying the mines. On 26 October 1917 the Admiralty designated two distilleries in Scotland, one at Inverness and the other nearby at Invergorden, as American mine assembly plants. The Americans commissioned Inverness as Base 18 on 9 February 1918 and commissioned Invergorden as Base 17 three days later. American naval personnel at the two mine bases assembled mines at a rate of thirty-five hundred per week, and American minelaying ships and crews arrived by 2 June to begin loading the assembled mines.

The British laid the first deep mines in Area B on 2 March 1918, but a safety defect forced them to sweep up all the mines three weeks later. The British had fitted their mines with a device that prevented them from exploding at any depth less than forty-eight feet, in keeping with their insistence that the barrage not interfere with the Grand Fleet's movements. The British discovered the device was faulty when the sloop HMS *Gaillardia* struck a mine that was faulty and too near the surface. The British investigation disclosed that faulty or not, several of their mines were too near the surface and they all had to be swept up.

Another change occurred that partially satisfied the Americans' ideas of how the barrage should be laid. The British abandoned the surface patrols in Area C, partly because hydrophones had proved to be less efficient than hoped, and in part because the British could not supply the large number of patrol craft required. The British now agreed to follow the American lead and plant both shallow and deep mines in Area C. The Americans felt good about this change, but they would have preferred that the entire barrage had been made dangerous from the surface to as great a depth as possible. Area B still had only deep mines.

The Americans and British carried out their first joint minelaying operation on 6 June 1918, the Americans in Area A and the British in Area C. The laying continued without cessation to 26 October. Resumption was scheduled for 30 October but bad weather and low visibility prevented any further minelaying.

By August 1918 it was apparent that the U-boats were avoiding Areas A and B and were passing through Area C or through Norwegian territorial waters. In addition to laying shallower mines in Area C, the British asked the Norwegians to mine their territorial waters. The British reminded the Norwegians that two royal decrees had forbidden all submarines to use Norwegian territorial waters, and mining them would make the decrees effective. The Norwegians were slow complying with the British request, and it was not until 29 September that Norway issued a warning that its waters would be mined and closed as of 7 October 1918.[4]

It would seem that at this point the Americans had achieved their goal of laying a coast to coast barrage, but that was not quite the case. A ten-mile-wide gap still existed off the Orkneys, and the British refused to close it unless it could be shown that U-boats were using the gap. The issue was the restriction on the Grand Fleet's movements that would result from closing the gap.[5]

The northern mine barrage was never fully completed, and laying operations continued steadily to expand the fields and to repair the holes that regularly appeared. The last minelaying operation took place on 26 October 1918, after which bad weather and low visibility prevented any further laying. But it did not matter since by that time the war was drawing to a close. On 27 October 1918, Kommodore Andreas Michelsen ordered all U-boats at sea to return home.[6]

The northern mine barrage was the largest mining operation undertaken during World War I. It is tempting to call it a Herculean undertaking. The U.S. Navy planted 56,611 mines in Area A, and the British planted 16,300 in Areas B and C. Even with those mines in place, the barrage was only about 85 percent complete. Area A needed 6,400 additional mines. Area B was never mined against surface craft; it was supposed to be patrolled around the clock. In practice, the patrols were not regularly maintained because the ships were needed elsewhere. Area C, off the Norwegian coast, was the weakest area. The area was not patrolled, there were no surface mines laid until August, and the deepest mines were at 125 feet. The biggest failing, however, was the unguarded passage through Norwegian territorial waters that provided the U-boats with a safe passage around the end of the barrage. That passage remained open until Norway finally mined it about 7 October 1918.

Was the northern mine barrage effective? That is a hard question to answer because the barrage was not completed and the war ended before the barrage was really tested. The Germans certainly knew it was there and they were able to monitor its growth fairly accurately. Many more U-boats passed through it than were destroyed in it. The British believed that the barrage would be "the operation most likely to give decisive results."[7] Their goal was to destroy the same number of U-boats per month in the northern barrage as they believed were being destroyed in the Folkestone–Gris Nez barrage. The Americans seem to have been more optimistic, believing that if it was done properly—the American way—the barrage would effectively seal off the North Sea. Using those two goals as a standard, it must be concluded that the barrage was not effective.

Had every mine in the barrage been 100 percent effective, a U-boat passing through on the surface or at periscope depth had a theoretical chance of one in three of making the passage safely. Below periscope depth and down to 250 feet, the U-boat had two chances in three of getting through safely. Considering the technical problems the mines suffered, the chances of a U-boat getting through were increased about two times.

On the other hand, its mere presence posed a serious threat to the U-boats. Henry Newbolt correctly said of the three areas, "even in their faulty state they were dangerous."[8] The degree to which the U-boat captains recognized the danger is demonstrated by the extended time it took for the U-boats to go from Germany to operations areas in the Irish Sea and the English Channel. The barrage had an effect on the U-boat crews' morale, an effect that is evident by the fact that U-boat commanders were unanimous in saying that mines were their greatest fear. If measuring the barrage's effectiveness by the degree to which it made the U-boat's job more difficult, it was very effective.

How many U-boats did the barrage destroy? The Americans claim six U-boats sunk and add that many were damaged. The British claim that five were destroyed in September 1918 alone. The Germans believe that five probably were destroyed in the barrage and two were damaged.

The northern mine barrage was the last ASW effort made in British home waters before the war ended on 11 November 1918. The antisubmarine war around Great Britain had been a British versus German struggle with the British running the ASW campaign and the Germans running the U-boats. Anyone else who took part in the British home waters operations was really just a bit player. The war in the theaters outside British home waters, however, was a free for all in which all the participants had an ASW responsibility.

PART FIVE

Entente Countermeasures in the Mediterranean, the Black Sea, and the Baltic

April 1915–November 1918

23

The Developing Situation

In 1914 the naval situation in the Mediterranean favored the French and the British. Italy was neutral, the Austrian navy was unwilling to come out of the Adriatic for much the same reasons that kept the High Sea Fleet in the Helgoland Bight, and two German cruisers, SMS *Goeben* and SMS *Breslau,* were bottled up in the Marmara Sea. As a result, until May 1915 the French and the British had virtually unhindered use of the Mediterranean.

The situation started to change when the Turks and the Germans bombarded Odessa and Sevastopol on 29 October 1914. The Russians declared war on Turkey on 2 November, with France and England following suit three days later. With Turkey in the war the Allies' route to Russia through the Dardanelles, across the Marmara Sea, and into the Black Sea was closed. It was this state of affairs that caused the British to launch an assault on the Gallipoli Peninsula that opened on 19 February 1915 and ended on 9 January 1916. The resulting blood bath is known simply as Gallipoli.

The British goals in the Gallipoli Peninsula campaign were to force Turkey to capitulate and thus reopen the Black Sea route to Russia. Although the Dardanelles campaign did not go the way the British hoped it would, the Turks immediately felt pressured and asked the Germans to send U-boats to the Mediterranean. The Turks wanted the U-boats to attack the British warships that were bombarding the Turkish defenses on the Gallipoli Peninsula.

In response to Turkish requests for support the Admiralstab dispatched U-21 to the Mediterranean. On 25 April 1915 Kapitänleutnant Otto Hersing in U-21 departed Germany and proceeded to the Austrian naval base at Cattaro in the Adriatic. On 20 May he departed Cattaro en route to Constantinople and on 27 May he torpedoed the battleships HMS *Triumph* and HMS *Majestic* at the entrance to the Dardanelles. The Allies suddenly found themselves confronted with a U-boat problem and no resources with which to fight it.

Between 20 March and 15 July 1915 the Germans shipped four UB and four UC boats by rail to Pola where they were assembled. Combined with U-21, the UB and UC boats formed the Halbflotilla Pola under Kapitänleutnant Adam, who answered directly to the Admiralstab. The Germans also established a detached halbflotilla at Constantinople, which became the Mittelmeer Division.

On 23 May 1915 Italy declared war on Austria-Hungary but not on Germany. From this date forward the Italians, supported by the British and the French, netted the Otranto Straits, which formed the passage between the Adriatic and the Mediterranean. The Italians established the Otranto Straits patrol headquarters at Brindisi. This meant that German and Austrian U-boats operating from Cattaro had to pass through the Entente defenses to reach their operations areas in the Mediterranean. The Admiralstab dealt with this touchy situation by directing U-boats to treat Italian warships as enemy vessels, but not to reveal the U-boats' German identity. If spotted on the surface, the German U-boats were to display the Austrian flag.[1]

In the meantime, U-21 arrived on 5 June 1915 in Constantinople from Cattaro and effectively became the first unit of the halbflotilla at Constantinople. This group remained very small and largely ineffective throughout the war because the British defenses at the Dardanelles' west entrance created a choke point for operations into the Aegean Sea. Although the base at Constantinople provided German access to the Black Sea and Russian targets, operations there had little effect on the course of the war.

In August and September 1915 the more powerful U-33, U-34, U-35, and U-39 arrived in the Mediterranean and the U-boats established bases at

Bodrum, Drak, and Smyrna (Izmir). With the arrival of the large U-boats, and the completed assembly of the smaller UB and UC boats, the Germans were ready to open an anti-shipping campaign in the Mediterranean.

At about the same time the Germans were preparing to open their anti-shipping campaign, the British and French opened a joint campaign to aid the Serbs with landings at Salonica. This new undertaking was started just as the British Gallipoli campaign was faltering. The Salonica operation took on added importance on 6 October 1915 when the Germans and Austrians under Field Marshal August von Mackensen launched an offensive against the Serbs. The Bulgarians joined the offensive on 11 October, causing a crisis among the Entente Powers. The Central Powers' offensive threatened to establish a rail link between Germany and Constantinople that would allow the Germans to supply the Turks with large amounts of artillery ammunition; this situation would seriously jeopardize the already failing British campaign on the Gallipoli Peninsula.

Britain and France had been concerned about Serbia's ability to resist Austria since early 1915. Because of national interests and internal politics, the French favored supporting Serbia with a landing at Salonica and a thrust through the Vardar River Valley. The combined British and French forces were designated the Army of the Orient and were placed under the command of Gen. Maurice Sarrail, former commander of the French Third Army.[2]

The British-French advance parties started landing at Salonica between 23 September and 2 October with the main landing on 3 October 1915, three days before the Austrian-German offensive against Serbia opened. The joint British-French force at Salonica attempted to relieve the Serbs, but it was a hopeless gesture. While the Central Powers were crushing the Serbs, the British were forced to give up their Gallipoli campaign and evacuate the Gallipoli Peninsula in January 1916. The Army of the Orient remained in place, however, and spent the bulk of the war wasting away on the beach at Salonica. Despite its inactivity, the Salonica beachhead had to be supplied and reinforced, which meant that the U-boats found plenty of targets there and along the supply routes into the Aegean.

Coincidental with the British and French landings at Salonica, the Germans opened their anti-shipping campaign in three clearly defined areas. They divided the Mediterranean into two areas, the eastern half and the western half, which were separated by Sicily. Because the Allied ASW efforts were concentrated in the eastern half of the Mediterranean, the

Germans achieved their largest successes in the western half. With the Allied landings at Salonica, the German boats operated in the Aegean on the approaches to Salonica and Kavalla, interdicting supplies to the French and British forces there. They operated around the entrance to the Dardanelles, attacking warships when the opportunity occurred and interdicting the supply lines to the British forces there. During the first three months of their campaign, September–December 1915, the U-boats sank ninety-nine ships, nearly all of them according to the Prize Regulations.

The political and diplomatic advantage the Germans enjoyed while operating in the Mediterranean was freedom from worrying about U.S. opinion and reaction. There were not very many American flag vessels in the Mediterranean and very few American citizens aboard passenger ships. The Germans recognized that U.S. indignation over the sinking of a passenger ship was in direct relation to how many, if any, Americans were killed or injured in such an attack. Nevertheless, the inevitable did happen when Kapitänleutnant Max Valentiner in U-38 sank the Italian passenger ship SS *Ancona* on 7 November 1915. Among the three hundred passengers who died were twenty Americans; in this case, the Germans were able to shove responsibility onto the Austrians and dodge the American bullet.[3]

With operations around Britain curtailed because of the ongoing dispute between the German navy and the civilian government over how to run the U-boat campaign, the Admiralstab sent more boats to the Mediterranean. During the period from January to April 1916 six U-boats—UB-42 through UB-47—were sent in sections to Pola and assembled. They went into service from 23 March to 4 July 1916. Initially the boats accomplished little. As the rules regarding attack without warning were relaxed, they sank more ships and their captains profited from their war experience.[4]

By mid-summer 1916 the Germans had increased their strength in the Mediterranean to fifteen U-boats. Three were at Constantinople and twelve were at Cattaro. During the last six months of the year the Admiralstab sent more U-boats to Cattaro, bringing the total to twenty. Throughout 1916 the number of boats at sea varied from three to five, and the Germans varied their zones of operation from week to week, but they preferred the western Mediterranean.

The ineffectiveness of the Allies' countermeasures is evident in the figures comparing U-boat losses to the number of ships and tonnage sunk. From 13 May 1915 to 31 December 1916 the Germans lost five boats:

UB-7, UB-44, UB-46, UC-12, and UC-13. The Austrians lost four: U-3, U-6, U-12, and U-16. Of those numbers, enemy action accounted for the four Austrian boats and one German boat. Even more significant is the fact that the only German boat known to have been lost due to enemy action, UB-46, was destroyed by a Russian mine, not by British, French, or Italian countermeasures in the Mediterranean.

The ineffectiveness of the Allied countermeasures is also illustrated by the successes accomplished by one German U-boat commander, Kapitän-leutnant Lothar von Arnauld de la Periere. In just two months, during June and July 1916, von Arnauld de la Periere in U-35 sank over forty ships, half of them large steamers. In August 1916 he operated between the northeast coast of Spain and the Gulf of Genoa where he sank over fifty-four steamers, amounting to ninety-one thousand tons. Representing two-thirds of the tonnage destroyed worldwide, it was accomplished in just three weeks. Significantly, the overwhelming majority of his attacks were carried out according to the Prize Regulations.

The Allied antisubmarine defenses in the western Mediterranean were not as strong as in the eastern section and along the regular transport routes. Even the steamers were more lightly armed. These conditions allowed Kapitänleutnant Valentiner to sink fifty-four ships according to the Prize Regulations and allowed Kapitänleutnant Walter Forstmann in U-39 to destroy twenty-one steamers totaling 61,339 tons between 5 July and 1 August 1916. Both captains racked up their victories in the western Mediterranean.[5]

The U-boats that were doing the most damage in the Mediterranean were operating out of the Austrian harbors at Pola and Cattaro in the Adriatic. Most of the ships sunk in the Mediterranean were Italian, then British, and then French. Until the close of 1916 the Germans torpedoed only armed steamers without warning, operating under the Prize Regulations in all other cases. Obviously armed steamers were also attacked with gunfire with fairly good results.[6]

The Entente Powers would have to respond to this developing disaster.

24

The Mediterranean Theater

The three ASW goals—confine the U-boats, shield the targets, and destroy the U-boats—were as important in the Mediterranean as they were anywhere else. To accomplish those goals, the Entente Powers used antisubmarine measures similar to those used in the Dover Straits, the English Channel, and the waters around Britain. Efforts to accomplish the goals took three forms: bottle up the U-boats in the Adriatic by closing the Otranto Straits; close the west entrance to the Dardanelles, initially to protect forces on the Gallipoli Peninsula and later to prevent U-boats from entering the Mediterranean from the Marmara Sea; and protect military and commercial traffic throughout the Mediterranean.

Until mid-1917 the Entente focused ASW efforts in three locations: the Otranto straits, the west entrance to the Dardanelles, and the Aegean Sea. The Otranto Straits were the most important and the place where the Entente made the greatest effort in terms of resources deployed.

THE OTRANTO STRAITS

With the Germans and Austrians operating from Pola, Cattaro, and Durazzo in the Adriatic, it was obvious to the Entente that they had to close the Otranto Straits. Their attempt to accomplish that with a forty-four-mile-long mobile net barrage that stretched from the Italian coast

to Fano Island was doomed to fail. The Otranto Straits' three hundred to
five hundred fathom depth made it too deep to seal with nets and far too
deep to use mines. Even with a maximum diving depth of only 160 feet,
the U-boats were capable of passing below the nets.

The Otranto Straits defense was a multinational operation with British,
French, and Italian units deployed in patrol lines that reached from the
Italian shore to about Fano Island. British drifters made up the majority
of the patrols. The first sixty British drifters arrived at Otranto in September 1915 and by December 1915 the British had ninety-two drifters
based at Brindisi. To these they added thirty motor launches in 1916.

The initial intention was to create a mobile net barrage so broad that
the U-boats would be forced to remain submerged until their batteries
were exhausted and they had to surface to recharge them. This was the
same plan the British used in the North Channel in the Irish Sea. The
British drifters shot their nets along a line that extended from Otranto to
Fano Island. South of the net line the British stationed a line of armed
drifters and motor launches, keeping them out at night to force returning
U-boats to dive into the nets. Farther south a line of French vessels, including submarines, operating out of Corfu, was supposed to provide support but they were not always there. On the north side of the net line
the Italians were supposed to station their auxiliary vessels with the purpose of forcing the outbound U-boats to dive into the nets. They were also
supposed to station a line of submarines beyond the pickets to torpedo
any surfaced U-boat that came along.

Even if the water had been shallow, closing the Otranto Straits with
drift nets would have been a hopeless task because the distance to be covered was too long. The British tried to reduce the inevitable gaps that
developed between the drifters by deploying nets up to eight hundred
yards long. With nets that large, each drifter covered about a half mile,
which meant that with a maximum effort the most they could cover was
thirty-five out of forty-four miles. In practice the British did not have
enough drifters in 1915 and 1916 to do that. There was also the fact that
the strong tidal flow and unpredictable currents played havoc with the
oversized nets, reducing them to a tangled mess.

Another problem was that the French and Italians were lax in sending
out their patrols. The Italians were also supposed to provide destroyers
to support the small craft, but that did not happen either. The Italians
adopted a firehouse approach to supporting the drifters by keeping their

destroyers in harbor, waiting to be called out by the drifters. The Italian policy was flawed because most of the drifters lacked radios. E. Keeble Chatterton commented after the war, "Frankly, the Italian naval units were something of a disappointment to us; they lacked that enterprise which had been expected."[1]

The British produced the drift nets that the Entente patrols used in the Otranto Straits during 1915 and 1916. The net panels were one hundred yards wide by thirty feet deep, but as the war progressed the British manufactured deeper nets. In most cases the U-boats passed through the Otranto Straits at night on the surface. When they did submerge, they ran at about 65 to 135 feet, which was well below the nets. With one exception the U-boats that did foul the nets did so when they were near the surface, either after diving or when they rose to periscope depth to fix their location, which meant that any strike was a purely happenstance occurrence.

There were four confirmed net strikes in the Otranto Straits during 1916 and one of them resulted in the destruction of the Austrian U-6 on 3 May 1916. Commanded by Linienschiffsleutnant von Falkenhausen, U-6 was a small boat less than one hundred feet long and powered by twin Körting engines. It had no deck gun. On the night of 13 May it was running on the surface when the British drifter *Calistoga* forced it to dive. U-6 almost immediately became entangled in the drifter's net. The drifter *Dulcie Doris* came on the scene in response to flare signals and U-6 fouled its nets too. The nets became entangled in U-6's starboard propeller, which forced von Falkenhausen to surface to clear away the net.

Both the *Calistoga* and the *Dulcie Doris* were unarmed, but a third drifter, the *Evening Star II*, soon arrived armed with a 12-pounder gun. The *Evening Star II* immediately opened fire at close range, scoring hits on the hull and the conning tower. Immobile and outgunned, von Falkenhausen ordered his crew to scuttle U-6 and abandon ship. The drifters rescued the captain and his thirteen crewmen.[2]

The second strike occurred on 17 December 1916 in heavy weather. The Austrian U-20 fouled nets towed by the British drifter *Fisher Girl*. U-20 was a new boat, but with an overall length of 130 feet, it was relatively small and underpowered. When the U-boat struck, the drifter's captain, A. H. Sage, immediately summoned help by hoisting the submarine signal and sounding the steam whistle. A fisherman, Sage tried to haul in the trapped boat, but the weight was far too great for his machinery.[3]

Shortly, the drifters *Guerdon* and *D.H.S.* arrived, and Captain Sage slacked off his tow, allowing the net and its contents to sink. Both the *Fisher Girl* and *Guerdon* dropped depth charges and a *Guerdon* crewman threw a lance bomb, which was ineffective. The *D.H.S.* exploded its sweep. Nothing happened. Having expended their ordnance, the drifters settled in to wait for the next development.

It was storming that night and the seas were very rough, but the drifters stayed on the scene until morning. They discovered that the net's tow rope was "tight as an iron bar," which meant that something was still entangled in the net below. The fishermen spent the morning trying to get slings under U-20, but the strain finally told and the wires parted. The crews of the three drifters were convinced they had destroyed a U-boat. However, U-20 was only shaken. After the drifters departed, it surfaced, and the crew cleared away the net as best they could. U-20 then returned to Cattaro.[4]

Five days after the Austrian U-20 stuck the nets, Max Valentiner in U-38 did the same thing. U-38 was on the surface, inbound to Cattaro and approaching the outer patrol line. Two destroyers suddenly loomed up ahead. Valentiner ordered the boat to crash dive, and went down to sixty feet. At 2200 he rose to periscope depth to fix his position and that was when he struck the net.

The first warning he had was when the port propeller stopped turning, indicating that the shaft was fouled. Valentiner said that after the port motor was shut down he heard noise indicating a net. He described the noise as "a disgusting music made by the steel strands scraping along the hull."[5] Valentiner ordered full power ahead on the starboard motor and dove to 120 feet. The purpose of that maneuver was to add the boat's weight to the forward thrust in an attempt to tear through the net. It worked and U-38 tore free in one attempt.

The last strike in 1916 occurred on 23 August when UB-47, commanded by Oberleutnant zur see Steinbauer, struck a net at 140 feet. Steinbauer went ahead at full power and tore through the net without difficulty. UB-47 had struck the lower edge of the net and was never completely entangled, which made the boat's escape fairly easy.[6]

The British had increased the depth of the nets to 140 feet on 16 April 1916, and had submerged the top of the net 12 feet below the surface so that the foot was 152 feet deep. In view of the fact that the British had determined through tests that a net 40 feet deep was the largest a drifter could handle, the 140-foot giants used in the Otranto Straits are amazing.[7] But it is impossible to deny the existence of these deep nets in light of Oberleutnant zur See Steinbauer's log entry that he fouled a net at 140 feet.

The inherent gaps in the British drift net line caused the French and Italians to advocate laying a heavy fixed net across the Otranto Straits. The British resisted the idea because their experience with fixed nets in the Dover Straits showed how difficult they were to maintain in the open sea. The French and Italians insisted, however, and in April 1918 they undertook to lay a fixed mine-net south of the established patrol lines from Cape Santa Maria di Leuca to Fano Island. The top of the net was 24 to 30 feet below the surface and the net hung down to 180 to 200 feet. The work moved forward slowly and the net was not completed until the end of September, about six weeks before the war ended.[8] An American sailor described the net:

> The nets were anchored at intervals and floated by means of large glass balls, thousands fastened to the steel mesh. Huge steel drums acted as the buoyant force to hold up the heavy net cables. These drums were tethered to the net thirty to fifty feet below the surface, although at other places we found them almost at the surface. Festooned along the coarse mesh of the net were mines, dangling like Christmas tree ornaments.[9]

On 3 August 1918 Oberleutnant zur See Sprenger in UB-53 struck the French-Italian mine-net. UB-53 had departed Pola on 1 August for a patrol in the Adriatic and as the U-boat approached the Otranto Straits Sprenger dove to pass under a destroyer line. Surfacing beyond the destroyer line, U-53 was immediately forced to dive to avoid a drifter line. Remaining submerged, Sprenger laid a course for the middle of the straits because he believed that the French-Italian net, then under construction, extended only about a third of the way out from the Italian coast.

At 1700, running at two hundred feet in a position approximately midway between Cape Maria di Leuca and Fano Island, Sprenger heard the unmistakable sounds of a wire dragging along the hull. Sprenger's order to go ahead full in an attempt to tear through the net was instantly followed by two powerful explosions at the stern. Sprenger described what happened next.

> The after ballast tanks flooded and the stern torpedo was blown back through the inner doors into the after torpedo room without exploding.

The watertight door to the torpedo room held and the room quickly
flooded causing the UB-53 to assume a radical stern down attitude. The
batteries spilled, the motors quit and the boat sank below 300 feet. I
ordered the tanks blown and brought the boat to the surface, but we were
unable to start the engines or pump out the water. Because I expected to
be quickly discovered by patrols, and my boat was not maneuverable, I
ordered the valves opened and charges set. We scuttled the UB-53 and
went into the water.[10]

Several hours later the HMS *Martin* and the drifter *White Abbey* picked
up twenty-four survivors.

Despite the presence of the newly laid French-Italian mine-net, the surface patrols remained as the principal barrier across the Otranto Straits.
On 7 June 1918 American subchasers joined the surface patrols and the
Otranto Straits became the scene of most of the American activity in the
Mediterranean. The U.S. Navy's ASW organization, the subchasers'
design, and their equipment were aimed at taking offensive action against
the U-boats. On 12–16 June 1918 the Americans conducted their first hunting patrol. Divided into alternating groups of eighteen subchasers each,
the Americans remained on station for six-day shifts during which they
alternately drifted and actively hunted. By the end of October the subchasers had carried out thirty-seven patrols without sinking a U-boat.

Submarines also played an active antisubmarine role, but until October 1917 the French and Italian boats carried most of the load in the Adriatic. The French and Italians stationed their submarines on patrol lines
across the Otranto Straits and sent them into the Adriatic to attack U-boats
as they left and entered the harbors at Pola and Cattaro.

The British had three H-class submarines based in Venice, but most of
their submarines were based at Malta and operated in the central and
eastern Mediterranean. In October 1917 the British took a more active
role in the Adriatic and based their E-class boats at Corfu to cover the line
from Cape Santa Maria di Leuca to Fano Island. Later the British moved
all their boats to Brindisi and placed them under the operational command of the Italians; the patrol area became a line between Cattaro and
Durazzo. In 1918 the offensive against the U-boats remained the top priority for the Entente Powers' submarines.[11]

The British, French, and Italian submarines made several contacts
with U-boats and fired torpedoes that often missed and sometimes hit

without exploding. Their collective success accounted for just three U-boats. The French *Circe* sank UC-24 off Cattaro on 24 May 1917 and a year later H-4 sank UB-52 in the same place. The Italian submarine F-12 torpedoed the Austrian U-20 off Venice on 4 July 1918.

THE DARDANELLES

The west entrance to the Dardanelles was another focal point for Entente ASW operations. During the Gallipoli campaign the primary defenses consisted of strong surface patrols and mobile indicator-nets. Kapitän- leutnant Otto Hersing went through the Dardanelles in July 1915 and reported very strong antisubmarine measures at the west entrance. He said he encountered destroyer and trawler patrols equipped with all ASW devices found in the Dover Straits and English Channel. The patrols were so strong that Hersing saw little chance for success in attempting to oper- ate out of Constantinople into the Mediterranean. He added that the typ- ically mirror flat sea and crystal clear water allowed the enemy to see a U-boat well below the surface.[12]

Hersing's pessimistic appraisal was underscored when UB-14 tangled with a drift net one month later on 22 August. Kapitänleutnant Heino von Heimburg was attempting to pass through the Dardanelles at periscope depth when he fouled the net and the indicators disclosed his position. The patrols attacked UB-14 with explosive sweeps and for a moment von Heimburg seriously considered surrendering. He later wrote:

> It appeared to me that it was all over. I went to my cabin to clean up and put on a white uniform so that the enemy would know who among the crew was the captain. I continued to try to figure a way out while the crew prepared the boat for surrender. As it worked out, things were not quite that serious yet. It suddenly occurred to me that a net that wound around a shaft going astern would unwind from a shaft going forward.[13]

Returning to the control room, von Heimburg tried going ahead at full power, risking serious damage to the starboard electric motor. The maneu- ver worked, and UB-14 tore free of most of the net. He took UB-14 down to 150 feet to escape the sweeps, and turned away from the Dardanelles.

By 13 September 1915 the British had succeeded in closing the Dar- danelles to the U-boats with nets and mines. On that date Hersing in U-21 attempted to enter the Dardanelles to return to Constantinople, but found the way barred by strong surface patrols and a dense net barrage.

Hersing withdrew and radioed Constantinople that the Dardanelles were closed, and requested that he be allowed to proceed to Cattaro. The request was granted. A week later UC-13 made a reconnaissance of the new barrage and reported it to be impassable. As a result of the two reports, Constantinople ordered its remaining boats to conduct operations only in the Black Sea, leaving the Cattaro boats to attack targets around the Dardanelles entrance. This is the only example during World War I when a net defense actually closed a passage to the enemy's submarines.[14]

THE AEGEAN

The character of the naval war in the Mediterranean changed after the evacuation of the Gallipoli Peninsula in December 1915. There were 400,000 men in the Mediterranean theater, and the British naval forces outside of the Otranto Straits shifted their attention to the Aegean while maintaining a reduced watch at the Dardanelles. The British ASW forces' primary goal was to protect the supply lines to the Army of the Orient that was spread out across the beach at Salonica.

The Germans' reaction to the Entente shift in focus varied, depending upon the commander and the circumstances he encountered on any given day. Because the Allies were spread very thinly, the strength of their ASW countermeasures in any locality often varied from day to day. Kapitänleutnant Waldemar Kophamel in U-35 reported no patrols in the Aegean and only light patrols around the main enemy strong points: Otranto Straits, Gulf of Salonika (Thessaloniki), the Mudros (Moudhros) Bight, and the Dardanelles.

Forstmann in U-39 reported strong patrols in the Aegean and around the Dardanelles. He also warned that the exceptional visibility in the Aegean allowed the surface patrols and coast watchers to see and report his movements. He believed these reports were sent to the enemy and the freighters were held in port. Added to those reports were similar observations from U-33 and U-39 that the exceptional visibility in the Aegean and the mirror flat sea made operations in those narrow waters impractical, and they suggested operating in the approaches west and east of Crete.[15]

ZONE DEFENSE TO THE CONVOY SYSTEM

The Entente forces tried to shield their commercial and military traffic from attack with little success. On 3 December 1915 representatives of the three powers met in Paris and divided the Mediterranean into eighteen zones, each to be covered by roving ASW patrols. Four zones—the Gibraltar Straits, the south Coast of Sicily, the Dardanelles, and the Aegean—were assigned to the British. The Italians took responsibility for the Adriatic, the Otranto Straits, and the Ionian Sea and the waters around Sicily. The French were assigned ten zones, mostly in the western Mediterranean off the coasts of France and North Africa.

In March 1916 the Entente Powers redistributed the zones and reduced them to eleven. At the same time they rejected the convoy system and opted for controlled routes with escorts reserved for special cases. A drop in sinkings during the first quarter of 1916 followed the changes and gave the Allies a false sense of security.

Despite the organizational changes, it was evident by the end of June 1916 that Entente ASW measures in the Mediterranean were not working. Losses were rising and the Germans had lost only two U-boats, UC-12 and UB-44, neither of which was attributed to enemy action. The situation continued to deteriorate in the second half of 1916 when the Mediterranean U-boats sank 32 percent of the total Entente tonnage lost worldwide.

Once loose in the Mediterranean the U-boats met little opposition because the British, French, and Italians lacked an efficient ASW capability during 1915 and 1916. For a time in early 1917 the British and French used two different systems that depended on dispersion and patrolled routes. The British favored dispersion over patrolled routes, whereas the French believed the U-boats were operating from secret bases around Crete and in Asia Minor and insisted on designated, patrolled routes.

The patchwork protection reflected the lack of Entente unity, which left each nation responsible for ship movement and protection according to its own plan in its own zones. As a result, ships were routed through the different zones according to the policies adopted by the nation that had responsibility for the zone. Occasionally the British and French would provide an escort for a particularly valuable ship, such as a troop transport. The escorting vessels went only to the zone boundary where they were supposed to hand off the troop transport to the next escorts. In many cases the escorts that were supposed to accept the hand-off did not show up and the troopship went on alone, unescorted and easy prey for a U-boat.[16]

The idea of the convoy came up occasionally, but was rejected for several reasons, including the lack of Entente cooperation. In late 1916 the

British rejected the convoy system in favor of a ports of refuge plan. Under this scheme ships laid up during the day in netted safe harbors and traveled close inshore at night. When possible they made use of Spanish territorial waters.

None of the schemes to protect shipping had worked and losses were rising. On 1 May 1917 the Entente replaced the patrolled route system with a mixed scheme of convoys and patrolled coastal routes. More important, from this point forward the British effectively commanded the ASW operations in the Mediterranean. On 22 May 1917 the first convoy ran from Malta to Alexandria, but through the summer of 1917 there was still no organized convoy system in the Mediterranean.

Pressure to institute convoys was building, particularly in view of the increasing success of the Atlantic convoy system. At a London conference held on 4–5 September 1917 the Entente gave precedence to Gibraltar-Genoa coal convoys, followed by Egyptian-Bizerte convoys and France–North Africa convoys. Adm. Henry T. Mayo, commander in chief of the U.S. Atlantic Fleet, attended the conference with the result that the United States provided ships in the Atlantic approaches to Gibraltar.

The Mediterranean convoy system grew after mid-October 1917 when the British introduced convoys between Britain and Port Said. The British used the same control system for Mediterranean convoys that they used for the Atlantic convoys. OE (outward eastern) and HE (homeward eastern) convoys ran every sixteen days using ships that could make at least ten knots. The convoys averaged sixteen to twenty ships.[17]

The Mediterranean convoys were not as spectacularly successful as were the Atlantic convoys because virtually the entire Mediterranean was a war zone. That meant that instead of dealing with a three hundred to four hundred mile offshore danger zone at the end of the trip, a Mediterranean convoy faced threats throughout the entire trip. The sea conditions in the Mediterranean gave the U-boats more opportunities to carry out multiple attacks, and the Mediterranean escorts used depth charges less aggressively than did their Atlantic counterparts. Despite the differences, the convoy system worked well in the Mediterranean.

The introduction of the convoy system created a fourth focal point for ASW in the Mediterranean. Focal points were defined by the amount of resources, effort, and priority the Entente forces assigned to specific operations. The weapons used were the same throughout the Mediterranean theater, although in smaller supply than were available to the ASW forces around Great Britain. The Otranto Straits patrols made extensive use of hydrophones in 1918, and aircraft were particularly effective in the Adriatic even though they did not sink any U-boats.

THE DEPTH CHARGE

The first Entente success using depth charges in the Mediterranean took place on 17 October 1916 and was largely accidental. The Austrian U-16 was in the Otranto Straits just south of Valona when it torpedoed the Italian destroyer *Nembo*. As the destroyer was sinking, U-16 surfaced and moved toward the site, apparently to gather information. Moments after the destroyer disappeared below the surface, the depth charges in the racks on the stern exploded and the blast sank U-16. The Italian Q-ship *Bormida* arrived on the scene later and picked up the survivors from the destroyer and the Austrian U-boat.[18]

The Austrians lost three other boats to Italian depth charges. On 29 April 1917 the Austrian U-30 was sunk as it approached the Otranto Straits from the Mediterranean. The Italian destroyer *Airone* sank U-23 between Brindisi and Vlone on 21 February 1918 and the *Ardea* sank U-40 on 24 April 1918 in the same area.

The Japanese navy operated eight destroyers in the Mediterranean under Rear Adm. Kozo Sato. The Japanese arrived in February 1917 with orders to cooperate with the British but to take no orders from any of the European admirals. Given the circumstances the British asked the Japanese to act as escorts. On 11 May 1917 the Austrian U-27, commanded by Linienschiffsleutnant Robert Teufl von Fernland, torpedoed the IJN *Sakaki,* killing the destroyer's captain and sixty-four crewmen. The *Sakaki* did not sink and its consorts subjected U-27 to a six-hour depth charging that shattered lights, smashed the compass, and sprung shaft glands. Shaken but alive, von Fernland and his crew limped back to Cattaro.[19]

GUNFIRE-ARMED MERCHANT SHIPS

There were fewer armed merchant ships in the Mediterranean than there were in the British home waters, simply because there were not enough guns to go around. Nevertheless, armed merchant ships were a problem for the Mediterranean U-boats, yet most U-boats were well enough armed to deal with them. Both the U-boats and the UB boats carried an 88 millimeter gun; in 1916 some of the U-boats started carrying two 88 millimeter guns. Toward the end of 1916, the U-30 class boats replaced the after deck guns with a more powerful 105 millimeter gun. Despite the U-boats' strong armament, better than 50 percent of the armed merchant ships they attacked escaped by driving off the U-boat. However, no armed merchant ship was ever able to sink a U-boat.[20]

DECOYS

By far the most dangerous encounter a U-boat could experience was with a decoy. In autumn 1915 the Admiralty converted four colliers—*Penhallow, Saros, Werribee,* and *Remembrance*—to decoys and based them at Malta. The Admiralty also sent the *Baralong,* renamed the *Wyandra,* and the Italians deployed the *Citta di Sassari.* During 1916 there were eight confirmed engagements between Q-ships and U-boats, but no U-boats were lost as a result of the engagements.[21]

RAMMING

Ramming played a small part in the Allies' ASW countermeasures in the Mediterranean. The Admiralty order of January 1915 was still in effect, but the U-boat captains in the Mediterranean were considerably more experienced now. Additionally, the U-boats were heavily armed, and an attempt to run down a surfaced U-boat could be very dangerous. Nevertheless, there were two recorded instances in which surface ships rammed U-boats.

The Austrian U-3 fired a torpedo at the Italian decoy *Citta de Palermo* on 12 August 1915 in the Otranto Straits between Otranto and the island of Saseno. The torpedo missed and the *Citta de Palermo* ran down the torpedo wake and rammed U-3 as it was trying to go deeper. The blow ruptured the conning tower and partially flooded the boat. Just a few minutes later an Italian destroyer exploded a sweep that opened seams in the pressure hull and U-3 found itself in serious trouble.

Fortunately for the U-boat the destroyer and the *Citta de Palermo* left the area. After they were gone U-3 surfaced and limped toward Cattaro. Damage to the boat had reduced the maximum speed to less than three knots, so the 135 nautical mile stretch back to Cattaro was a long way. In fact, it was too long. Two days later the French destroyer *Bisson* caught the damaged U-boat on the surface and opened fire on it. U-3's captain, Linienschiffsleutnant Karl Strnad, knew at once that resistance was pointless. He ordered his crew to scuttle the boat and abandon ship. The *Bisson* fished all seventeen survivors out of the water.[22]

The war's most bizarre ramming incident took place on 4 December 1916 when Kapitänleutnant Fischel in U-65 torpedoed the steamer SS *Caledonia* without warning. As the ship was sinking, its captain ran the *Caldonia* down the torpedo wake and rammed the submerged U-boat, driving it down to 260 feet. U-65 recovered and surfaced in time to watch the *Caldonia* go down. There was no damage to the pressure hull, but the casing was badly damaged and the badly shaken Fischel broke off his patrol and returned to Cattaro.[23]

MINES

Mines played a small role in the Allied ASW countermeasures in the Mediterranean, although they were used extensively in the Adriatic and the Black Sea. Mining was confined almost exclusively to harbor entrances and across the entrance to the Dardanelles. After the evacuation of Gallipoli in January 1916, the British laid a series of shallow minefields across the entrance to the Dardanelles to catch U-boats and surface ships trying to come out. On 18 June 1916 UB-42 reported heavy mining in the entrance to the Dardanelles, which made passage impossible. By the end of 1916 these fields had been washed away by storms and swept up by the Turks. The only two confirmed losses to a mine laid by anyone other than the Russians were the Austrian U-12 that struck a mine off Venice on 8 August 1915 and the Austrian U-10 that hit a mine in the northern Adriatic on 9 July 1918. All the other losses were probably due to Russian mines in the Black Sea.[24]

25

The Black Sea and the Baltic

Russian ASW was different from that used by the other Entente Powers. There was never any cooperation between the Russian ASW forces and any Entente forces in the Black Sea or the Baltic because Russia was effectively cut off from the west. In a nutshell, Russian ASW was terribly ineffective. They had excellent mines, but that was about all they had, and their surface forces appeared to be unmotivated. Awful weather in the Baltic and meager targets in both the Baltic and the Black Seas troubled the U-boats more than any Russian ASW threat.

THE BALTIC

U-boats sank 26 vessels totaling 15,939 tons, and took two prizes totaling 1,690 tons in the Baltic from 16 August 1915 to 31 December 1916. The average target was a 630-ton vessel. The Germans lost only two U-boats during the same period: U-26 sometime after 11 August 1915 and U-10 in May or June 1916. Both boats simply vanished without a trace. While it is probable that each one hit a Russian mine there is no conclusive evidence that Russian countermeasures actually destroyed them.[1]

In the Baltic the U-boats patrolled into the Gulf of Riga, the Gulf of Finland, and the Gulf of Bothnia. The operational season was roughly April to early November and then the U-boats went into port for the winter. Russia's most potent ASW countermeasure was the vicious winters, combined with a paucity of targets.

Mines

The Russians had very good mines and they used them in large numbers, especially near the entrances to their harbors. There were two types. One featured a Herz horn that fired a 160-pound charge. The Russians had designed that mine prior to 1900. The second was a better mine that had an inertia system that fired a 280-pound charge. The Russians had developed that mine from a 1912 design.[2]

Nets

The Russians used fixed nets, suspended from anchored buoys. Construction details for the Russian nets are not available in English or German, but there are enough clues to provide some detail. Russian nets were suspended from large, anchored buoys and they apparently reached down to depths of 100 to 150 feet. This latter assumption is based on the fact that UC-27 encountered a net somewhere between 100 and 130 feet. That being the case, the nets were probably made with a fairly light strand similar to the British and German drift nets. Light construction would be necessary in order for buoys to support nets the size the Russians were using.[3]

Mine and Net Barrage

In 1916 the Russians laid two enormous barriers across the Gulf of Finland. The first barrier, known as the outer barrier, was about fifty miles long and ran from the Island of Dagö (Hiiumaa) to Hangö on the Finnish side. It consisted of several rows of mines laid at different depths in front of a net barrier supported with buoys. The second barrier was called the inner barrier and it was laid about seventy miles east of the first barrier. The inner barrier was a mine barrage that stretched nearly forty-four miles from Revel on the Russian side to Helsingfors (Helsinki). Gates at both ends of each barrier allowed the passage of commercial traffic.[4]

Most of the U-boats avoided the barriers by passing through the gates at each end, but some went right through the barrier. Kapitänleutnant Johannes Spiess in U-19 described his 10 September 1916 passage through the outer barrier, which was marked by large, red buoys.

Diving, we continued our way at various depths. We listened anxiously for the grating of nets or mine cables on the hull, but we penetrated the outer

mine barrage safely at considerable depth. Shortly before dawn we surfaced to ventilate the boat and to recharge batteries, but it soon became
light and we had to disappear. We could not cruise the whole day submerged because we had used up too much of our batteries breaking
through the barrier, so we found a place to rest on the bottom until dark.[5]

The Russians divided the seventy-mile-wide area between the barriers
into three zones: the forward zone, the central zone, and the rear zone.
Within those zones, the Russians had planted more minefields and
deployed specially organized antisubmarine patrols consisting of torpedo
boats and auxiliary patrol vessels. The patrols were more heavily concentrated in the central zone than anywhere else.

Once past the outer barrier, the U-boats transited the interior security zones during daylight at 100 to 150 feet, depths so deep that some
boats sprung leaks due to the pressure and others popped rivets when the
hulls scraped along the bottom. At night, they tried to find a place where
they could safely remain on the surface to recharge their batteries. Spiess
described the technique that was most commonly used.

After thirteen hours submerged cruising we came up in the fresh evening
air and drifted about during the night while the batteries were being
charged, the propellers idle. I used this method every night in that vicinity in order to minimize the danger of running into a mine barrier. One
drifted about somewhat, but still the boat remained closer to one place
than would have been the case with the propellers revolving.[6]

Despite the apparently strong patrols in the area between the barriers,
the Russians were extremely lax; U-boats rarely had the feeling that they
had been seriously hunted. In the two or three instances in which patrol
boats spotted a surfaced U-boat, the patrol vessels retired quickly after
firing a few shots. It is notable that the German log books report very few
encounters with Russian ASW patrols.

Aircraft

The Russians used both lighter than air and heavier than air aircraft for
patrol and antisubmarine work. There were two recorded instances of
aircraft dropping bombs on U-boats, but no damage resulted. Both
occurred west of Dagö Island in 1916.

Surface Responses

Surprisingly, the Russians usually made little or no response to a U-boat sighting, even if that sighting was associated with a torpedo attack. Spiess twice entered Russian harbors and made his presence known without attracting any countermeasures. The first time was at Uto on 12 August 1916 when he attempted to torpedo a Russian submarine and the second was in Moon Sound on 14 August 1916. What responses the Russians did make were inefficient and showed no strong motivation on the crews' part. Typical of such an encounter is the experience Spiess had after he had torpedoed the SS *Elizabeth* on 12 September 1916 just inside the outer barrier.

U-19 dove to avoid a half flotilla of destroyers that came out of Revel at high speed and then cruised about the vicinity on zigzag courses. Spiess wrote, "In those innocent times this procedure was known as submarine chasing. They did not disturb us."[7] Spiess and his crew had little to worry about in the presence of the Russian destroyers, because the Russians operating in the Baltic apparently did not have depth charges in 1916. They may have been equipped with an explosive sweep similar to the British or German devices but there was no evidence they were using them in the Baltic.[8]

THE BLACK SEA

When Kapitänleutnant Otto Hersing in U-21 arrived in Constantinople from Cattaro on 5 June 1915 there was no intention of conducting a war against shipping. His assignment was to support the Turks in the Dardanelles campaign. By September that had changed and the Germans in Constantinople turned their attention to the Russian-controlled Black Sea. From September 1915 to January 1917 the U-boats sank ten steamers and four sailing vessels for a total of 19,572 tons. That was about two thousand tons more than the boats in the Baltic had accomplished.[9]

The Germans, however, lost five boats in the Black Sea compared to two in the Baltic. Of the five boats, UC-13 was lost due to equipment failure that resulted in the boat running aground, UB-45 and UB-46 hit Russian mines, and UC-15 and UB-7 simply vanished without a trace. UC-15 had gone to the mouth of the Sulina to lay mines and never returned; there is a possibility that it blew up on its own mine, a fairly common occurrence with UC boats. It is also possible that UC-15 hit a Russian mine, since it was operating in an area where the Russians had laid lines, or that it suffered a diving accident.

The disappearance of UB-7 is the more interesting mystery. Leaving Vara on 27 September 1916 to patrol off Sevastopol, it never came back.

Although there is no firm evidence to explain its disappearance, there was speculation that a Russian seaplane bombed and sank it. Erich Gröner believed that was the case and Bodo Herzog shares that opinion. According to Herzog, the seaplane bombed the boat near the Khersonese Lighthouse at 44°30'N, 35°15'E. E. Keeble Chatterton adds that the Germans captured a Russian aviator who told his captors that a U-boat had been bombed off Khersonese Lighthouse in October 1916. Whether the Russian aviator was taking credit for the kill or simply reporting the event is not clear. Other authorities are less certain and simply list the cause as unknown.[10]

Russian ASW in the Black Sea was limited almost entirely to defensive mining. There were surface patrols along the commercial routes and some vessels were convoyed, but the U-boats rarely encountered them. When an encounter did occur, the U-boat simply dove and the Russian patrol vessel quickly cleared the area. The absence of a persistent search is indicative of poor motivation, which was probably a result of the social and political unrest that was growing in Russia.

A rare exception occurred on 2 July 1916 when Kapitänleutnant Max Valentiner in U-38 torpedoed the British steamer, SS *Rockliffe*. U-38 was submerged near the east shore of the Black Sea when the first officer reported three steamers escorted by a destroyer and a steam yacht. Valentiner maneuvered his boat and fired one torpedo at a range of about fourteen hundred yards. While the torpedo was streaking toward its target the destroyer wheeled and bore down on U-38.

To avoid being rammed, Valentiner ordered U-38 to dive, but a solid blow shook the boat before the order could be executed. U-38 was firmly grounded in less than thirty-three feet of water. As the destroyer charged across the stranded U-boat, the Russians exploded a sweep that exploded too far away to seriously damage U-38. Valentiner wrote:

> The force of the explosion knocked me back off my feet, the lights exploded and water squirted through a loosened rivet in the conning tower. I soon heard the report that the engine telegraph was damaged and saw that the machine had been ripped from its mount. A check of all stations revealed that the hull was still tight.[11]

While Valentiner tried to get U-38 off the sand, the Russian destroyer made two more passes, each farther away. There was silence after the third detonation. Valentiner took a chance and extended his periscope.

He saw that the Russian had turned his attention to rescuing the survivors of the torpedoed ship, apparently satisfied that he had driven off the U-boat. While the Russian was occupied with other matters, Valentiner went ahead at full power, taking U-38 into deep water.

The nature of the attack tells more than simply what happened. The sweep failed to do serious damage to the stranded U-38, illustrating how difficult it was to place a sweep within killing range. The U-boat was essentially stuck at the point from which the torpedo was launched, which meant the torpedo wake gave an accurate indication of the boat's location. It is possible that the Russian captain did not know that U-38 was stranded, and assumed it was under way and going deep. As he approached what he thought was its last probable position, he fired his sweep at a point to which he thought the U-38 had moved. Of course, that spot was close enough to rattle the boat severely, but not close enough to really damage it. This theory is supported by the fact that he fired the next two charges farther away, apparently following U-38's presumed track.

The winds of political change would soon reduce Russia's limited ASW effort to zero. With the start of the Russian revolution on 6 November 1917, the Russian boats were no longer in the war.

PART SIX

The Central Powers' Countermeasures

1914–1918

26

Weapons

Germany played essentially the same role within the Central Powers that Britain played in the Entente Powers. Germany took the lead in developing an ASW capability; therefore any measurement of Central Powers' ASW accomplishments relies largely on the Germans' experience. Although the submarine problem was never as large for the Germans as it was for the British, the Germans reacted to it more quickly than the British. The German response to the threat was essentially the same as the British response. With the exception of nets, German ASW technology was never as sophisticated as the British technology, nor did the Germans produce the variety of devices and systems that the British produced. It is, however, a fact that the Germans used depth charges earlier than the British.

The Central Powers conducted ASW operations in five areas: the Baltic, the Helgoland Bight, the Adriatic, at the west entrance to the Dardanelles, and the Marmara Sea. The Germans were responsible for operations in the Baltic and the Helgoland Bight, the Austrians handled the Adriatic, and the Turks were concerned with the Dardanelles and the Marmara Sea. The Turks relied exclusively on German-produced nets and mines, while the Austrians drew on German supplies and to a lesser extent their own resources. By far, the most active area for ASW operations was in the Baltic where the Germans developed an efficient ASW force.

The Germans divided ASW measures into three categories: stationary devices, including mines, anchored nets, and mine-nets; mobile devices, including guns, ramming, towed nets, depth charges, and explosive sweeps; and the so-called helpers, which were hydrophones, smoke apparatus, and the convoy system. Like the British, the Germans found that the convoy system was the most effective antisubmarine measure.[1]

In 1914 the Germans established the *Technische Versuchskommission* (TVK), responsible for developing ASW weapons and devices. By spring 1915 TVK had placed production orders for depth charges and explosive sweeps, and was developing hydrophones. By the end of the year the Germans had ordered examples of all the ASW weapons, including indicator-nets and antisubmarine mines.[2]

STATIONARY DEVICES AND MEASURES

Mines

The standard German mine was the E-mine, which carried a 330-pound charge.[3] This was the mine the British copied in 1917. Although it was primarily intended for use against surface vessels the Germans also laid them across suspected submarine routes. The antisubmarine U-mine carried a 44-pound charge and weighed considerably less, but was only a little smaller than the E-mine. Both the E-mine and the U-mine featured the Hertz horn method of detonation. U-mines were in production in 1915, but quantity production was not reached until 1916.

The German doctrine for antisubmarine minefields differed radically from British doctrine as it evolved in 1918. The Germans believed that an antisubmarine minefield could look after itself and needed no surface patrol. This was a marked difference to the British experience, which showed that an antisubmarine minefield was only effective if patrols could force U-boats to dive into the minefield. The German view was probably based on the fact that they lacked the resources to maintain standing patrols over their mine barriers.

Throughout the war the British and Russians lost a total of eight submarines to German mines. There were six Russian and ten British submarines that simply disappeared. Most of them probably struck mines, but there is no evidence to prove that. The losses to mines all appear to have been due to striking a full-size E-mine rather than the underpowered U-mine.

Anchored Nets

A postwar German naval officer commented, "Nets proved worthless except for harbor defense."[4] Nevertheless, by 1917 the Germans had developed an anchored net that they felt was strong enough to prevent any submarine from breaking through. Strength alone was not enough to ensure the barrier's success, however, and the Germans believed that to be effective, any fixed net system had to be laid in two parallel lines spaced 100 to 150 feet apart. They also recognized that a surfaced submarine could cross the barrier by stopping its engines and fore-reaching across the net. Their solution was to add a surface cable that ran along the tops of the buoys.

Regardless of how heavily built the net was, all the German anchored nets suffered from wind, storms, and high seas to the point that no net system had a life expectancy of more than five months. Additionally, the Germans were plagued with neutral fishing and commercial vessels that blundered into the nets. Because of the cost in resources to patrol and maintain the nets, the Germans replaced as many as possible with minefields. The realities of the situation, however, forced the Germans to rely on net barriers almost to the end of the war.

On 26 October 1914 the Germans laid anchored nets, without indicators, in seven locations in the western Baltic. Early in 1915 they took up the old nets and replaced them with nets that did have indicators, and they added four new locations. The Germans experienced the same problems as the British with their indicator-nets. The indicator buoys ignited when they were not supposed to, the panel clips failed, and storms tore away the nets. The Germans had one problem that the British did not have. In the Baltic the storms tore up the sea grass, which clogged the nets. This put such a strain on the panels that the clips failed and the panels gave way. In a 1918 report, the Germans concluded:

> Experience had shown that the indicator-net was not suitable for use in a long-term, fixed position. Current and seas drifted the nets and tore them apart, and the indicators illuminated unintentionally, causing consternation along the patrol line. Attempted improvements to the nets and indicators were not successful and the indicator-nets were eliminated in early 1918.[5]

The only instance in which an enemy submarine fouled a German anchored net occurred on 2 October 1915 off Bornholm when E-19, commanded by Lt. Comdr. Francis N. Cromie, fouled a German net patrolled by SMS *Sylvana*. E-19 ran full into the net and became entangled by its hydroplanes to the extent that the crew lost control of the boat for an hour and a half. Twice during that time E-19 broke surface and *Sylvana* fired on it without scoring any hits. E-19 finally tore free and escaped. Cromie later commented that the German nets were "far stronger steel wire nets than the Turks had at the Dardanelles."[6]

Mine-Nets

Anchored mine-nets were in use in autumn 1915, with development continuing until April 1916.[7] They were never popular. In 1917 the German navy completely rejected mine-nets because they were too dangerous to handle—the mines were too sensitive—and the maintenance system was too complicated.

MOBILE DEVICES AND MEASURES

Gunfire and Ramming

Like their enemies, throughout the war the Central Powers relied on gunfire and ramming to attack submarines. Both methods, however, were weapons of opportunity and ramming could be as dangerous to the attacker as it could be to the submarine. From 1914 to 1918 the Central Powers destroyed eight submarines with gunfire. In five cases the submarine was stranded and the other three were destroyed in conjunction with a net, ramming, or an explosive sweep.

Towed Indicator-Nets

The Germans first deployed towed indicator-nets in 1915.[8] They made some improvements to their nets throughout the war, but their towed nets were never satisfactory. The biggest complaint was that the deck gear used to handle the nets functioned too slowly. Second, the indicator sleds ignited when they were not supposed to, especially when the nets were shot or being hauled aboard. Third, the nets were not buoyant enough.

The Germans produced their towed nets in individual 800-foot by 80-foot panels. Each drifter carried four panels that were clipped together to create a 6,600-foot panel of lightweight netting. Unlike the British, the

Germans did not use single drifters to tow the nets astern. German practice was to stretch the net between two drifters to create a forward moving wall eighty feet deep with the head about three to six feet below the surface. The towing speed was one to one and a half knots. The Germans preferred to use their towed nets in water less than one hundred feet deep to prevent submarines from passing below the net.

The Germans were able to reef their nets for use in shallow water, but the net had to be reefed before it went into the water. This was a time-consuming, difficult task on a drifter's small deck. Reefed or not reefed, the Germans could shoot their nets fairly quickly, but hauling them in under any condition was another time-consuming effort. It took the crew two hours to haul in a four-panel net and four hours if the net was reefed.

The Germans tried three different tactics for deploying their towed nets. Initially they had the idea of surrounding the submarine with nets so that no matter which way a boat turned, it would strike a net. That tactic proved to be unworkable. Next, they tried deploying the drifters in line abreast with a line of attack boats following them. That left gaps in the line between the pairs of net-towing drifters. Finally, they developed a checkerboard formation with a second line of drifters whose nets overlapped the gaps in the forward line. There are no recorded instances, however, in which an enemy submarine fouled a German mobile net.

Depth Charge

The Germans used only the C15 depth charge during World War I.[9] Carbonit Gesellschaft, a private company, developed the 200-pound C15 during the winter of 1914 and the German navy started issuing the depth charge in the spring of 1915. According to the Germans the C15's 110-pound charge gave it a thirty-five-foot destructive radius.

Like the British Type A and the American Mark I, the C15 operated on the float and line principal. When the C15 hit the water, the float remained on the surface as the depth charge sank, paying out a lanyard, the length of which determined the depth at which the depth charge would explode. When the depth charge reached the end of its lanyard, the tension pulled the pin and detonated the charge. The C15 had a back-up firing device that was timer activated. If the lanyard failed to pull the pin a preset timer would explode the charge.

The C15 failed to explode about 50 percent of the time. One of the reasons was that vibrations associated with handling and transporting the

C15 at sea caused the picric acid in the detonator to leak out. Another weak spot was the joint where the lanyard was attached to the float. Typically the joint failed, leaving the float on the surface while the unarmed depth charge and its lanyard plunged to the bottom. There were also instances in which the lanyard remained firmly attached to the float, but failed to pull the pin. That left the equally firmly attached depth charge dangling below the float. Despite the fact that the depth charge was supposed to be unarmed in those circumstances, the Germans made no attempts to recover a dud. They disposed of it by sinking the float with gunfire.

The Germans were not happy with the C15 for several reasons, especially its failure rate. Its total weight to charge weight was too high, its design prevented mass production, and it sank too slowly. As a result, the Germans considered the C15 to be at best only marginally useful and only 2,256 were produced during the war.

The C15 went into service in April 1915 and by April 1916 depth charges were in general use. The supply was limited and not all vessels received them. Throughout the war destroyers and torpedo boats received no more than six and all the smaller auxiliaries were limited to two or four each. Supply limitations prevented the Germans from adopting the saturation tactic and they accepted the reality that destroying a submarine with just a few depth charges was a matter of luck. At the same time they recognized that dropping even a few depth charges—provided that they exploded—drove off the submarine and allowed the target to escape.

Explosive Sweeps

TVK's early experiments with trailed charges led to the development of two devices: the *Spenganker* (explosive anchor) and the *U-Bootsdrachen* (UD).[10] Both were produced and issued to destroyers and auxiliary patrol vessels.

The explosive anchor was very similar to Jeffrey's traveling torpedo, which the British developed in 1914–15. The German version consisted of a grappling hook attached to the end of a wire cable and a kite for maintaining depth. Two drifters, spaced fifty meters apart, towed the grappling hook at depths down to thirty feet. When the grapple hooked an obstruction it activated a pilot line that jerked the explosive charge off the deck of one of the towboats and guided it to the obstruction. A timing device that was based on the depth of the hook detonated the charge. The explosive anchor was a makeshift device that was used only during 1916 when the explosive sweeps were in short supply. There are no recorded instances in which it made contact.

The Germans' explosive sweep, the UD, was as ineffective as its British counterpart. The Germans developed it in two versions, but only issued one version, the UD15, a 200-pound charge towed at the end of a 300-foot line and capable of descending to eighty feet. A kite maintained the desired depth and the charge could be towed at speeds from six to twenty-one knots. The tow cable also carried the electric cable that supplied current to the detonator. The UD15 was designed so that when it struck a submarine, the circuit was closed and the charge fired, but there was no provision for firing the charge manually from the deck.

The UD15 was not a reliable weapon and the list of complaints was long. The maximum towing speed was too slow. The electrical firing system was too complicated, which resulted in frequent failures to fire. The most disconcerting problem was that at speeds above twenty-one knots it rose to the surface, planed, and exploded. Another vexing problem was that the combination tow and electrical cable was too weak and parted under strain. Also, UD15's eighty-foot maximum depth was too shallow to be effective because submarines usually went deep or lay on the bottom. In either case, the UD15 could not reach them.

The UD15 was all the Germans had so they developed a specific tactic for deploying the device called the Berghoff curve, code name USV, which stood for *U-Bootssuchverfahren,* literally U-boat search procedure. The attacking UD-equipped vessels formed a line abreast and followed a spiral pattern that was based on or very near the point at which the submarine was last known to be. Maintaining their line abreast formation, the group followed an expanding spiral course outward from that point. Theoretically, it was mathematically impossible for the submarine to avoid being struck by at least one of the charges. The patrol vessel's captain used a specially designed cardboard course indicator to navigate along the spiral, using as his base reference a buoy that had been dropped on the spot that represented the submarine's last known position.

Despite theoretical certainty of success, the Germans correctly concluded that the UD15 was simply a weapon of chance. Many Germans believed the UD had enormous potential, which would be realized when an effective hydrophone was developed; the two devices could be used in concert. In practice the Germans destroyed one submarine with the UD device, the Russian submarine *Bars* on 21 May 1917.

Hunter Groups

Like the British and the Americans, the Germans believed that deploying hydrophone-equipped hunter groups was the best way to fight the submarine.[11] The hunter groups that started to appear late in 1915 were organized on an ad hoc basis; formally constituted groups appeared in the spring of 1916. The only difference between German hunter groups and their Entente counterparts was that the German groups were much larger and included drift nets. German hunter groups were even less successful than the British and American groups.

Decoys

Starting in October 1915, the Germans launched a decoy operation that functioned very much like its British counterpart.[12] The Germans commissioned seven decoys consisting of three steamers, three sailing vessels, and one steam lighter, and gave each decoy an alpha designation. For example, the former SS *Kronprinz Wilhelm,* a 1,550-ton coastal steamer, became SMH *K.*

In January 1916 the German decoys started operating along the German and Swedish coasts and in the Skagerrak. Because the British and Russians conducted only a very brief anti-shipping campaign during October 1916, five of the German decoys never saw an enemy submarine, one made a sighting and no contact, and one engaged the enemy three times. The only decoy to engage an enemy submarine was SMH *K,* once while acting as a decoy and twice while acting as a convoy escort.

Aircraft

The Germans made extensive use of seaplanes and rigid airships for anti-submarine patrols. Like all airmen, they made more sighting reports and claimed more damage done to the enemy than actually occurred. German aircraft were hampered to some degree by the prohibition on flying over neutral territorial water, and their opportunities were further limited because the Allies did not have very many submarines in the Baltic. But German aircraft made a strong showing in the Baltic, and in mid-June 1916 Lieutenant Commander Cromie told the Admiralty that British boats were seeing nothing but aircraft and patrols. Cromie also stated that the Germans were very active with ASW.[13]

U-Boats versus Submarines

The Germans made limited use of their U-boats in the ASW role both in the Baltic and in the Helgoland Bight. In the Baltic the only specific instances occurred in October 1914 when Grossadmiral Prince Heinrich ordered five U-boats to undertake antisubmarine patrols in Kiel Bay and again in February 1915 when he assigned a boat to a station west of Bornholm. In the Helgoland Bight the Germans used U-boats in the ASW role as early as 1914 and continued the practice off and on until the end of the war. But those were exceptions because German policy was to use their U-boats against surface targets and to sink submarines when the opportunity presented itself.[14]

During the war there were seven confirmed instances in which a German U-boat torpedoed an enemy submarine; in only one instance was the U-boat operating in an ASW role. In the other six instances the sinkings resulted from an opportune encounter. Austrian U-boats sank two enemy submarines; in both cases the Austrian boats were working as ASW units. The breakdown of the losses was five British, two Italian, and two French.[15]

HELP DEVICES AND MEASURES

Hydrophones

Like the other ASW devices, the Germans did not develop the hydrophone to the degree that the British and the Americans did, and they produced only two types.[16] The first type developed was the UGE, which stood for *Unterwassergeräuschemfänger* or underwater sound receiver. The other was called the SS for *Schwimmschalle,* or swimming shell. Both were towed devices.

The UGE, often called the "flying" hydrophone, was a nondirectional hydrophone that could only be used when the ship was stopped, and there was no way to rotate the device from inside the ship. That meant that the ship's heading had to be changed to find the direction from which the sound was coming. The procedure was to stop, shut down, and listen and then move on, turning the patrol boat in the direction indicated by which ear the listener thought was receiving the loudest sound. For example, if the listener heard the loudest sound in his right ear, the boat turned right. When the patrol boat was on the proper heading, it stopped and the listener took a new bearing. The boat continued the turn and stop procedure until the sound was centered in the listener's ears. At that point the patrol boat would be pointed directly at the target.

The SS was a disk-shaped directional hydrophone designed to operate at a depth of about fifteen feet while suspended from a buoy. The towing cable was attached to the buoy and was paid out from a drum that passed the line through two specially designed davits mounted on the stern. An electrical cable that connected the listener to the microphones was attached to the towing cable and led aft to the SS.

A microphone was located on each side of the disk inside. Changing the ship's heading allowed the listener to center the sound until the bow was pointed directly toward the source. The SS was intended to be used while being towed at ten to twelve knots, but in practice it could only be towed at very low speeds; even then the towing vessel's engine, wave, and propeller noises made using the device very difficult. In practice, the SS vessel had to stop just like the UGE vessel did.

The Germans did not establish hydrophone shore stations during the war because the drain on material resources needed to manufacture and maintain the equipment was too great. However, they did establish fixed listening positions at sea using the UGE hydrophone. The defenses at the entrances to the western Baltic featured fixed hydrophone positions at sea. The arrangement consisted of a large, anchored buoy with the UGE streaming away from it with the tide. An electrical cable descended from the buoy to the bottom and then ran along the seabed to a vessel anchored in the area.

The fixed positions were not successful for several reasons. Because there was no way to remotely alter the position of the UGE unit, the listener was unable to tell from which direction the sound was coming. All he knew was that something somewhere near the buoy was producing a sound. Also, the equipment kept breaking down because of a weak connection where the electrical cable was attached to the buoy. The attachment chafed the line as the buoy tossed and rolled in the sea, until the insulation was broken and seawater destroyed the circuit. The Germans abandoned the system in July 1917 due to repeated failures.

Ships Reporting Post

The Germans developed and deployed a variation of the Bragg loop. Called the SMP for *Schiffsmeldepost,* or ship's reporting post, the device was a cable that lay on the seabed and ran from Nordenny to Helgoland to Eidermünde. The cable was charged with direct current. Whenever a steel ship crossed over the cable, anywhere along its length, the passage was noted on a gauge in the shore station. The problem with the SMP was that there was no way to tell at which point the ship crossed the cable.[17]

Smoke Devices

With the introduction of the convoy system in early 1916, the Germans recognized the need for a smoke apparatus that would obscure the submarine's target. They created two versions. The first was the smoke buoy, designated NB for *Nebelboje,* that the escort vessels dropped in the water between the attacking submarine and the convoy. The other was a deck-mounted smoke drum, called the NT for *Nebeltrommel,* that was carried aboard merchant ships and some escorts. The Germans were generally satisfied with both types, although the NB was effective only when used in large numbers. Used alone or in small groups, it produced a thin blanket of smoke that was not effective.[18]

Convoy System

The Germans began convoying their iron ore trade in April 1916, more than a year earlier than did the Entente Powers. When the British and Russians opened their anti-shipping campaign in October 1915, the German shipping companies pressed the navy to adopt a convoy system. Prince Heinrich was reluctant to adopt the convoy system and used the same arguments the British opponents of the convoy system used in 1917. Specifically, Prince Heinrich said that the Baltic forces lacked sufficient escorts to do the job, and convoys made better targets than individual ships. He also took notice that the British and the Russian submarines were operating according to the Prize Regulations rather than torpedoing their targets without warning. Ships in convoy would be fair targets for being torpedoed without warning. As an alternative solution, Prince Heinrich directed that German ships should steam as much as possible inside neutral territorial waters or sail at night through the open sections.

German naval officers also opposed the convoy system, claiming that submarine captains would welcome convoys because the size of a convoy alone would preclude adequate escort protection. They also objected to the fact that the slowest vessel in the convoy set the convoy's speed. A large slow-moving convoy would be an easy target for a submarine; and even if the shot missed its intended target, it would almost certainly hit another ship in the convoy. U-boat captains, whose opinions the naval staff solicited, agreed with the arguments against convoys. The U-boat captains' views would change dramatically two years later.

In addition to taking advantage of neutral waters and sailing at night, the Germans established fixed positions and regular patrol beats along the shipping lanes. Every twenty hours two destroyers left Libau and patrolled to Landsort, stayed there eighteen hours, cruised down to Segerstad, and then back across the Baltic to Libau. Auxiliary patrol boats patrolled the German coast.

In 1916 Prince Heinrich was persuaded to the benefits of the convoy system but he could not legally compel the shipping companies to cooperate. Several German shipowners opposed the convoy system for the same reasons the British ship owners opposed it a year later. The German owners objected to the delays and cited the danger of collisions. Prince Heinrich overruled them and the first iron ore convoy sailed on 7 April 1916. From that time until the end of the war convoys sailed three times a week along the shipping lanes from Gjedser Strait to the Sound, the Swedish coast, and Schweinemünde. Another group sailed from Schweinemünde to the Sound and Sweden, and another to Danzig-Pillau-Memel-Libau.[19]

ORGANIZATION AND TACTICS

By 1916 the Germans had grouped their ASW forces in three categories: hunting groups, convoy escorts, and general purpose ASW forces. The hunting groups and the convoy escorts were specifically detailed to carry out antisubmarine warfare. The goal of the hunting groups was to find and destroy submarines, a goal they did not once achieve. The convoy escorts' goal was simply to protect the convoy; if in the process they sank a submarine, so much the better. For them, simply preventing a submarine from reaching its target was a success. And the convoy escorts were very successful. The general purpose groups patrolled specific areas, stopped and searched merchant ships, patrolled net lines and maintained the nets, swept up mines and laid new ones, and acted as pilot boats. They were jacks of all trades.

The German ASW weapons, tactics, and organization were similar, but not identical, to their British counterparts. However, they never achieved the efficiency that the British did.

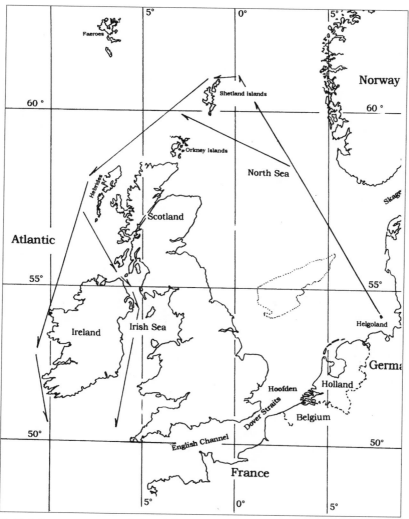

British home waters and the Helgoland Bight, showing the northern route used by the German High Sea Fleet's U-boats after 10 April 1915.

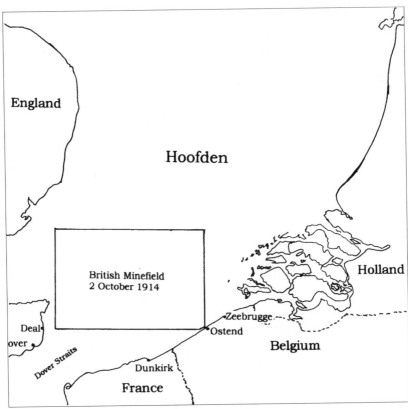

The 2 October 1914 British minefield.

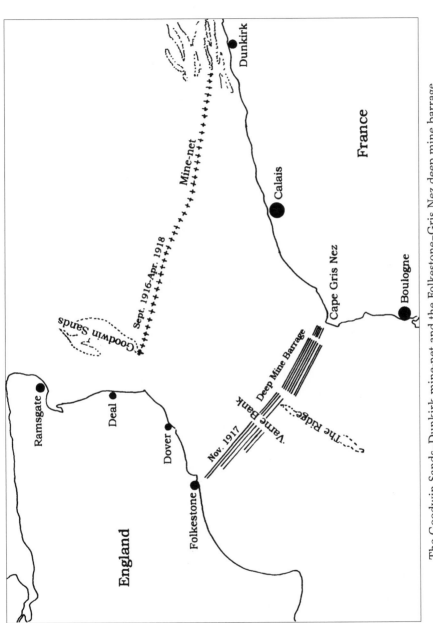

The Goodwin Sands–Dunkirk mine-net and the Folkestone–Gris Nez deep mine barrage.

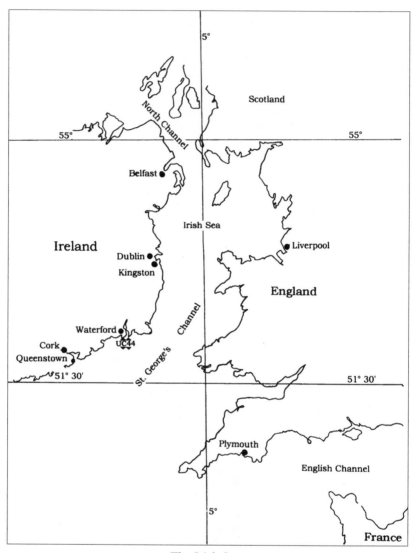

The Irish Sea.

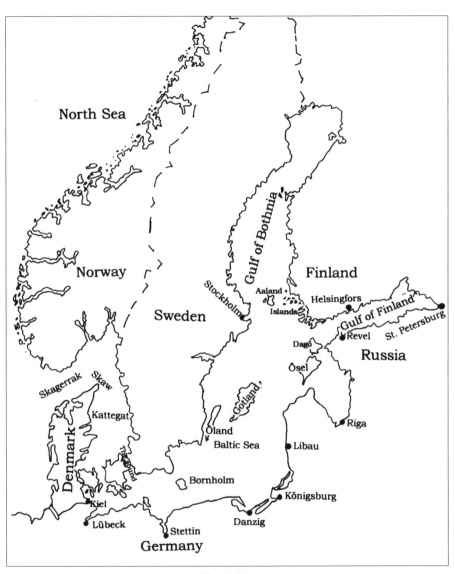

The Baltic.

The entrance to the Baltic.

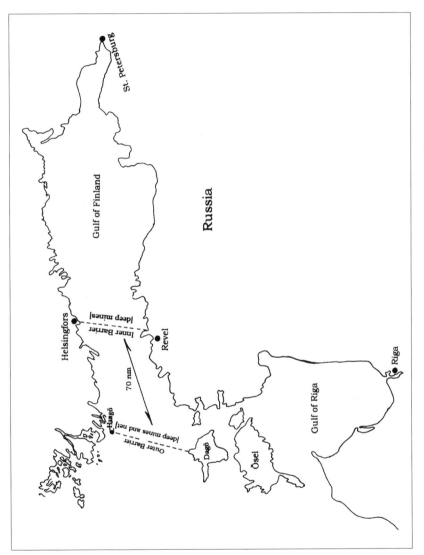

Russian mine and net barriers in the Gulf of Finland.

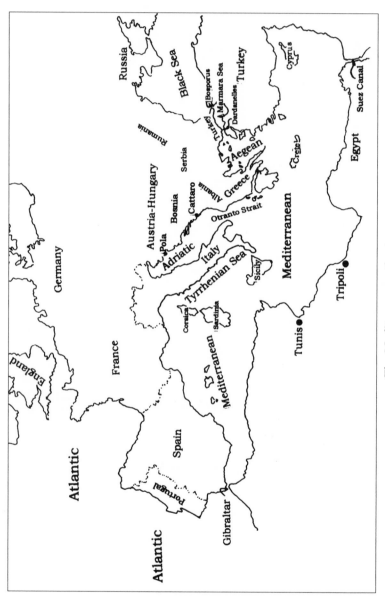

The Mediterranean theater.

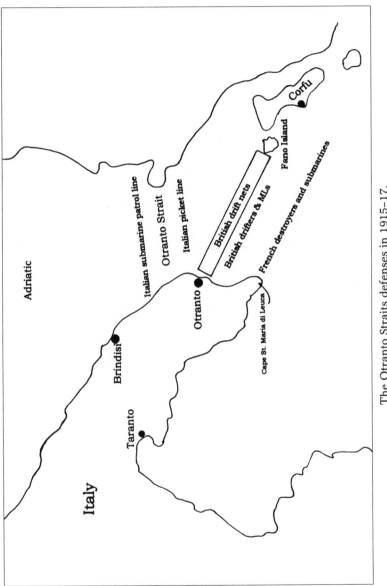

The Otranto Straits defenses in 1915–17.

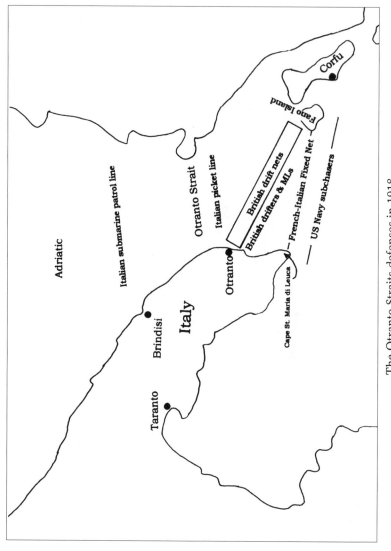

The Otranto Straits defenses in 1918.

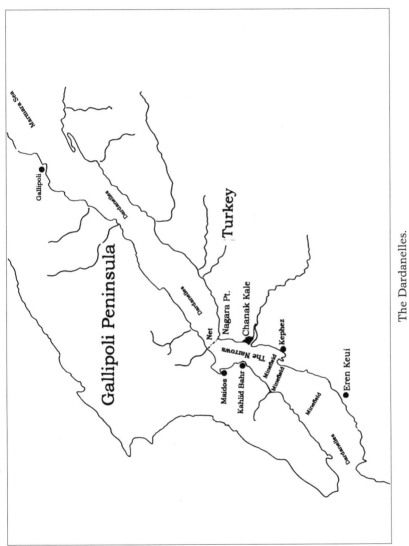

The Dardanelles.

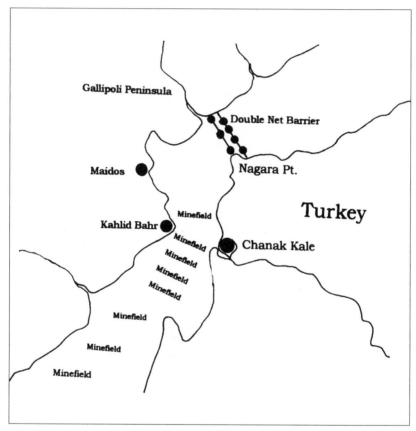

Turkish defenses in the Dardanelles.

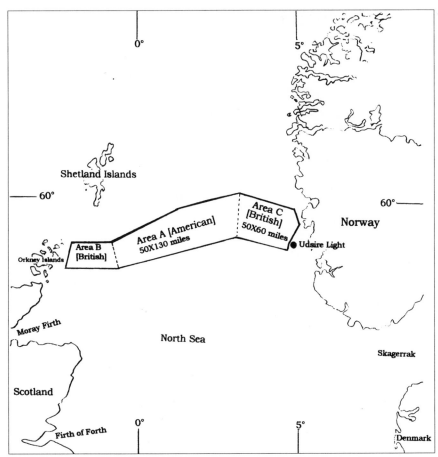

The Northern mine barrage.

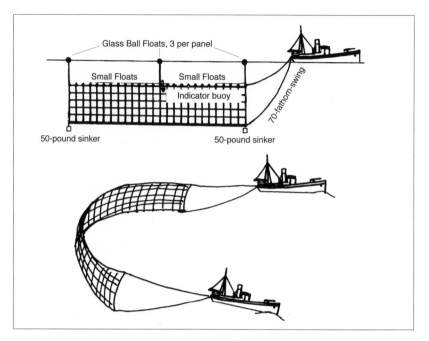

Towing a Net. There were two ways to tow a net: single tow and double tow. The British tried both, but preferred the single tow. The Germans used the double tow exclusively. In both methods the net was submerged six to thirty feet, and the foot reached down to about one hundred feet.

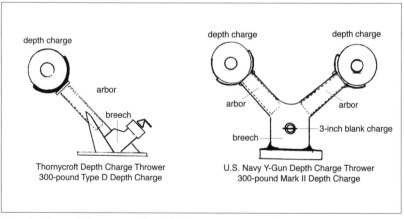

Depth Charge Throwers. The left illustration is a Thornycroft depth charge thrower for a 300-pound Type D depth charge. The right illustration is a U.S. Navy Y-gun depth charge thrower for a 300-pound Mark II depth charge.

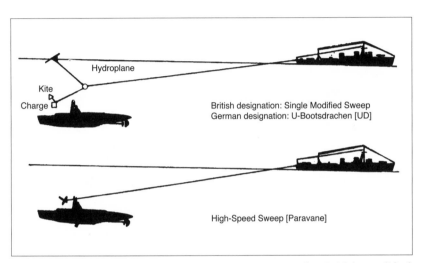

Hydroplane

Kite

Charge

British designation: Single Modified Sweep
German designation: U-Bootsdrachen [UD]

High-Speed Sweep [Paravane]

Explosive Sweeps. The upper illustration represents the British modified explosive sweep. It was identical in principle and very similar in appearance to the German *U-Bootsdrachen* (UD). The lower illustration represents the high-speed sweep, or paravane, which was less complicated and easier to deploy and control than the modified sweep. The British produced the paravane in two versions: a high-speed model for destroyers and a low-speed model for trawlers.

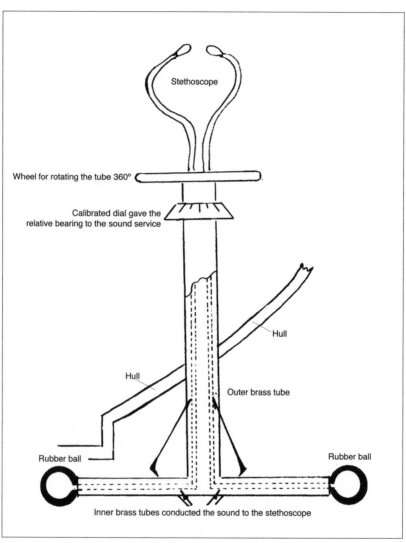

Stethoscope

Wheel for rotating the tube 360°

Calibrated dial gave the
relative bearing to the sound service

Hull

Hull

Outer brass tube

Rubber ball

Rubber ball

Inner brass tubes conducted the sound to the stethoscope

SC-Tube Hydrophone. The U.S. Navy's first successful hydrophones were the C-tube and the SC-tube. The SC-tube was identical to the C-tube except that the SC-tube was through-hull mounted whereas the C-tube was simply dropped over the side. Both versions were simple mechanical devices that were inexpensive to build and easy to use.

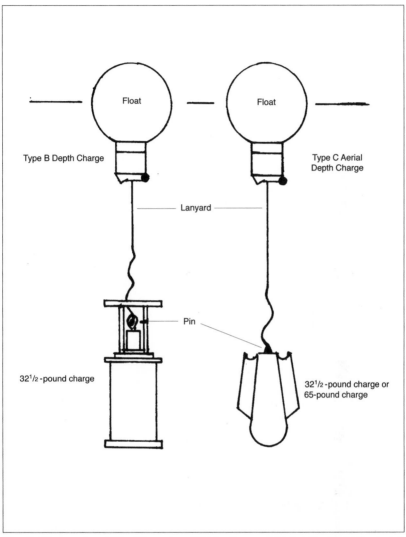

Depth Charge Assembly. These two illustrations represent the basic float and line, or pull-off pistol, principle for detonating a depth charge. The British Type B was identical in operation to the American Mark I and the German C15. The length of the lanyard determined the depth at which the depth charge exploded. British models B and C were available in two lengths: 40 and 80 feet. The Germans' C15 was the largest and had a 110-pound charge.

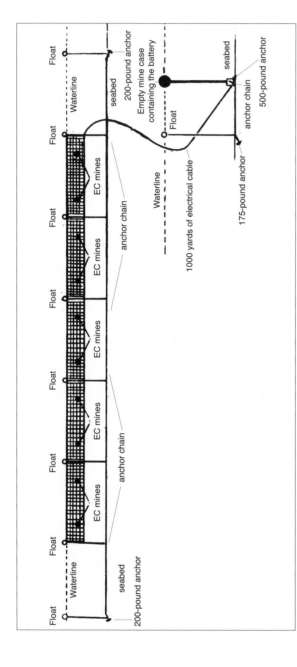

Anchored EC Mine-Net. Illustrating a mine-net laid near the surface, this EC mine-net's panels were three hundred feet wide by seventy-five feet deep. The method used to moor this net is identical to the method used to moor any anchored net. Depending on the circumstances, the top of the net could be submerged to about thirty feet, but the supporting buoys were always visible on the surface as was the mine case that contained the battery.

27

The Baltic and the Helgoland Bight

The Baltic was the scene of the most highly developed and concentrated German antisubmarine effort, and it was there that they deployed their most efficient antisubmarine forces. That was because the western Baltic was the training ground for the German navy and Kiel Bay held the same position with the German navy that Scapa Flow did for the Royal Navy. There was also the critical importance of the iron ore trade between Sweden and Germany. Also, harbors in the three Nordic countries served as arrival points for cargoes that successfully evaded the British blockade.

The German supreme commander in the Baltic was Grossadmiral Prinz Heinrich von Preussen, better known to Americans as Prince Heinrich. He organized his forces into four separate commands, each of which had at least some ASW responsibility. The Coast Defense Division, commanded by Konteradmiral Mischke, was charged with guarding the entrances from the Kattegat into the western Baltic and protecting the waters west of Bornholm. The Reconnaissance Division, commanded by Konteradmiral Hopman, was responsible for the middle and eastern Baltic. Both commands shared a general ASW responsibility. In the autumn of 1915 Prince Heinrich created the antisubmarine flotilla under Korvettenkapitän von Rosenberg who organized his command into hunting groups. And beginning in April 1916 Konteradmiral Schultz's Trade Protection Division provided convoy escorts.

There were outside factors that aided the German ASW effort. Most important, the Russian Baltic Fleet's primary mission was to defend the Russian capital at Saint Petersburg by holding the Gulf of Finland. With the exception of a brief anti-shipping campaign in October to December 1915, and spotty efforts in 1916 and 1917, the Russians ignored German shipping. Another factor was that international law and the Baltic's geography limited the British and Russian submarines' access to merchant shipping. A merchant ship could complete long stretches of its passage inside neutral waters and as long as the British and Russians observed the provisions of the 1909 Declaration of London the ship was immune from attack. A third factor was that the exceptionally hard winters limited submarine activities to the months of May through November. German shipping was also spared heavy losses because both the Russians and the British had torpedo problems. British torpedoes often ran too deep or failed to explode on contact, whereas the Russian captains tended to fire their torpedoes at long range, which gave the German ships time to evade the torpedoes and resulted in a high number of misses.

PHASE I, OCTOBER 1914–FEBRUARY 1915

The first British boats, E-1 and E-9, entered the Baltic on 17 and 18 October 1914 and joined the Russians at Lapvik. Clearly the arrival of British submarines in the Baltic boded ill for the Germans who at that time still lacked the weapons and the destroyers, aircraft, and small auxiliary vessels needed to fight the submarines. Prince Heinrich's first reaction was a plan to lay mines in the Sound, but the Admiralstab vetoed the plan for two reasons: they did not believe that mines would be effective against submarines and the mines would interfere with commercial traffic.[1]

The Germans' lack of an ASW capability in October 1914 is illustrated by the attempt to close the Fehmarn Belt, which is the east entrance to the Kiel Bight. The Germans used herring nets because their purpose-built, steel mesh antisubmarine nets were still under development. The hope was that the herring nets might at least foul a propeller. Between 23 and 27 October the Germans laid twenty-one miles of fishing nets in what proved to be a futile gesture. On 29 October a storm tore away the nets, balled them up, and washed them ashore.[2]

While the nets were being laid in the Fehmarn Belt, Prince Heinrich ordered five U-boats to undertake antisubmarine patrols on a line between Marienleuchte and Hyllekorg. During the day the U-boats patrolled in assigned quadrants at periscope depth looking for submarines. At night they recharged their batteries and rested on the bottom. The effort was at best a shot in the dark and Prince Heinrich recalled the boats on 27 October.[3]

Fortunately for the Germans, Adm. Nicholas O. von Essen, commander of the Russian Baltic Fleet, ordered the British boats to attack German warships rather than the iron ore trade. In doing so, Admiral von Essen made a major contribution to the success of Germany's ASW effort. The Germans used the time to develop their ASW capability. TVK developed the Germans' first usable antisubmarine nets, the depth charge, and the explosive sweep. The Germans also culled their fishing fleet for trawlers and drifters that could be converted to auxiliaries. By January 1915 there were sixty German auxiliary patrol boats in the Kiel Bight, operating around the clock and in all weather.[4]

PHASE II, APRIL 1915–JANUARY 1916

The British and Russian submarines reopened their campaign against German warships on 28 April 1915. By this time the Germans had a limited supply of depth charges, explosive sweeps, and towed antisubmarine nets available for use. Although the Germans were hardly prepared to deal with a serious submarine threat, Russian policy and British technical problems hid the Germans' deficiencies.

The Germans' biggest worry was that the British and Russian submarines would attack the iron ore carriers that ran between Sweden and Germany. The Germans were relieved when the 1915 season opened and the Russians and British continued to focus on German warships rather than on the iron ore trade. The situation was similar to what had happened in the Dover Straits during the Germans' prolonged period of indecision, but the Russian policy was grounded on the tactical situation rather than politics. In May 1915 the German advances in the Gulf of Riga and their offensive into Kurland threatened the Russian naval defenses in the Gulf of Finland, the key to the defense of Saint Petersburg. In response to that threat the Russians made every effort to blunt the German advance by attacking German warships.[5]

How did the Germans respond to attacks on their warships? Until September 1915 only a few German destroyers carried depth charges and others carried only explosive sweeps. Most had neither. As a result the Germans could do little more than dodge torpedoes, fire at the periscope, or try to ram. Two destroyers unsuccessfully hunted E-9 with sweeps on 11 May, and SMS *G135* attacked the Russian submarine *Okun* with a sweep on 3 June. *G135* exploded its sweep and rammed the submarine at the same time, rolling the boat on its beam ends, springing rivets, and bending the periscope at a right angle. The *Okum* returned home safely. But those were rare instances, and destroyers without depth charges were more of a nuisance than a serious threat to the Russian and British submarines.[6]

In mid-August the British sent E-8 and E-13 to reinforce the boats in the Baltic and handed the German ASW forces their first victory. The Germans take credit for destroying the E-13, but its loss was due as much to poor luck as it was to German ASW. While entering the Baltic on 18 August, E-13's compass malfunctioned and the British submarine ran aground well inside Swedish territorial waters. That is where the matter should have ended with the boat interned for the duration. Instead, on the following day SMS *G132* moved in close and destroyed the stranded boat with gunfire, killing and injuring several of the crew. The attack was a flagrant violation of international law and Sweden protested loudly, but the Germans had one less submarine to worry about.[7]

E-8 also negotiated the Sound during the night of 18 August, avoiding German patrols until exiting the Sound where a German destroyer caught it on the surface. In a desperate attempt to escape, E-8 crash dived, hit bottom at nineteen feet, bounced along the rocky bed, and sheared off its starboard propeller. Crippled, E-8 managed to reach deep water, but the destroyer dogged it through the night. Nevertheless, E-8 reached Revel on 23 August 1915.

E-8's narrow escape illustrates the disadvantage the German surface forces suffered when trying to destroy a submarine. The German destroyer had no depth charges and no explosive sweeps. Its only hope was to either ram E-8 or sink it with gunfire while the submarine was still on the surface. Even when E-8 was bouncing along the bottom in shallow water, the destroyer had no way to get at it. In fact, in the dark, the destroyer could not even find it.

Following the August entry of British submarines into the Baltic, Prince Heinrich mined the Sound entrance and later he added nets.

Everyone agreed that it was impossible to actually close the Sound because enemy submarines could use neutral territorial waters for much of the passage. The Germans believed, however, that nets and mines would make entry into the Baltic more difficult as well as reducing the area of open water to be patrolled. At the same time the Germans beefed up their surface patrols behind the newly laid barrier.[8]

On 9 and 10 September, the British demonstrated the impossibility of closing the Sound. On 8 September, acting on a report that five British submarines were coming south from the Kattegat, the Germans stationed three destroyers, five picket boats, and nine auxiliaries to intercept them. SMS *Amazone* and SMS *G136* spotted E-18 on 9 September but the submarine dove too quickly for them to engage. A short time later the submarine broke the surface and *Amazone* fired on it, the rounds landing so close that the explosions shattered lights and loosened cork insulation inside the submarine. Neither *Amazone* nor *G136* had depth charges, but *G136* deployed its sweep without making contact.[9]

E-19 cleared the Flint Channel on 10 September, but again *Amazone*, now operating with the destroyer *S122*, spotted it. E-19 dove, maneuvered to attack, and fired a torpedo at *S122*. The torpedo ran deep and the destroyer followed the torpedo wake to its source and dropped four depth charges without effect. Later the airship M-IV dropped two 110-pound aerial depth charges on a suspected periscope wake without results.[10]

The German reaction to the new entries was immediate and illustrates how difficult—virtually impossible—it was in 1915 to locate and destroy a submarine. The Germans knew exactly when the boats had entered the Baltic, they had accurate position reports on both of them, and they knew exactly where they were going. The destroyers in the 16th Half Flotilla took up positions in line abreast across the predicted track and remained there for twenty-four hours without making contact. The entire 8th Flotilla was stationed farther north monitoring strong British radio traffic. Despite RDF plots and the boats' known destination, no contact was made.[11]

In mid-September the Germans started equipping all minesweepers and picket boats with depth charges, placed an order for five hundred depth charges, and increased the production of explosive sweeps. The German build-up was none too soon. On 28 September 1915 *Bars*, E-8, and E-19 sailed from Revel to attack German merchant shipping between Sweden and Germany. Until the boats arrived in their patrol areas on 1 October, Russian and British submarines had not operated in the middle

Baltic, having limited their operations to the eastern Baltic. The anti-shipping campaign had a powerful effect on the Germans, who reacted immediately.

The Germans became aware that British boats were in the Kiel Bight when E-19 fouled an anchored net off Gedser on 2 October. E-19 broke surface twice and the auxiliary vessel SMS *Sylvana* fired on it before E-19 managed to tear free. The next day E-19 attempted to stop the ore ship SS *Svionia* off Stubbenkammer, but the attack misfired when the *Svionia* refused to stop and turned away. E-19 opened fire on the fleeing ore carrier with the deck gun and then fired two torpedoes. The first torpedo ran a short distance and sank; the second passed under the ship. In its panic to escape, the steamer ran aground in neutral waters where E-19 could not legally attack it. E-19 was forced to break off the attack. The Germans were able to salvage the *Svionia* and its cargo three days later. Two days later E-8 sank the 400-ton SS *Margarette* with gunfire according to the Prize Regulations.[12]

On 10 October E-19 stopped and tried to sink the 2,250-ton SS *Lulea* fifty miles from Lübeck. After the crew left the ship E-19 fired four torpedoes at point-blank range at a ship that was abandoned and dead in the water. The first torpedo suffered a gyro failure and ran off in the wrong direction. The second slammed into the *Lulea*'s hull but failed to explode. The third torpedo passed under the ship and the fourth missed ahead. In the meantime the *Lulea* drifted onto a reef where the Germans were later able to recover it and its cargo.[13]

These British embarrassments were followed by a string of successes, starting on 11 October when E-19 sank five ships in one day. The last of these sinkings illustrates that the British were just as willing to ignore international law as the Germans. The incident involved the 1,900-ton ore carrier, SS *Germania*.

As with the other four victims, the *Germania* had come down the Kalmar Sound through Swedish territorial waters between Öland and the Swedish mainland. Clearing Öland's south point, the *Germania* entered international waters and became fair game. That was when E-19 jumped it. Instead of stopping, the *Germania* went about and fled back into Swedish territorial waters, finally running aground two miles off the coast.

E-19 chased the steamer, firing at it right up to the point that it went aground. As the crew abandoned the ship, E-19 went alongside and fired directly into the hull, starting a fire in the engine room. British sailors went aboard the hulk and placed a charge in the boiler room that finished the job. The Swedish government filed a strong protest over the violation of its territorial waters. The British denied the charge, claiming that E-19 had simply fired shots to warn the *Germania* that it was standing into danger. The explosion, they said, was a boiler explosion that occurred after the fire room crew abandoned the ship.[14]

The last ore ship lost in 1915 was the 1,300-ton SS *Friesenberg*, sunk on 4 December. During the brief two-month campaign, the Germans lost sixteen ships totaling 31,000 tons. With the exception of three or four attacks made in neutral waters, the British and the Russians had acted within the restrictions of international law. No ships had been torpedoed without warning, and there was no loss of life among the merchant crews.

By the end of the year, when the British-Russian anti-shipping campaign petered out, the Germans began to feel that their ASW organization was becoming efficient. What the Germans did not know was that poor training, faulty equipment, and internal politics substantially eroded the enemy submarines' potential effectiveness. Despite satisfaction with their ASW performance, the Germans did not slacken their efforts to prevent a repeat of the 1915 shipping losses.

Early in 1916 Prince Heinrich assigned strong forces to patrol the shipping lanes and the Germans laid more anchored nets and minefields throughout the Baltic. The German net and mine systems were much more numerous than what the British laid, and they were heavier. The German net defenses, however, never achieved the prominence that some of the British systems did because, with one exception, submarines never fouled the German nets.

Like the British experience, the Germans' fixed net defenses represented an enormous expenditure in resources, time, and manpower for little apparent gain. Nets were something the Germans thought they could not do without. Nevertheless, the nets' failure to produce a measurable result and their huge cost prompted one officer to write, "Nets were useless except for harbor defense."[15]

Early in 1916 Prince Heinrich established the Submarine Search Flotilla under Korvettenkapitän von Rosenberg. The flotilla consisted of slow herring drifters divided into six groups of twelve drifters each. Every drifter was armed with a deck gun, depth charges, explosive sweeps, and enough net to create a 6,600-foot-long barrier. Additionally, every drifter was equipped with a UGE hydrophone. Each twelve-drifter group, led by an old destroyer, could protect a stretch of seaway about ten nautical miles long.[16]

The quality and quantity of Germany's antisubmarine devices were never very high. Their depth charges were too few, too small, and too unreliable; their explosive sweeps suffered the same drawbacks; and their hydrophones were only marginally useful. Had the Russians and their British allies made a serious attempt to sink German ore carriers in 1915, the Germans would have suffered large losses. The measure that made up for their weapons' shortcomings was the convoy system that the Germans initiated on 7 April 1916. The convoys were so successful that British and Russian submarines did not sink any German ship that was in convoy throughout the remainder of the war.

PHASE III, MAY–OCTOBER 1916

When British and Russian submarines came out again on 14 May 1916, their targets were again primarily warships. E-18 and E-1 hunted German warships between the Pomeranian and Swedish coasts without success while *Volk*, E-9, and E-19 were sent to report on German movements. *Volk* was not limited to those narrow orders, however, and on 16 May 1916 it sank three German ore ships east of Häfringe in the Bay of Norrkoping.

At this point the Germans deployed their first submarine hunting units under Korvettenkapitän von Rosenberg, but the hunting groups were unable to locate and destroy any submarines. Part of the problem was that there were too few enemy submarines for the Germans to find. The other problem was that the Germans had not developed an efficient hydrophone. Searching vast expanses of water with no way of effectively searching below the surface was a futile task.

The Germans also deployed their decoy vessels in the Central Baltic and along the Swedish coast. The heavily armed German decoys changed their names, appearances, and colors frequently and hung around in areas where submarines were suspected to be located. From 7 to 16 July 1916 the Germans even set a decoy using a tug towing a small sailing vessel, a ruse similar to the British sailing ship–submarine decoy trap scheme.

SMH *O* was a sailing pram armed with two 105-millimeter guns, one forward and one aft. A seagoing tug towed the *O* and maintained communication with the pram through a phone cable connected to the *O*'s forward gun. The plan called for the tug to cast off the tow and run for safety, leaving the *O* in the lurch. When the submarine was very close, *O*'s gunners would open fire. When the submarine sank or dove, the tug would return and drop depth charges over the spot. No contacts were made. In a similar scheme SMH *A* towed the submerged U-66 with the same tactical plan the British had used with their submarine traps.[17]

The only instance in which a German decoy vessel acting as a decoy made contact with the enemy occurred on 12 August 1916. SMH *K*, the former 1,550-ton freighter SS *Kronprinz Wilhelm*, was operating as a decoy six nautical miles south off the Anholt lighthouse when a lookout spotted a surfaced submarine steaming on a parallel course one and a half nautical miles distant. While the bridge crew watched through their binoculars, the submarine raised the international signal to stop.

At this point everything looked right for the decoy to sink the submarine. Armed with four 105-millimeter guns, all the decoy had to do was wait until the submarine came in close enough and then overwhelm it with gunfire. Instead of stopping, putting a panic party in boat, and waiting to draw in the submarine, the Germans opened fire immediately. Predictably, the submarine pulled the plug and disappeared below the surface.

The Germans later claimed that they scored a hit forward of the conning tower on the third salvo and a conning tower hit on the fourth salvo. After the second hit the boat dove with the signal flag still flying. The *K* turned hard to starboard and crossed the dive position, dropping five depth charges. Three exploded and two did not. It then dropped two more that exploded simultaneously. The submarine was never identified and no Russian or British boats were reported damaged or destroyed on or about that date. There is no doubt the Germans saw a submarine, but they let it get away.[18]

The German decoys failed because they did not attract submarines. Convoys, on the other hand, did attract submarines. SMH *K*, acting as a convoy escort, made the first contact on 27 May 1916. At 1017 a lookout spotted a periscope 45 degrees off the port bow one hundred yards away. Kapitänleutnant Lauterbach ordered the *K* to full speed, put the helm hard over to ram, and hoisted the battle flag. At 1022 a hard blow shook the ship as *K* rammed the submerged *Gepard*. Moments later a periscope appeared to starboard very close to the *K*, and then it immediately disappeared. *K* dropped one depth charge, which did not explode, and opened fire on a rapidly expanding oil slick. *K*, which was taking water through its damaged bow, broke off the search and returned to the con-voy while the crew congratulated themselves for having sunk a subma-rine. In fact, the *Gepard* suffered only minor hull damage and returned safely to Revel.[19]

The next day the *K* spotted the Russian submarine *Bars* on the surface as the Russian was closing on the convoy at high speed. Apparently the submarine's captain thought the *K* was part of the convoy because the *Bars* fired a torpedo at it. The shot was made at long range and the tor-pedo passed astern of the *K*. Again, Lauterbach did not wait until the *Bars* came closer before he opened fire. After several shots were fired, the *Bars* dove and the *K* dropped a depth charge on the spot. The depth charge did not explode.

In his action report Lauterbach wrote that the *K*'s gunners had seen three direct hits on the submarine, two of which hit the conning tower. The lookouts even claimed they saw pieces fly off and a large smoke cloud erupt from the boat. In fact the *Bars* was not hit and returned to port safely. Even though it did not sink any submarines, the *K* was by far Germany's most successful decoy simply because it was the only decoy that encountered the enemy.[20]

The 1916 operations period was limited to May and June for the British boats. In mid-June the senior British submarine officer, Lt. Comdr. Fran-cis N. Cromie, complained to the Admiralty that the Russians were using them principally for reconnaissance and called 1916 the wasted year; it is interesting that the U-boaters were saying the same thing about 1916. Although the British were largely immobilized after June by the unfold-ing political events in Russia, some of the Russian submarines carried on. From August to November Russian boats attacked four German convoys and sank two lone freighters.

During August 1916 the British sent C-26, C-27, C-32, and C-35 to Rus-sia. The British removed the boats' batteries and towed the boats to Archangel where they were loaded on barges and shipped to Saint Peters-burg, arriving there on 9 September. The batteries arrived eleven days later, in a damaged condition as a result of sloppy packing. C-35 went out on 18 October and C-32 on 25 October, but they accomplished nothing.

For the British and the Russians, 1916 ended on a low note. The sub-marines did not repeat their 1915 successes, largely due to the convoy system, and there was growing friction between the Russians and the British boat crews. For the Germans, 1916 ended on a high note.

The efficiency of the German ASW forces, combined with Russian command decisions and Russia's descent into revolution, limited German shipping losses to six vessels during 1916. The Germans safely delivered over four million tons of iron ore and zinc, enough to meet all wartime needs. They also successfully delivered foodstuffs from south Sweden and Denmark, as well as twenty-two thousand horses, without loss. In August alone, the commercial traffic between Sweden, Denmark, and Germany exceeded 650 trips, and the ferry service between Germany and Sweden continued virtually without interruption. The seaborne supply train for the left wing of the German army in the east moved up and down the German coast without difficulty and was as fast and punctual as railroads.[21]

PHASE IV, MAY 1917–APRIL 1918

During the first few months of 1917 the British submarines had few opportunities to attack the enemy. The Russians kept E-boats on watch off Libau or to seaward of the Irben Straits. The C-boats supported the Russian navy in the Riga Gulf, and for them the summer of 1917 was endless patrols without a glimpse of the enemy. In the meantime, the Germans sank the Russian submarine *Bars*. The action provides an example of how German convoy escorts operated against a submarine attack.

A convoy composed of four escorts and two freighters scored the success on 21 May 1917 five nautical miles east of Arkö. The trawlers M-37, M-38, *Hamme*, and *William Jürgens* were escorting the SS *Stern* and SS *Britannica*. The convoy formation had the four escorts placed one ahead, one astern, and one on each side of the two freighters. The *William Jürgens* was the point vessel and its job was to lead the steamers away from the attack and into neutral waters.

M-37, one thousand yards from the convoy, saw a periscope three hundred yards off the starboard bow. M-37 sounded the siren alarm, hoisted the submarine sighted signal, and turned toward the periscope. As it charged down on the position the crew dropped one depth charge and deployed an explosive sweep. The depth charge, set for thirty-five feet, failed to explode. The periscope reappeared close aboard to starboard, inside M-37's turning circle. The trawler, still trailing its explosive sweep, passed close to the spot and entered a Berghoff curve that spiraled outward from the last sighting position. M-38 and the *Hamme* both deployed their sweeps and entered the Berghoff curve, keeping station on the

M-37. In the meantime, the point vessel, *William Jürgens,* led the *Stern* and *Britannica* toward neutral territorial waters.

As the *William Jürgens* led the freighters toward safety M-37's sweep struck bottom and exploded, bringing mud and silt to the surface. M-37 immediately broke out of the curve and moved off to rig a new sweep. Returning to the curve, M-37 and M-38 each dropped one depth charge simultaneously. Both depth charges failed to explode. Moments later *Hamme's* explosive sweep, towed at 65 feet, exploded in 150 feet of water, bringing oil and debris to the surface. The explosion in deep water, followed by the appearance of oil and debris on the surface, indicated that *Hamme's* sweep had hit a submarine. M-37 and M-38 passed over the site and each dropped one depth charge. Both depth charges exploded. The *Hamme* then came around and dropped one depth charge that was a dud. The three escorts had now expended their depth charges, and after a short wait to see what might happen, they returned to the convoy.

Based on postwar examination of Russian navy records, the Germans had correctly concluded that the escorts had sunk the Russian submarine *Bars.* Further examination led the Germans to conclude that *Hamme's* explosive sweep had destroyed the submarine or had damaged it so badly that the two depth charges dropped by M-37 and M-38 had finished the job. This was the only confirmed instance in which the Germans sank a submarine with an explosive sweep.[22]

Winter shut down all submarine operations and essentially ended the naval war in the Baltic. The 6 November revolution and the 17 November armistice isolated the British boats and took the Russian boats out of the war. On 3–5 April 1918 the British destroyed their boats at Helsingfors (Helsinki) where they had gone following the revolution. The antisubmarine war in the Baltic was over.

THE HELGOLAND BIGHT

Although smaller in number and less well equipped than forces in the Baltic, German ASW units in the Helgoland Bight were active from 1914 until the last day of the war. British submarines maintained so-called diving patrols in the Helgoland Bight and kept watch off the mouths of the German rivers from the start of the war. Whenever the opportunity presented itself, the British submarines attacked German warships, a practice that kept the Germans continually on the alert and caused them to establish regular patrol lines using destroyers and auxiliary vessels. More important, the Germans made extensive use of their dirigibles and seaplanes for antisubmarine patrols. During October 1914, German picket boats, destroyers, and aircraft reported many submarine sightings in the Helgoland Bight. However, lacking any sort of a weapon with which to attack a submerged submarine, the Germans could only hope to catch one on the surface. That did not happen.

When depth charges, explosive sweeps, and hydrophones became available in 1915 and 1916, the German navy issued them to the patrol vessels and destroyers operating in the Bight. None of the units scored any success with depth charges or explosive sweeps but the Germans had better luck with torpedoes.

The first use of a U-boat to hunt a submarine occurred in October 1914. On 18 October U-30 and U-27 were stationed off Borkum Reef with U-27 having the additional responsibility of covering the mouth of the Ems. At 1245 Kapitänleutnant Bernhard Wegener saw what he at first thought was a buoy, but it turned out to be the E-3. He and his watch officer both examined the submarine carefully to be sure that it was not a U-boat. What they thought was a large "83" painted on the conning tower was actually "E3." At 1322, Wegener fired one torpedo from three hundred yards, dead abeam of E-3. The torpedo's run to target was twelve seconds followed by "a 100-foot high water column filled with shrapnel, chunks of steel and debris. The boat broke amidships, and both stern and bow rose up. Before the water column collapsed, the boat had disappeared."[23]

The Germans laid one net barrier near the Borkum Reef Lightship. Like all nets, it was difficult to maintain and virtually ineffective. The only boat to strike the net was E-16. On 25 July 1915 Lt. Comdr. C. P. Talbot became aware of the problem at 1415 when E-16 abruptly became heavy forward, began to sink gradually, and then developed a steep down angle by the bow. Just as Talbot blew the main ballast two depth charges exploded with no effect; the jolt told him there was at least one patrol vessel on the surface. Talbot stopped blowing the tanks and allowed E-16 to settle to the bottom in eighty feet. He tried going ahead and astern, but all he accomplished was to lift the stern at a large angle. At 1440 Talbot blew the forward tanks, hoping that the bow would tear free as it rose. Instead, E-16 rose stern first, surfacing with everything forward of the conning tower still below the surface. When Talbot opened the conning tower hatch he saw to his horror that a Zeppelin was directly overhead.

He quickly dove. Back on the bottom, Talbot again tried going forward and astern until suddenly the boat shot upwards. The crew checked the rise and restored trim before E-16 broke surface.[24]

Mines were the most effective ASW measure in the Helgoland Bight and the Germans laid several antisubmarine minefields west of Helgoland. The minefields accounted for four confirmed sinkings and possibly as many as eleven others. One British officer commented, "By the middle of 1916 the Helgoland Bight was so thickly strewn with mines that to put a foot wrong meant certain death."[25]

Compared to the German ASW forces in the Baltic, the ASW forces in the Helgoland Bight accomplished little. The Germans were not concerned with protecting commercial traffic in the Helgoland Bight and no convoys operated there. As a result, they operated on a firehouse response basis, sending out units whenever a submarine was reported, with the result that the submarine was gone before the ASW units arrived. Enemy aircraft and strong surface units posed a far greater threat to German ASW units in the Helgoland Bight than was the case in the Baltic so that the Germans were restricted in their movements.

Could the Germans have developed a more effective ASW capability? They certainly had the technological capability of perfecting better ASW weapons and devices, but they were not motivated to do that. Their shipping losses in the Baltic were very low, which led them to believe that their countermeasures were adequate and did not warrant further development. The same situation existed in the Helgoland Bight.

28

The Mediterranean

The Central Powers carried out ASW operations in the Mediterranean theater: German and Turkish operations in the Dardanelles and the Sea of Marmara, and Austrian operations in the Adriatic. The Central Powers' ASW forces enjoyed more success in the Mediterranean theater than anywhere else. The combined German and Turkish ASW forces accounted for nine submarines: four French and five British. The Austrians sank thirteen enemy boats: five French, six Italian, and two British. The number of successes would appear to imply a highly developed and sophisticated ASW capability, but in fact the Austrians and the Turks did not develop or deploy the variety of weapons and devices that the Germans used in the Baltic.[1]

Of the twenty-two enemy boats destroyed or captured, mines accounted for five, stranding eliminated five, torpedoes sank four, nets accounted for four, gunfire claimed one, ramming accounted for one, and aircraft got two. Gunfire figured prominently in nine of the sinkings, particularly in the Dardanelles where the Turks had dozens of shore batteries. The Turks and the Germans used aircraft to a much smaller degree than the Austrians. In fact the greatest concentration of aircraft in the Mediterranean Theater was in the Adriatic. Austrian and German U-boats attacked enemy submarines as the opportunity presented itself, but in October

1915 German U-boats had a specific ASW responsibility in the Sea of Marmara. Mines played a much smaller role throughout the theater although they were important in the Dardanelles and the Adriatic where the five losses attributed to mines occurred. Stranding was simply a matter of geography and navigational error, but in the Dardanelles stranding became a natural ASW feature that, combined with nets, created a formidable but not entirely effective barrier.

GERMAN AND TURKISH ASW

In October 1914 the British established a mixed naval force base on Tenedos and a larger base at Mudros on the island of Lemnos. Three old British submarines—B-9, B-10, and B-11—plus three French boats operated from the island throughout October. The British established a close blockade across the entrance to the Dardanelles to prevent the SMS *Goeben* and the SMS *Breslau* from coming out of the Sea of Marmara, and on 5 November Britain and France declared war on Turkey.[2]

The Turks were forced to develop an ASW capability in January 1915 when the British attacked at Gallipoli. French and British submarines supported the Gallipoli campaign by passing through the Dardanelles and conducting an anti-shipping campaign in the Sea of Marmara. Between 15 April 1915 and 2 January 1916 twelve French and British submarines attempted to pass through the Dardanelles. Designated Turkish ASW forces sank eight of the twelve (66.6 percent), three of them French. During the Gallipoli campaign, which lasted from 25 April 1915 to 9 January 1916, British submarines sank 1 old Turkish battleship, 6 smaller warships, 55 merchant ships, and 148 sailing vessels.[3]

The focal point of the Turkish-German ASW effort was in the Dardanelles. The Dardanelles is twenty-seven miles long, is very narrow and very deep, and makes two right angle turns. The narrows between Chanak Kale and Kilid Bahr are three-quarters of a mile wide and just a mile wide between Nagara Point and Boghali Kale, which is three and a half miles east. The current that flows from the Marmara Sea through the Dardanelles and into the Mediterranean runs three to four knots and changes direction at various depths. Navigation through the Dardanelles is a headache during peacetime; in a submerged submarine during wartime it is a nightmare.[4]

The first British submarine to enter the Dardanelles was B-11. It went up to Chanak Kale and torpedoed the old Turkish battleship *Messudie* on

13 December 1914. The French submarine *Saphire* tried to get through on 25 January 1915, but ran aground off Chanak Kale. Turkish shore batteries destroyed it, killing most of the crew. On 17 April the British sent E-15 out to attack shipping in the Sea of Marmara, but it grounded at Kephez Point and the Turks destroyed it with gunfire. Following those failures, British boats made twelve round trips between 27 April 1915 and 2 January 1916. Although the Turks managed to destroy four more boats in the Dardanelles and two in the Sea of Marmara, they failed to close the Dardanelles to submarines.[5]

The British had three good reasons for sending submarines through the Dardanelles to attack shipping in the Sea of Marmara. First, the Turkish army fighting on the Gallipoli Peninsula was entirely dependent on seaborne supply. The Turks were almost entirely dependent on Germany for arms and munitions. German arms and munitions, however, could not reach Turkey by land because Serbian resistance to the Austrian offensive blocked rail communications between Germany and Turkey. Second, the British campaign on the Gallipoli Peninsula blocked sea access to Constantinople. Third, coal that was needed to supply the Turkish navy was available only from the Turkish mines at Sunguldak on the Black Sea; ships had to deliver that coal to Constantinople. Understandably, the defense of the Dardanelles became a major concern and the Germans sent experts to Turkey in September 1914 to help build the defenses.[6]

Stationary Measures

Mines

The Turks used a mine that was commercially manufactured by the Carbonit Gesellschaft, the same company that produced the German depth charge. The Carbonit mine was a moored contact mine that featured a very accurate hydrostatic depth setting device, enabling it to be laid in water three hundred feet deep. Five Herz horns, fitted to the top of the mine, fired the 220-pound TNT charge.[7]

The Turks laid eleven minefields starting from just above the narrows at Chanak Kale and Kahlid Bahr down to Eren Keui Bay, a distance of about nine miles. They numbered the fields sequentially from north to south and the number of mines in each barrage varied. Minefield number 8 had the fewest mines at sixteen and minefield number 1 had the most at fifty-three. The total number of mines used was 395, which does not sound like many, but the mined area was only three-quarters of a mile wide at minefield number 1 and just two miles wide at minefield number 10.[8]

The Turks laid their mines fifteen to fifty feet below the surface, expecting to destroy submarines that tried to pass through the Dardanelles at periscope depth or slightly deeper. They could and should have planted them deeper because the British submarines passed beneath the mines at seventy or eighty feet, rising to periscope depth only briefly to obtain a position fix. Although the British were able to safely negotiate the minefields, each trip was a terrifying experience in which the crews listened apprehensively to the mine anchor cables scraping along the hull. There were five recorded instances in which a submarine's forward hydroplanes fouled mine anchor cables without exploding the mine. The following is a typical example.

E-11, commanded by Lt. Comdr. Martin Nasmith, passed through the Dardanelles en route to the Sea of Marmara on 19 May 1915. Nasmith dove as he approached minefield number 10, which consisted of twenty-nine mines, and entered the field at eighty feet. He and his crew could hear the mine cables scraping along the hull. Nasmith carefully kept his speed under four knots. He believed that the mine would not detonate unless it was craned down so that the horns on top of the mine struck the boat. The four-knot speed was intended to prevent that from happening. On the way up the Dardanelles it worked.[9]

Coming back on 7 June 1915, E-11 fouled a mine cable off Kahlid Bahr in minefield number 1 at seventy feet. The situation was serious. The mine cable had jammed in the port forward diving plane so that E-11 was carrying the whole mine, cable, and anchor assembly. The mine was hooked to the upper end of the cable above E-11 while the anchor dangled below. The pressure of the boat's forward motion craned the mine back toward the conning tower. If the weight of the mine anchor dragged the cable downward, the mine would be pulled down to the point that it would strike the conning tower. Nasmith could see the mine clearly through the conning tower scuttle, and as the boat moved forward the mine oscillated left and right and dipped down toward the conning tower, which was just ten feet away. Nasmith had a good look at the top of the mine, which confirmed that the horns were indeed on the top.

How do you get rid of something like that? The truth was that in his present position Nasmith could not. He had to carry the mine through ten more minefields until he reached a place where he could safely surface and dispose of it. Despite the odds, E-11 made it and Nasmith used a tricky piece of seamanship to unhook his boat from the mine. He had the crew blow the after tanks while E-11 went full astern. That kept the bow down and the force of the boat going astern freed the cable from the hydroplane. The mine sank and E-11 surfaced safely.[10]

Despite the threat the mines posed to submarines trying to pass through the Dardanelles, the Turkish mine defenses sunk only two submarines during the war. On 1 May 1915 the French submarine *Joule* struck a mine in barrage number 11. There were no survivors. The second victim was E-14, which hit a mine on 28 January 1918 while rounding Nagara Point. There were nine survivors.

Anchored Nets

The Germans made the decision to net the Dardanelles in June 1915, after it became apparent that British submarines were routinely passing through the minefields and entering the Sea of Marmara.[11] They chose to lay the net at Nagara Point, about three miles north of Chanak Kale, but there were several technical problems to overcome. The water is over three hundred feet deep off Nagara Point and the current through the narrows there often exceeds four knots. The strong current and rocky bottom made it difficult to anchor the net securely. Natural obstacles, however, were not the only problems the Germans faced.

The Turkish military commander at the Dardanelles refused to cooperate and remained uncooperative. He argued that there were insufficient materials for the project and that the quantities needed were unobtainable. The Turk had a point because the required materials were not immediately available and there was no way to obtain them from Germany. The Germans had to use their imagination and the nets used in the Dardanelles were classic examples of field expediency.

Led by Leutnant der Reserve Hoefer, German sailors scrounged quantities of discarded one-inch-diameter power cables and other scrap wire from industrial sources. From scrap wire the Germans produced two hundred foot by one hundred foot panels with heavy bolt lines and a thirteen-foot mesh. They combed the Turkish naval arsenal for discarded anchor chain, shackles, wire hawsers, and buoys that "had lain buried for many decades under piles of rubbish." They lifted ship's mooring buoys from the harbor at Constantinople and took them with their cables and anchors to Nagara Point. They scrounged hundreds of seventeenth-century stone cannon balls, old anchors, and discarded stone ballast and took that to Nagara Point too.

Having gathered their odds and ends, the Germans began construction on 27 June and completed the barrier on 26 July 1915. The Germans supported the net with the ship's mooring buoys spaced at intervals of two hundred feet and added empty mine cases between the buoys for more buoyancy. They used the stone cannon balls and old anchors as weights along the bottom of the net to keep the panels in a nearly vertical position. It was a formidable barrier, but the submarines got through it anyway.

In August the Germans laid a second net parallel to the original. By that time the supply of scrap material in Turkey was nearly depleted, but they found a large supply of scrap one-inch-diameter steel wire in Bulgaria. They had an even harder time locating enough large buoys to support the heavier, deeper net panels. The new net was 1,550 yards long and consisted of 28 large buoys supporting 25 net panels that reached down to 230 feet.

Maintaining the double barrier and replacing damaged sections of the net was an ongoing struggle. The Germans had used up the available supply of wire and buoys. There was also a serious anchor shortage. The Germans partly resolved the anchor shortage by resorting to everything from wood stock anchors from old sailing ships to a few modern, two-ton types. The size of the problem is illustrated by the fact that the Nagara nets required fifty buoys, seventy anchors, nine thousand yards of anchor chain, and eighty-one miles of wire.

The Germans soon discovered that the submarines were taking the net at about the same location, and they laid a short net across that spot. The patch was just over 100 yards long and 265 feet deep, with a 10-foot mesh. This short net was made of the best obtainable materials. Even two rows of heavy net and a steel patch did not stop the submarines from getting through, but it slowed them down a bit.

The net scored its first success on the day it was completed. On 26 July the French submarine *Mariotte* stuck the net and became entangled. Unable to tear free, it was forced to surface. Turkish shore batteries opened fire on it at virtually point-blank range. The submarine sank and most of the crew was captured.[12]

The only other boat that the net destroyed was E-7, which struck the triple-layer defense on 4 September. Lt. Comdr. A. D. Cochrane had made one round trip through the Dardanelles before the Germans had completed the Nagara net, but going and coming he had passed through the area while the net was under construction. He struck the reinforced net at 0600 at one hundred feet and had torn partially through when a wire fouled E-7's starboard propeller. Anchored to the net, E-7 swung with the current, came broadside against the net, port side to, and became more firmly entangled.[13]

Turks in the patrol boats knew exactly where the boat was, but not its exact depth, and could tell that it was badly tangled in the net. Because neither the Germans nor the Turks had any depth charges, there was no way of getting at it. Not willing to let the boat work its way free, the Turks groped in the depths with grapples trying to snare the boat. Apparently using lines that were too short, they were also hampered by the strong current and repeated false reports as the grapples caught the net rather than the E-7. At 0830 and again at 1030 they exploded small charges attached to lines without effect. By 1400 E-7's batteries were nearly exhausted and Cochrane ceased his efforts to tear free. On the surface, the secession of activity below made it appear that the submarine had escaped.

At about 1400 Oberleutnant zur See Heino von Heimburg, captain of the UB-14, and Karl Herzig, his cook and explosives expert, arrived at the scene. About three hours later a shout went up from one of the gunboats that the grapple had something at 130 feet, and a fleet of small boats gathered around. Von Heimburg and Herzig had been onlookers up to this point, but now they took a greater interest. Von Heimburg asked Herzig if he had any ideas and Herzig suggested a solution similar to the explosive anchor. He proposed to rig a charge with a timed fuse and attach it to the grapple line so that the charge would slide down the line to the submarine where it would explode. The trick was estimating how much time it would take the charge to slide down 130 feet, and set the fuse accordingly. Apparently, Herzig's calculations were correct and the charge exploded at 1840.

Inside E-7 the explosion was so violent that Cochrane thought a mine had gone off close aboard. The blast smashed the electric lights, knocked loose cork insulation and paint, and ruptured small fittings. Hoping the explosion had also damaged the net, Cochrane used his remaining battery power to break loose, but it did not work. Fifteen minutes later, while Herzig was preparing a second charge, Cochrane blew the tanks and surfaced. Following a brief flurry of gunfire, the crew was able to surrender while inside men set charges to scuttle E-7.

In addition to netting the Dardanelles, the Germans and Turks also laid a net across the Bosporus. Started on 28 July and completed on 6 August 1915, the Bosporus net was about 650 yards long. It consisted of eleven panels suspended from fourteen anchored buoys. The panels extended down to nearly the bottom. Depth and current were less a problem here than at the Dardanelles, which allowed for lighter construction. There were no enemy encounters with this net.

Mobile Devices

Gunfire

Neither the Germans nor the Turks had depth charges in the Dardanelles or in the Sea of Marmara.[14] The underwater explosions that British submarine captains reported were either mines exploding or the sounds of artillery exploding on the surface. With the exception of the makeshift underwater explosives used against E-7, the Turks were limited to gunfire as an offensive measure against submarines.

The shore batteries in the Dardanelles got plenty of experience firing at submarines and periscopes, and there were occasional instances in the Sea of Marmara whereby a warship spotted a submarine on the surface and got off a few rounds in its direction. There was only one instance, however, in which a Turkish surface unit sank a submarine with gunfire and that happened in the Sea of Marmara on 30 April 1915. In an apparently empty sea, the Australian submarine AE-2, commanded by Lt. Comdr. H.G. D. Stoker, was having trim problems. Without warning the bow shot up and the submarine broke the surface. By pure chance the Turkish torpedo boat *Yar Hissar,* commanded by Lt. Ali Risa, was a mile away. When the submarine suddenly appeared on the surface the *Yar Hissar* turned toward it but the submarine dove before the *Yar Hissar* could get off a shot. Lt. Risa remained in the area, circling, hoping the submarine would appear again.

AE-2's trim problems worsened. Down sharply by the bow, it was rapidly approaching its maximum rated depth when Stoker ordered the motors full astern and blew the main ballast tanks. AE-2 shot toward the surface stern first. At one hundred feet Stoker reflooded the tanks and went ahead in an attempt to regain control, but it was too late. AE-2 broke surface stern first at 0940 and it was out of control. The *Yar Hissar* opened fire with its single 37-millimeter gun, scoring three hits in the engine room. The submarine momentarily disappeared below the surface, quickly reappeared, and the crew poured out on deck. AE-2, its sea valves open, settled and sank while the *Yar Hissar* picked up the crew.

Decoy Vessels
The Turkish navy deployed twenty lightly armed sailing craft in the Sea of Marmara as decoys, but the navy crews did not wear naval uniforms. The Turks alone took the initiative for this program without informing Konteradmiral Wilhelm Souchon. When he became aware of the operation in mid-June 1915 he ordered it stopped, fearing British treatment of German submarine crews in retaliation. Thereafter, the Turks operated decoys only in the Black Sea.

Despite the order, some British submarine captains reported engaging Turkish decoys in the Sea of Marmara. If the vessels they mentioned were actually decoys, they were not very effective. Unlike their British counterparts, there was no stopping and feigning panic to draw in the submarine. Instead, the ships the British encountered ran for the cover of shore batteries, or ran to gain distance before coming about and attacking.[15]

U-Boats
There were a few occasions when U-boats were specifically detailed to sink submarines. UB-14 was given its assignment on 4 November after the French submarine *Turquoise* ran aground near the Nagara net and was captured intact. Among the papers the Turks found inside the *Turquoise* were detailed instructions for a planned rendezvous with E-20 on 6 November. Konteradmiral Souchon ordered von Heimburg to take UB-14 to the rendezvous. E-20 kept the appointment and UB-14 torpedoed it, killing all the crew except for the captain, two officers, and six men who were either on deck or in the conning tower.[16]

Help Devices

Convoy
The Turks instituted the convoy system in the Sea of Marmara on 26 April 1915, two years before the British started using them and one year before the Germans started using convoys in the Baltic. The principal convoy route was from Constantinople to Gallipoli City and the return route. The convoys were made up of two to eight troop ships and freighters traveling at six to eight knots, escorted by one to three old destroyers. Convoys were also run down the Dardanelles from Gallipoli City to the smaller

ports nearer to the front. The return convoys carried wounded or the ships were in ballast.

The objections the Germans raised against using convoys in the Baltic, and that the British raised against them in home waters, were fully realized in the Sea of Marmara. German officers and enlisted gunners assigned to the convoy escorts reported serious difficulties with Turkish watch officers not understanding visual and flag signals and failing to follow the procedures for a submarine attack. The Turkish merchant captains and their crews were poorly trained and panic ensued whenever a submarine alarm was sounded.

British submarine attacks on convoys were often successful, although their score was usually just one ship. The Turkish escorts had nothing more than deck guns and sharp bows with which to attack the submarine, and those were worthless when a boat was submerged.[17]

AUSTRIAN ASW IN THE ADRIATIC

The Adriatic is a roughly rectangular body of water, about four hundred miles long and one hundred miles wide. During World War I, Italy formed one side of the Adriatic and Austria-Hungary formed the other. The only way in and out was through the Otranto Straits, and the British and Italians held the straits. Because of the restricted area and the geography, submarines played a large role in the Adriatic. The Austrian ASW was very basic and lacked the scope, variety, and sophistication that the Entente forces had. Austrian ASW was also much less developed than what the Germans used in the Baltic.[18]

Stationary Devices

Nets

The Austrians deployed no offshore nets, but they did net the entrances to Pola and Cattaro. Austrian harbor defense nets were conventional heavy wire panels with a twelve-foot mesh and were supported by large buoys. The panels reached almost to the harbor floor and small auxiliary vessels and net tenders were stationed near the nets. Like all harbor defense nets, those at Pola and Cattaro had a gate that the net tenders could open and close.

The only success occurred on 20 December 1914 when the French submarine *Curie* attempted to enter the harbor at Pola and fouled the net. The *Curie,* commanded by Lieutenant de Vaisseau O'Byrne, struck the net at sixty feet and the crew could hear the chains and cables scraping and rattling along the hull. As O'Byrne rose to periscope depth the *Curie* became so thoroughly entangled that he stopped the ascent and made violent fore and aft maneuvers trying to tear free. All he accomplished was to foul both shafts and burn out the electric motors. At 1630 the *Curie* assumed a steep down angle by the bow, the batteries spilled, and chlorine gas quickly developed. O'Byrne ordered the tanks blown and surfaced.

Lookouts ashore and in patrol boats had been watching the net thrash, jerk, and sag as the submarine flailed around trying to escape. When the *Curie* surfaced, the Austrian patrol boats opened fire immediately but did little damage before the French crew scuttled it. The *Curie* sank and the Austrians took the entire crew prisoner. A few weeks later the Austrians raised the *Curie,* reconditioned it, and commissioned the boat as the Austrian U-14 on 10 August 1915.[19]

Mines

The Austrians used a mine that was nearly identical to the German E-mine. Mines accounted for three submarines off Cattaro and one off Trieste. The Italian submarine *Jalea* hit a mine off Trieste on 15 August 1915. There were no survivors. On 15 July 1916 the British H-3 became the first boat lost to a mine off Cattaro, and the Italian W-4 suffered the same fate a year later. The last boat lost to a mine off Cattaro was the French *Bernouilly* in February 1918.[20]

Several submarines passed through minefields safely but the British B-10 had a scary experience in June 1916. Commanded by Lt. K. Mitchell, B-10 was submerged off Fiume (Rijeka) when it fouled a mine at fifty feet. The water was so clear that Mitchell could clearly see the mine through the periscope, at first floating six feet above the bow, as B-10 was turning to starboard. He watched as the boat's motion caused the mine to crane down and touch the port forward hydroplane. Because the horns were up it did not explode.

Mitchell stopped the starboard turn and the mine rose until it was again six feet above the bow. B-10 was in a tight spot. It was too close to the heavily defended shore to surface, and even if it did surface the mine would come down onto the boat. If B-10 carried on as it was, the forward movement would surely crane the mine down against the hull. Mitchell took a chance. He ordered the bow planes hard up and went ahead full.

His maneuver worked and the mine's anchor cable parted, sending the mine to the surface.[21]

Mobile Devices

Aircraft

Because the Adriatic is relatively narrow, aircraft played a large role in the area. The Austrians used seaplanes to attack enemy harbors and for antisubmarine patrols. The aircraft were not equipped with depth bombs, but their conventional bombs accounted for two submarines. On 15 September 1915 Austrian seaplanes L-132 and L-135 bombed the French submarine *Foucault* while it was at periscope depth ten miles off Cattaro. The bombs were big enough that when they hit the surface and exploded, the shock waves caused an electrical short that started a fire in the *Foucault*. The boat dove out of control to 250 feet, then came back to 80 feet, at which point the electric motors quit. Without power and filled with smoke, the *Foucault* surfaced and its crew scuttled it. Austrian destroyers called to the scene picked up the survivors.[22]

Austrian ASW forces actually did not sink the other submarine that is credited to bombing, but the result was the same. Having survived its June 1916 encounter with a mine, B-10 was laid alongside a depot ship in Venice when Austrian aircraft bombed the harbor on 9 August 1916. One of the bombs landed squarely on B-10 and it simply disappeared.[23]

U-Boats

Austrian U-boats operating as submarine hunters scored two victories in 1915. U-11, formerly the German UB-15, torpedoed the Italian *Medusa* off Venice on 10 June. Five Italian crewmen survived to be taken prisoner. U-5 torpedoed the Italian submarine *Nereide* off Pelagruz Island on 5 August and there were no survivors.

Gunfire

On 5 December 1915 the French submarine *Fresnel* ran aground off Durazzo. Before the crew could get it off, the Austrian destroyer *Warasdiner* appeared and destroyed the *Fresnel* with gunfire, killing the captain. The rest of the crew became prisoners of war.

Two weeks later the French submarine *Monge* attacked the Austrian cruiser *Helgoland* and missed. The destroyer *Balaton* rammed the submerged submarine, slashing a hole in the pressure hull over the engine room, causing the *Monge* to sink to two hundred feet before the crew blew the tanks and dropped the exterior ballast. The *Monge* shot to the surface where the *Balaton* shelled it as the crew jumped into the water.[24]

Explosive Sweep

The only recorded instance in which an explosive sweep was used in the Adriatic occurred on 14 July 1916. The Austrian destroyers *65* and *66* caught the Italian submarine *Balilla* on the surface and drove it under with gunfire. Both destroyers deployed their sweeps and towed them across the *Balilla*'s suspected tract with the sweeps set at sixty-five feet. One of the Austrian destroyers got lucky when its sweep connected with the *Balilla* and exploded. There were no survivors.[25]

Epilogue

When World War I ended, the political matters were not settled and many sons of the men who had fought in the first war would fight in the second war. Many historians look at the period from August 1914 to August 1945 as the Thirty Years War, with World War II being simply a continuation of the first war. That view is well founded and is illustrated by the fact that the belligerents in World War II used essentially the same ASW devices and measures they had used in the first, with some improvements.

Hydrophones were greatly improved and were surpassed by sonar, which is an active detection system. Equally important was the wartime development of surface and airborne radar. These technological developments did much to deprive the U-boats of their underwater invisibility and limited their surface operations.

The depth charge underwent some improvements but remained essentially the same device that the Americans and the British used in World War II. The Germans abandoned their three-part C15 depth charge and adopted the British Type D for use in World War II. The Americans' Mark II depth charge rack, with minor improvements, became the world's standard. The Y-gun was unchanged in World War II and was supplemented with the Hedge Hog projector. During World

War II, the combination of sonar and the depth charge created a truly formidable ASW system.

Radio intelligence played a large and important role in World War II. The British broke the Germans' Enigma codes early in the war, and capitalized on their World War I experience to create a truly efficient service. The Germans failed to learn from their World War I experience and their U-boats continued to use the radio excessively, providing British intelligence with a wealth of information that the Allies used to sink the U-boats.

Aircraft became much more efficient during World War II. They had much greater range. When equipped with airborne radar and aerial depth charges they were very effective in the ASW role. The Americans produced blimps in large numbers and used them as convoy escorts and for offshore antisubmarine patrols. The U.S. Navy claims that no ships under escort by blimps were lost to a U-boat attack during World War II.

All the belligerents used the convoy system during World War II, but the Germans had learned from their World War I experience. Although the convoy system worked the second time, losses among convoys were much higher because the Germans had adopted the wolf pack tactic for attacking convoys. Had they done that in World War I the outcome might have been different.

Antisubmarine nets were used by the belligerents during World War II, but only for harbor defense. Mines were again used in enormous numbers and were very effective. The variety of mines used during World War II was almost mind boggling, and each one was much more reliable and deadly than the earlier versions. As an antisubmarine weapon mines were still limited to use in relatively shallow choke points and posed no threat to U-boats and submarines that operated on the high sea.

Put in the proper perspective, the ASW devices and measures used during World War I do not look so primitive after all. Some were ineffective, others were only marginally effective, and a few were downright deadly. In 1914 ASW was an entirely new undertaking. By 1918 it was a well-developed military science, the principles of which remain unchanged.

Appendix A: Rank Equivalents during World War I

Central Powers

German Navy[1]	Austro-Hungarian Navy[2]	U.S. Navy[1]
Grossadmiral	—[3]	—
Generaladmiral	—	—
Admiral	Admiral	Admiral
Vizeadmiral	Vizeadmiral	Vice Admiral
Konteradmiral	Konteradmiral	Rear Admiral
Kommodore	—	Commodore
Kapitän zur See	Linienschiffskapitän	Captain
Fregattenkapitän	Fregattenkapitän	Commander
Korvettenkapitän	Korvettenkapitän	Lieutenant Commander
Kapitänleutnant	Linienschiffsleutnant	Lieutenant
Oberleutnant zur See	Linienschiffsfähnrich	Lieutenant (jg)
Leutnant zur See	—	Ensign

Entente Powers

Royal Navy[1]	French Navy[1]	Italian Navy[1]	U.S. Navy
Admiral of the Fleet	—	—	—
Admiral	Vice-Amiral	Ammiraglio d'Armata	Admiral
Vice Admiral	Vice-Amiral	Ammiraglio d'Squadra	Vice Admiral
Rear Admiral	Contre-Amiral	Contrammiraglio	Rear Admiral
Commodore	—	—	Commodore
Captain	Capitaine de Vaisseau	Capitano di Vascello	Captain
Commander	Capitaine de Frégate	Capitano di Fregata	Commander
Lieutenant Commander	Capitaine de Corvette	Capitano di di Corvetta	Lieutenant Commander
Lieutenant	Lieutenant de Vaisseau	Tenente di Vascello	Lieutenant
—	Enseigne	—	Lieutenant (jg)
Sub-Lieutenant	—	Sottotenente di Vascello	Ensign

[1]*Source:* U.S. Naval Academy, *Naval Phraseology,* Annapolis, Maryland, 1934.
[2]*Source:* Claudia Ham, Ph.D., Heeresgeschichtliche Museum, Vienna.
[3]No equivalent rank.

Appendix B: Gun Caliber Equivalents

Size	Metric Equivalent	U.S. Equivalent
1-Pounder	37 millimeter	1.457 inch
3-Pounder	47 millimeter	1.85 inch
6-Pounder	57 millimeter	2.244 inch
10-Pounder	73 millimeter	2.75 inch
12-Pounder	76 millimeter	3 inch
13-Pounder	76 millimeter	3 inch
15-Pounder	76 millimeter	3 inch
18-Pounder	84 millimeter	3.3 inch

Sources: Aberdeen Ordnance Museum to author, 26 April 1998; I. V. Hogg and L. F. Thurston, "Gun and Carriage Data," in *British Artillery Weapons and Ammunition, 1914–1918*, 233–34.

Notes

Translation note: Unless otherwise noted, all translations from German to English were done by the author. Translations that appear in the work cited are denoted by the phrase "including translation."

Chapter 1   The Prize Regulations

1. "Declaration Concerning the Laws of Naval War, 208 Consol. T.S.338 (1909)."
2. Arno Spindler, *Der Handelskrieg mit U-Booten,* 1:172.
3. Sir Julian S. Corbett and Henry Newbolt, *History of the Great War: Naval Operations,* 1:75.
4. Ibid., 2:15, 216.
5. Ibid., 1:158.
6. Hermann Bauer, *Als Führer der U-Boote im Weltkrieg,* 129.
7. Corbett and Newbolt, *History of the Great War,* 1:92.
8. Otto Groos and Walter Gladisch, *Der Krieg in der Nordsee,* 2:130.
9. Ibid., 131.
10. Ibid., 156, including translation.
11. Corbett and Newbolt, *History of the Great War,* 1:182.

12. Groos and Gladisch, *Der Krieg in der Nordsee,* 2:152.
13. Ibid., 163, including translation.
14. Ibid., 154.
15. Ibid., 156, including translation.

Chapter 2   The German Awakening

1. Paul G. Halpern, *A Naval History of World War I,* 21–22.
2. Corbett and Newbolt, *History of the Great War,* 1:180.
3. Ibid., 2:133.
4. Ibid., 1:182; Spindler, *Der Handelskrieg mit U-Booten,* 1:177.
5. Spindler, *Der Handelskrieg mit U-Booten,* 1:177.
6. U17 KTB, 1–23 October 1914, T-1022, Roll 32, PG61523, in *Records of the German Navy, 1850–1945* (hereafter cited as *RGN*).
7. Corbett and Newbolt, *History of the Great War,* 1:247–48.
8. U24 KTB, 12–28 October 1914, T-1022, Roll 13, PG61548, *RGN.*
9. Corbett and Newbolt, *History of the Great War,* 2:132; and Spindler, *Der Handelskrieg mit U-Booten,* 1:35.
10. Spindler, *Der Handelskrieg mit U-Booten,* 1:35–36.
11. The preceding account was taken from ibid., 1:78–80; Walter Görlitz, *The Kaiser and His Court,* 62.
12. Bauer, *Als Führer der U-Boote,* 185.
13. Corbett and Newbolt, *History of the Great War,* 2:133, 3:270.
14. Ibid., 2:131.
15. Ibid., 3:270.

Chapter 3   Channel Defenses, Mines, and Radio Intelligence

1. Groos and Gladisch, *Der Krieg in der Nordsee,* 2:165.
2. E. Keeble Chatterton, *Fighting the U-Boats,* 23.
3. Groos and Gladisch, *Der Krieg in der Nordsee,* 2:162, 207.
4. Corbett and Newbolt, *History of the Great War,* 2:7–8.
5. Ibid., 18.
6. Bauer, *Als Führer der U-Boote,* 61.
7. Groos and Gladisch, *Der Krieg in der Nordsee,* 2:153.
8. Ibid., 154.
9. Admiral Sir Reginald Bacon, *The Dover Patrol, 1915–1917,* 1:69–70; Captain J. S. Cowie, *Mines, Minelayers and Minelaying,* 47–48.
10. Bacon, *Dover Patrol,* 1:69–70.

11. Kapitänleutnant Freiherr von Spiegel, *Kriegstagebuch U202*, 65-74; Spindler, *Der Handelskrieg mit U-Booten*, 2:54-56, 128.

12. Spindler, *Der Handelskrieg mit U-Booten*, 3:40.

13. Bacon, *Dover Patrol*, 1:69-70.

14. R. H. Gibson and Maurice Prendergast, *The German Submarine War, 1914-1918*, 38-39.

15. Viscount Jellicoe, *The Crisis of the Naval War*, 50.

16. E. Keeble Chatterton, *The Auxiliary Patrol*, 38-39, 62.

17. Spindler, *Der Handelskrieg mit U-Booten*, 1:172.

18. The following is taken from Alberto Santoni, "The First Ultra Secret," 99-110; and Patrick Beesley, *Room 40*, 90-92.

Chapter 4   Ramming, Gunfire, and Decoys

1. Spindler, *Der Handelskrieg mit U-Booten*, 1:171-72.

2. Erich Gröner, *Die deutschen Kriegsschiffe, 1915-1945*, 1:342-72.

3. Gibson and Prendergast, *German Submarine War*, 3.

4. The following account is based on four sources, none of which exactly agrees with the other three. Chatterton, *Fighting the U-Boats*, 40-41; Gibson and Prendergast, *German Submarine War*, 17-18; Groos and Gladisch, *Der Krieg in der Nordsee*, 3:15-20; "Bericht des Kommandenten von U18, Kapitänleutnant von Hennig, über die letzte Unterhehmung des boots, 17-23 November 1914," T-1022, Roll 32, PG61526, *RGN*.

5. "Bericht des Kommandenten von U18, Kapitänleutnant von Hennig, über die letzte Unterhehmung des boots, 17-23 November 1914," T-1022, Roll 32, PG61526, *RGN*.

6. Corbett and Newbolt, *History of the Great War*, 2:274-76.

7. Ibid., 275.

8. Spindler, *Der Handelskrieg mit U-Booten*, 2:29; U6 KTB, 28 February 1915, T-1022, Roll 6, PG61505, *RGN*.

9. Spindler, *Der Handelskrieg mit U-Booten*, 2:50-51.

10. Albert B. Hart, et al., eds., *Harper's Pictorial Library of the World War*, 10:265-69.

11. Spindler, *Der Handelskrieg mit U-Booten*, 2:82.

12. Ibid., 125-26; "Bericht von Kapitänleutnant Mühlau, 30 April 1918," T-1022, Roll 3, PG61519, *RGN*.

13. Spindler, *Der Handelskrieg mit U-Booten*, 2:117-18; Gibson and Prendergast, *German Submarine War*, 49-50; Lowell Thomas, *Raiders of the Deep*, 111-17.

14. Gibson and Prendergast, *German Submarine War,* 46–48; Spindler, *Der Handelskrieg mit U-Booten,* 2:130–32; Keeble E. Chatterton, *Q-Ships and Their Story,* 10.

15. U16 KTB, 20 July 1915, T-1022, Roll 3, PG61521, *RGN.*

16. Corbett and Newbolt, *History of the Great War,* 3:51; and Chatterton, *Q-Ships,* 13.

17. Gröner, *Die deutschen Kriegsschiffe,* 1:345; Spindler, *Der Handelskrieg mit U-Booten,* 2:119.

18. Chatterton, *Q-Ships,* 13–16; Spindler, *Der Handelskrieg mit U-Booten,* 2:119.

19. Spindler, *Der Handelskrieg mit U-Booten,* 2:213.

20. Corbett and Newbolt, *History of the Great War,* 3:131.

21. Ibid., 133; and Spindler, *Der Handelskrieg mit U-Booten,* 2:250–55.

22. Oberleutnant zur See Crompton, *Crompton U-41: Der zweite Baralong-Fall,* 47–54; Corbett and Newbolt, *History of the Great War,* 2:139–40; and Spindler, *Der Handelskrieg mit U-Booten,* 2:262–67.

Chapter 5   Nets

1. V. E. Tarrant, *The U-Boat Offensive, 1915–1945,* 17; Bacon, *Dover Patrol,* 2:393, 391–94; Ernest C. Fayle, *Seaborne Trade,* 2:21–22.

2. Corbett and Newbolt, *History of the Great War,* 2:271, 390.

3. Heino von Heimburg, *U-Boot gegen U-Boot,* 44; Max Valentiner, *300,000 Tonnen versenkt,* 151.

4. Admiralty Technical History Section, *Technical History and Index: A Serial History of Technical Problems Dealt with by Admiralty Departments,* Part 40 [TH40], "Anti-Submarine Development and Experiments Prior to December 1916," 50–52 (hereafter cited as TH40).

5. Bacon, *Dover Patrol,* 2:418.

6. TH40, 50–52.

7. Bacon, *Dover Patrol,* 2:418; Chatterton, *Fighting the U-Boats,* 50, 57.

8. "Aus dem KTB *UB10* vom 10 Juni 1915" and "Besprechung beim O.d.O mit Oblt.z.S. Steinbrink, U-Boots-Kommandant Flandern UB10, 8 Dezember 1915," T-1022, Roll 1284, PG40906, *RGN.*

9. Gibson and Prendergast, *German Submarine War,* 39–40; Corbett and Newbolt, *History of the Great War,* 2:388.

10. "Aus em KTB *UB10* vom 10 Juni 1915," T-1022, Roll 1284, PG90406, *RGN.*

11. Ibid.

12. The following account is taken from Corbett and Newbolt, *History of the Great War,* 2:275–76; Gibson and Prendergast, *German Submarine War,* 33; Spindler, *Der Handelskrieg mit U-Booten,* 2:24–28; "Bericht von Kptlt. Stoss," T-1022, Roll 23, PG61507, *RGN.*

13. Spindler, *Der Handelskrieg mit U-Booten,* 2:231.

14. U32 KTB, 3–17 April 1915, T-1022, Roll 14, PG61566, *RGN.*

15. Spindler, *Der Handelskrieg mit U-Booten,* 2:57; Bauer, *Als Führer der U-Boote,* 277.

16. Ibid., 276–82; Beesley, *Room 40,* 96.

17. Corbett and Newbolt, *History of the Great War,* 2:387.

18. Bacon, *Dover Patrol,* 1:19.

Chapter 6   Neutral Flags, Explosive Sweeps, and Lance Bombs

1. The foregoing was taken from Spindler, *Der Handelskrieg mit U-Booten,* 2:18–20.

2. Ibid., 15; Corbett and Newbolt, *History of the Great War,* 2:264.

3. TH40, 41.

4. Admiralty Technical History Section, *Technical History and Index: A Serial History of Technical Problems Dealt with by Admiralty Departments,* Part 7 [TH7], "The Anti-Submarine Division of the Naval Staff, December 1916–November 1918," 21 (hereafter cited as TH7).

5. TH40, 19–20.

6. U12 KTB, 11 November 1915, T-1022, Roll 31, PG61515, *RGN.*

7. TH40, 36–37, 46–47; TH7, 21.

8. The account of the U-12's loss is taken from "Übertrag der stenographischen Aufzeichnung des Steuermannes Rath von U12," T-1022, Roll 31, PG61516, *RGN;* Spindler, *Der Handelskrieg mit U-Booten,* 2:38–40; Corbett and Newbolt, *History of the Great War,* 2:278–80.

9. Letter, Seeburg to Spindler, 22 November 1928, T-1022, Roll 31, PG61516, *RGN.*

10. "Übertrag der stenographischen Aufzeichnung des Steuermannes Rath von U12," T-1022, Roll 31, PG61516, *RGN,* including translation.

11. Bacon, *Dover Patrol,* 1:115; Halpern, *A Naval History of World War I,* 3.

12. French Navy Historical Service, Chateau de Vincennes, Paris, via Evelyn DeBernado, Embassy of France in the United States, letter to the author, 13 June 2000 with enclosure, Document Code #1, No. CC 309, "Les Armes," 26.

13. TH40, 52–53; TH7, 22.
14. TH40, 53.
15. TH7, 22.
16. Charles W. Domville-Fife, *Submarine Warfare of Today,* 91.
17. William W. Nutting, *The Cinderellas of the Fleet,* 27.

Chapter 7   The Bombardments of Zeebrugge and Ostend, 1915

1. Captain Alfred F. B. Carpenter, RN, *The Blocking of Zeebrugge,* 11.
2. Corbett and Newbolt, *History of the Great War,* 3:148; Carpenter, *The Blocking of Zeebrugge,* 11.
3. Bacon, *Dover Patrol,* 1:76.
4. John Moore, ed., *Jane's Fighting Ships of World War I,* 63.
5. Ibid.; Bacon, *Dover Patrol,* 1:31, 75–80.
6. Bacon, *Dover Patrol,* 1:80.
7. Ibid., 86.
8. Ibid., 88.
9. Ibid., 31.

Chapter 8   German Indecision

1. U.S. Congress, House of Representatives, *The Problems of Neutrality when the World is at War,* Part I, *The Submarine Controversy,* 64th Cong., 2d Sess., Document No. 2111, 9 (Hereafter cited as HR Doc. No. 2111).
2. Ibid., 10.
3. Ibid., 11.
4. Spindler, *Der Handelskrieg mit U-Booten,* 1:129–30.
5. Bauer, *Als Führer der U-Boote,* 202.
6. Ibid., 271.
7. Ibid., 259.
8. Spindler, *Der Handelskrieg mit U-Booten,* 2:65.
9. Corbett and Newbolt, *History of the Great War,* 2:387.
10. Spindler, *Der Handelskrieg mit U-Booten,* 2:84.
11. Ibid., 136–37.
12. HR Doc. No. 2111, 41.
13. Ibid., 43.
14. Ibid., 138.

15. Görlitz, *The Kaiser and His Court*, 82.

16. Spindler, *Der Handelskrieg mit U-Booten*, 2:102.

17. Görlitz, *The Kaiser and His Court*, 83.

18. HR Doc. No. 2111, 52.

19. Görlitz, *The Kaiser and His Court*, 102.

20. Spindler, *Der Handelskrieg mit U-Booten*, 2:278.

21. Ibid., 286-87.

22. Spindler, *Der Handelskrieg mit U-Booten*, 2:9-13.

23. Bodo Herzog, *Deutsche U-Boote, 1906-1966*, 101-6; Halpern, *A Naval History of World War I*, 296, 299; Edwyn Gray, *The Killing Time*, 90; Spindler, *Der Handelskrieg mit U-Booten*, 2:77, 126, 128, 130, 242-44, 255-59.

24. Halpern, *A Naval History of World War I*, 303.

Chapter 9   Armed Merchant Ships, the Paravane, and the Depth Charge

1. Tarrant, *U-Boat Offensive*, 37.

2. Arthur J. Marder, *From Dreadnought to Scapa Flow: The Royal Navy in the Fisher Era, 1904-1919*, 4:90-91.

3. Ibid., 38.

4. Ibid., 229.

5. Corbett and Newbolt, *History of the Great War*, 4:330-31.

6. TH7, 21.

7. L. Cope Cornford, *The Paravane Adventure*, 87; *The Submarine Sweep as Fitted on Trawlers*, 2.

8. Cornford, *Paravane Adventure*, 131.

9. TH7, 21.

10. Cornford, *Paravane Adventure*, 277-78.

11. TH40, 54-56.

12. Spindler, *Der Handelskrieg mit U-Booten*, 3:107; Chatterton, *Q-Ships*, 40-42.

13. Tarrant, *U-Boat Offensive*, 27; Günter Krause, *U-Boot-Alarm*, 46.

14. Spindler, *Der Handelskrieg mit U-Booten*, 3:113.

15. Ibid., 112.

16. Ibid., 318; Gibson and Prendergast, *German Submarine War*, 119.

17. Spindler, *Der Handelskrieg mit U-Booten*, 3:318.

18. French Navy Historical Service, 27.

19. Ibid., 28.

20. All the technical information on the American Mark I and Mark II depth charges is taken from U.S. Department of the Navy, Bureau of Ord-

nance, *Navy Ordnance Activities, World War 1917-1918,* 98-102 (hereafter cited as Navy Department, *Navy Ordnance Activities*); TH7, 19.

Chapter 10   Indicator-Nets and Mine-Nets

1. Chatterton, *Fighting the U-Boats,* 176-77; Chatterton, *The Auxiliary Patrol,* 146-47.
2. Spindler, *Der Handelskrieg mit U-Booten,* 3:126; UB26 KTB, 4 April 1916, Abscrift Z14433/19, T-1022, Roll 55, PG61771, *RGN.*
3. Chatterton, *The Auxiliary Patrol,* 119-20.
4. Bacon, *Dover Patrol,* 2:419; Cowie, *Mines, Minelayers and Minelaying,* 52.
5. Bacon, *Dover Patrol,* 2:420.
6. Ibid., 1:146; Cowie, *Mines, Minelayers and Minelaying,* 54-55.
7. Bacon, *Dover Patrol,* 1:59, 2:394.
8. Ibid., 2:394.
9. Gibson and Prendergast, *German Submarine War,* 90-91; Cowie, *Mines, Minelayers and Minelaying,* 54.
10. Gibson and Prendergast, *German Submarine War,* 90-91; Chatterton, *The Auxiliary Patrol,* 243.
11. Bacon, *Dover Patrol,* 1:150.
12. Gibson and Prendergast, *German Submarine War,* 91.
13. Bacon, *Dover Patrol,* 2:420.
14. Spindler, *Der Handelskrieg mit U-Booten,* 3:57-58; UC5 KTB, 25 April 1916, T-1022, Roll 84, PG61899, *RGN.*
15. Bacon, *Dover Patrol,* 1:171.
16. Ibid., 2:395.
17. Ibid., 398.

Chapter 11   The End of German Indecision

1. Spindler, *Der Handelskrieg mit U-Booten,* 3:78.
2. Ibid., 26
3. Ibid., 70.
4. Ibid., 2:288-89.
5. Ibid., 3:70.
6. Gerhard Ritter, *The Sword and the Sceptor,* 3:243, 157-58.
7. Ibid., 73.
8. Ibid., 3:143-44.
9. Spindler, *Der Handelskrieg mit U-Booten,* 3:70.

10. Ritter, *The Sword and the Sceptor,* 3:158.
11. Spindler, *Der Handelskrieg mit U-Booten,* 3:71.
12. Ibid., 3:125.
13. Ibid., 125.
14. Ritter, *The Sword and the Sceptor,* 3:172–73.
15. Spindler, *Der Handelskrieg mit U-Booten,* 3:200, 203.
16. Halpern, *A Naval History of World War I,* 337–38.

Chapter 12   Ramming, Nets, and Decoys

1. UC26 KTB, 8 May 1917, T-1022, Roll 71, PG61934, *RGN.*
2. Ibid.
3. U48 KTB, 9 March 1917, T-1022, Roll 18, PG61604, *RGN.*
4. Spindler, *Der Handelskrieg mit U-Booten,* 4:121.
5. Ibid., 421.
6. Ibid., 143, 323–24.
7. UC33 KTB, 26 September 1917, T-1022, Roll 85, PG61945, *RGN.*
8. Spindler, *Der Handelskrieg mit U-Booten,* 4:308.
9. The figures are based on material found throughout Spindler, *Der Handelskrieg mit U-Booten,* vols. 2–4.
10. Chatterton, *Q-Ships,* 137–38.
11. Ibid., 230–33.
12. Spindler, *Der Handelskrieg mit U-Booten,* 4:499.
13. Ibid., 312; Chatterton, *Q-Ships,* 72–73.
14. Spindler, *Der Handelskrieg mit U-Booten,* 4:100.
15. Ibid., 105–6.
16. Ibid.; Chatterton, *Q-Ships,* 145–50.
17. Spindler, *Der Handelskrieg mit U-Booten,* 4:106.
18. Chatterton, *Q-Ships,* 266–69; Spindler, *Der Handelskrieg mit U-Booten,* 5:92–93.

Chapter 13   Hydrophones

1. Willem Hackmann, *Seek and Strike,* 5–6, 64–65.
2. U.S. Department of the Navy, *History of the Bureau of Engineering, Navy Department,* 63 (hereafter cited as Navy Department, *Engineering*).
3. Ibid., 45; Hackmann, *Seek and Strike,* 46.
4. TH7, 25, 43.
5. Ibid., 44; Hackmann, *Seek and Strike,* 60–61.

6. TH7, 25; Hackmann, *Seek and Strike,* 62.

7. TH7, 23-24.

8. Unless otherwise noted, the information dealing with American hydrophones is found in Captain L. S. Howeth, *History of Communications-Electronics in the United States Navy,* 302-9; Navy Department, *Engineering,* 47-64.

9. Nutting, *The Cinderellas of the Fleet,* 72.

10. Hackmann, *Seek and Strike,* 57-59.

11. Nutting, *The Cinderellas of the Fleet,* 72-74; Hackmann, *Seek and Strike,* 57-59.

12. Hackmann, *Seek and Strike,* 56-57.

13. Ibid., 58.

14. Nutting, *The Cinderellas of the Fleet,* 76.

15. Howeth, *History of Communications-Electronics,* 308-9.

Chapter 14   Patrols and Patrol Vessels

1. Hackmann, *Seek and Strike,* 68-69.

2. Spindler, *Der Handelskrieg mit U-Booten,* 4:145.

3. UB57 KTB, 28 September-21 October 1917, T-1022, Roll 68, PG61817, *RGN.*

4. UB40 KTB, 25 June-3 July 1917, T-1022, Roll 11, PG61798, *RGN.*

5. UC75 KTB, 4-23 June 1917, T-1022, Roll 59, PG61786, *RGN.*

6. All the following from Nutting, *The Cinderellas of the Fleet,* 15-19.

7. Bacon, *Dover Patrol,* 1:39.

8. All the following from Nutting, *The Cinderellas of the Fleet,* 55-79, 173-77.

9. Ray Millholland, *The Splinter Fleet,* 97-99.

10. Moore, *Jane's Fighting Ships of World War I,* 87; Corbett and Newbolt, *History of the Great War,* 5:116.

11. Moore, *Jane's Fighting Ships of World War I,* 87; E. Keeble Chatterton, *Danger Zone,* 72.

12. Ibid., 79.

13. Millholland, *The Splinter Fleet,* 122.

14. Foregoing taken from TH7, 22-24.

15. TH7, 23; Spindler, *Der Handelskrieg mit U-Booten,* 5:99.

Chapter 15   Aircraft

1. Spindler, *Der Handelskrieg mit U-Booten,* 5:259, 301, 423.

2. Ibid., 278.

3. UC16 KTB, 29 July 1917, T-1022, Roll 45, PG61920, *RGN.*

4. UB12 KTB, 6 September 1917, T-1022, Roll 79, PG61743, *RGN.*

5. Spindler, *Der Handelskrieg mit U-Booten,* 5:310.

6. TH7, 3–6.

7. Admiralty Technical History Section, *Technical History and Index: A Serial History of Technical Problems Dealt with by Admiralty Departments,* Part 4 [TH4], "Aircraft v. Submarines: Submarine Campaign 1918," March 1919, 5 (hereafter cited as TH4).

8. Alfred Price, *Aircraft versus Submarines,* 13–14, 20; Ces Mowthorpe, *Battlebags: British Airships of the First World War,* xix–xxvii.

9. Adrian Van Wyen, *Naval Aviation in World War I,* 27.

10. TH40, 55.

11. TH4, 9.

12. Navy Department, *Navy Ordnance Activities,* 144.

13. Ibid., 144–45.

14. TH4, 12; Van Wyen, *Naval Aviation in World War I,* 76.

15. Price, *Aircraft versus Submarines,* 24–25.

16. Spindler, *Der Handelskrieg mit U-Booten,* 5:95.

17. TH4, 12–15; Van Wyen, *Naval Aviation in World War I,* 23, 64, 76, 80–81, 88.

18. TH4, 14; T-1022, Roll 57, PG61783, *RGN;* Spindler, *Der Handelskrieg mit U-Booten,* 4:302.

19. TH4, 13; Gibson and Prendergast, *German Submarine War,* 303, 318; Herzog, *Deutsche U-Boote,* 95.

20. Van Wyen, *Naval Aviation in World War I,* 64, 76.

21. TH4, 9.

22. Ibid.

23. UC34 KTB, 17 June 1917, T-1022, Roll 85, PG61946, *RGN.*

24. TH4, 9–10.

25. "Unterseeboote und Unterseebooteabwehr," T-1022, Roll 2100, PG33380, *RGN.*

Chapter 16 Submarines versus U-Boats

1. Rear Admiral William Sowden Sims, USN, *The Victory at Sea,* 278–79.

2. Ibid., 279; TH7, 16–17; Lieutenant Commander Kenneth Edwards, RN, *We Dive at Dawn,* 292.

3. Sims, *Victory at Sea,* 274–76.

4. TH7 17; Norman Friedman, *Submarine Design and Development,* 23; Krause, *U-Boot-Alarm,* 31.

5. Edwards, *We Dive at Dawn,* 303–4.

6. Spindler, *Der Handelskrieg mit U-Booten,* 5:53.

7. Edwards, *We Dive at Dawn,* 304.

8. U81 KTB, 1 May 1917, T-1022, Roll 8, PG61662, *RGN;* Edwards, *We Dive at Dawn,* 292–93.

9. Edwards, *We Dive at Dawn,* 298–99.

10. Spindler, *Der Handelskrieg mit U-Booten,* 4:461.

11. Edwards, *We Dive at Dawn,* 293.

12. Spindler, *Der Handelskrieg mit U-Booten,* 4:108.

13. The following account is taken from U153 KTB, 11 May 1917, T-1022, Roll 64, PG61708, *RGN;* Edwards, *We Dive at Dawn,* 251–53.

14. U153 KTB, 11 May 1917, T-1022, Roll 64, PG671708, *RGN.*

15. Friedman, *Submarine Design,* 33; Moore, *Jane's Fighting Ships of World War I,* 80; TH7, 45.

Chapter 17   The Convoy System

1. Spindler, *Der Handelskrieg mit U-Booten,* 4:498.

2. Halpern, *A Naval History of World War I,* 69.

3. Jellicoe, *Crisis of the Naval War,* 103–14.

4. Sims, *Victory at Sea,* 76.

5. Jellicoe, *Crisis of the Naval War,* 109–10; Halpern, *A Naval History of World War I,* 251–52.

6. Jellicoe, *Crisis of the Naval War,* 119–20.

7. U52 KTB, 19 July 1917, T-1022, Roll 19, PG61611, *RGN.*

8. Spindler, *Der Handelskrieg mit U-Booten,* 4:244.

9. Jellicoe, *Crisis of the Naval War,* 120.

10. UC21 KTB, 26 April 1917, T-1022, Roll 69, PG61927, *RGN.*

11. Sims, *Victory at Sea,* 114–16.

12. Jellicoe, *Crisis of the Naval War,* 118; Sims, *Victory at Sea,* 133.

13. Sims, *Victory at Sea,* 111–14, 122–24, 129–38.

14. U94 KTB, 16 August 1917, T-1022, Roll 38, PG61677, *RGN.*

15. Spindler, *Der Handelskrieg mit U-Booten,* 4:407.

16. U94 KTB, 15 September–15 October 1917, T-1022, Roll 38, PG61677, *RGN.*

17. Spindler, *Der Handelskrieg mit U-Booten,* 4:370 and 503.

18. Friedman, *Submarine Design,* 35.

19. Thomas, *Raiders of the Deep,* 218–21.

20. Bauer, *Als Führer der U-Boote,* 458–60.

21. For the history of *U-Deutschland*/U-155 see Dwight R. Messimer, *The Merchant U-Boat: The Adventures of the Deutschland, 1916–1918.*

Chapter 18   Howitzers, Bomb Throwers, and Depth Charge Throwers

1. The material covering the development history is found in TH40, 61.
2. The technical material dealing with howitzers and bomb throwers is found in TH7, 10–11.
3. The material dealing with the Thornycroft depth charge thrower is found in Navy Department, *Navy Ordnance Activities,* 105; TH7, 18–20.
4. The material dealing with the Y-gun is found in Navy Department, *Navy Ordnance Activities,* 104–6; Nutting, *The Cinderellas of the Fleet,* 68.
5. The material dealing with the Mark I launching rack and destroyer tactics is found in Navy Department, *Navy Ordnance Activities,* 104; Sims, *Victory at Sea,* 98–100.
6. Ibid., 100.

Chapter 19   The Folkestone–Gris Nez Deep Mine Barrage

1. Details on the dispute between Bacon and Keyes and the initial laying of the barrier are found in Admiral Sir Roger Keyes, *The Naval Memoirs of Sir Roger Keyes: The Narrow Seas to the Dardanelles, 1910–1915,* 114–26; Halpern, *Keyes Papers,* 430–31; Lady Wester Wemyss, *The Life and Letters of Lord Wester Wemyss, Admiral of the Fleet,* 365; Bacon, *Dover Patrol,* 2:391–413.
2. Bacon, *Dover Patrol,* 2:408; Halpern, *Keyes Papers,* 438.
3. Cowie, *Mines, Minelayers and Minelaying,* 78.
4. Donald Maxwell, *The Naval Front,* 76–77.
5. TH7, 34.
6. UB35 KTB, 1 January 1918, T-1022, Roll 60, PG61791, *RGN,* including translation.
7. Spindler, *Der Handelskrieg mit U-Booten,* 5:5, 32, 49–70.
8. Ibid., 5:32–33.
9. Ibid., 5:68–69.
10. UB55 KTB, 22 April 1918, T-1022, Roll 68, PG61815, *RGN.*
11. Spindler, *Der Handelskrieg mit U-Booten,* 5:73–75.
12. Cowie, *Mines, Minelayers and Minelaying,* 76.
13. Spindler, *Der Handelskrieg mit U-Booten,* 5:98–99.
14. Ibid., 122.

Chapter 20   Trying to Block Zeebrugge and Ostend, 1918

1. Bacon, *Dover Patrol,* 1:261–89; Admiral Sir Roger Keyes, RN, *The Naval Memoirs of Sir Roger Keyes: Scapa Flow to the Dover Straits, 1916–1918,* 127–34.
2. The description of the two harbors are from Carpenter, *The Blocking of Zeebrugge,* 3–42.
3. Bacon, *Dover Patrol,* 1:145, 209.
4. Chatterton, *The Auxiliary Patrol,* 278–79.
5. Carpenter, *The Blocking of Zeebrugge,* 161–270.
6. Roy Humphreys, *The Dover Patrol, 1914–1918,* 166–67; Corbett and Newbolt, *History of the Great War,* 5:264.
7. Corbett and Newbolt, *History of the Great War,* 5:274.
8. Beesley, *Room 40,* 282; Corbett and Newbolt, *History of the Great War,* 5:274–75.

Chapter 21   Radio Intelligence and UC-44

1. Beesley, *Room 40,* 265.
2. Spindler, *Der Handelskrieg mit U-Booten,* 4:237.
3. Ernst Hashagen, *U-Boote Westwärts,* 116–21.
4. Herzog, *Deutsche U-Boote,* 98; Beesley, *Room 40,* 265–66.
5. Keyes, *Memoirs, 1910–1915,* 117–26; Robert M. Grant, *U-Boat Intelligence, 1914–1918,* 117–19.

Chapter 22   The Northern Mine Barrage

1. Unless otherwise noted all the details about the MKVI mine and the Northern Barrage are taken from Navy Department, *Navy Ordnance Activities,* 107–30; Cowie, *Mines, Minelayers and Minelaying,* 62–72; Robert C. Duncan, *America's Use of Sea Mines,* 38–63.
2. Duncan, *America's Use of Sea Mines,* 58.
3. Spindler, *Der Handelskrieg mit U-Booten,* 5:318, 334.
4. Corbett and Newbolt, *History of the Great War,* 5:349.
5. Cowie, *Mines, Minelayers and Minelaying,* 70.
6. Ibid.
7. Corbett and Newbolt, *History of the Great War,* 5:228.
8. Ibid., 362.

Chapter 23   The Developing Situation

1. Spindler, *Der Handelskrieg mit U-Booten*, 2:200–201.
2. S. L. A. Marshall, *World War I*, 188.
3. Spindler, *Der Handelskrieg mit U-Booten*, 3:28; Chatterton, *Fighting the U-Boats*, 165.
4. Spindler, *Der Handelskrieg mit U-Booten*, 3:168–69.
5. Ibid., 159–64.
6. Corbett and Newbolt, *History of the Great War*, 4:175, 173.

Chapter 24   The Mediterranean Theater

1. Corbett and Newbolt, *History of the Great War*, 4:288–90; Chatterton, *Fighting the U-Boats*, 161.
2. Konteradmiral Theodor Winterhalder, *Die österreichisch-ungarische Kriegsmarine im Weltkrieg*, 19; Chatterton, *Fighting the U-Boats*, 187–88.
3. Chatterton, *The Auxiliary Patrol*, 162.
4. Gibson and Prendergast, *German Submarine War*, 132.
5. Valentiner, *300,000 Tonnen versenkt*, 146–54.
6. Spindler, *Der Handelskrieg mit U-Booten*, 3:172; UB47 KTB, 23 August 1916, T-1022, Roll 17, PG61601, *RGN*.
7. Gibson and Prendergast, *German Submarine War*, 128.
8. Chatterton, *The Auxiliary Patrol*, 209–11.
9. Millholland, *The Splinter Fleet*, 123.
10. Spindler, *Der Handelskrieg mit U-Booten*, 5:201.
11. Michael Wilson and Paul Kemp, *Mediterranean Submarines*, 156–59.
12. Spindler, *Der Handelskrieg mit U-Booten*, 2:198.
13. The entire account is taken from Heimburg, *U-Boot gegen U-Boot*, 41–52; UB14 KTB, 22 August 1915, T-1022 Roll 64 PG61748, *RGN*, including translation.
14. U.S. Department of the Navy, Office of Naval Intelligence, *War in Turkish Waters*, 227–28 (hereafter cited as Navy Department, *War in Turkish Waters*).
15. Spindler, *Der Handelskrieg mit U-Booten*, 2:203, 206, 3:27.
16. Marder, *From Dreadnought to Scapa Flow*, 3:277.
17. Halpern, *A Naval History of World War I*, 392–95.
18. Jacob Rehder, *Die Kriegsschiffsverluste der fremden Flotten im Weltkrieg, 1914–1918*, 32.

19. Corbett and Newbolt, *History of the Great War,* 4:295–96; Wilson and Kemp, *Mediterranean Submarines,* 143.
20. Gröner, *Die deutschen Kriegsschiffe,* 343, 345; Marder, *From Dreadnought to Scapa Flow,* 3:274; Spindler, *Der Handelskrieg mit U-Booten,* 3:21–47, 154–75, 323–52.
21. Chatterton, *Fighting the U-Boats,* 163.
22. Winterhalder, *Die österreichisch-ungarische Kriegsmarine,* 22; Gibson and Prendergast, *German Submarine War,* 73; Rehder, *Die Kriegsschiffsverluste der fremden Flotten,* 32.
23. Spindler, *Der Handelskrieg mit U-Booten,* 3:338; U65 KTB, 4 December 1916, T-1022 Roll 36 PG61632, *RGN.*
24. Spindler, *Der Handelskrieg mit U-Booten,* 3:169; Corbett and Newbolt, *History of the Great War,* 4:287.

Chapter 25   The Black Sea and the Baltic

1. Spindler, *Der Handelskrieg mit U-Booten,* 3:176–79.
2. Cowie, *Mines, Minelayers and Minelaying,* 38.
3. Rudolf Firle, Heinrich Rollmann, and Ernst von Gagern, *Der Krieg in der Ostsee,* 3:90.
4. Johannes Spiess, *Sechs Jahre U-Boot-Fahrten,* 44; Firle et al., *Der Krieg in der Ostsee,* 3:90.
5. Spiess, *Sechs Jahre U-Boot-Fahrten,* 45; U19 KTB, 10 September 1916, T-1022, Roll 32, PG61529, *RGN.*
6. Spiess, *Sechs Jahre U-Boot-Fahrten,* 45.
7. Ibid., 46.
8. Firle et al., *Der Krieg in der Ostsee,* 3:90.
9. Spindler, Der Handelskrieg mit U-Booten, 2:195; Spindler, *Der Handelskrieg mit U-Booten,* 3:176–79.
10. Gröner, *Die deutschen Kriegsschiffe,* 1:362; Herzog, *Deutsche U-Boote,* 92; Chatterton, *Fighting the U-Boats,* 37.
11. Valentiner, *300,000 Tonnen versenkt,* 71.

Chapter 26   Weapons

1. "Unterseeboote und Unterseebooteabwehr," 21 March 1929, Roll 2100, PG33380, *RGN.*
2. Firle et al., *Der Krieg in der Ostsee,* 2:294.
3. The material on mines is from Rehder, *Die Kriegsschiffsverluste der fremden Flotten,* 16–35; "Algemeine Gesichtspunkte für die Bekämp-

fung der U-Boote in der Ostsee, Sommer 1916," 26 April 1916, T-1022, Roll 1284, PG90406, *RGN*.

4. The material on anchored nets is from "Entstehung und Entwicklung der Vorposten-Halbflottille, Kiel," T-1022, Roll 250, PG62830, *RGN;* "Algemeine Gesichtspunkte für die Bekämpfung der U-Boote in der Ostsee, Sommer 1916," 26 April 1916, T-1022, Roll 1284, PG90406, *RGN;* and "Kriegserfahrungen der Küstenschutzdivision der Ostsee, 10 April 1917, T-1022, Roll 994, PG76893, *RGN*.

5. "Entstehung und Entwicklung der Vorp. Halbflt. West Geschichte der Gjedser Bewachung durch Vorpostenboote bis End April 1918," T-1022, Roll 247, PG62837, *RGN*.

6. Edwards, *We Dive at Dawn*, 215-16.

7. The material on mine-nets is from "Algemeine Gesichtspunkte für die Bekämpfung der U-Boote in der Ostsee, Sommer 1916," 26 April 1916, T-1022, Roll 1284, PG90406, *RGN*.

8. The material on towed indicator-nets is from "Entstehung und Entwicklung der Vorp. Halbflt. West Geschichte der Gjedser Bewachung durch Vorpostenboote bis End April 1918," T-1022, Roll 247, PG62837, *RGN;* and "Bekämpfung der feindlichen Unterwasser-Fahrzeuge und Waffen," 24 April 1916, T-1022, Roll 1284, PG90406, *RGN*.

9. The material on depth charges is from "Unterseeboote und Unterseebooteabwehr," 21 March 1929, T-1022, Roll 2100, PG33380, *RGN;* "Bericht über den U-Bootsangriff in Quadrat 109 Betta," 11 August 1917, T-1022, Roll 1284, PG90406, *RGN;* and "Schiffs- und Bootsmaterial," 10 April 1917, B.Nr.G.1065AZ, T-1022, Roll 994, PG76893, *RGN*.

10. The material on explosive sweeps is from "Verteidigung gegen Unterseeboote durch Hindernisse," T-1022, Roll 1283, PG90406, *RGN;* "Entwurf einer Seekriegsanleitung für den Unterwasser-Such und Sicherungsdienst," 27 April 1916, T-1022, Roll 1284, PG90442, *RGN;* "Gesichtspunkte zur U-Bootsbekämpfung" T-1022, Roll 1284, PG90406, *RGN;* "Kriegserfahrungen der Küstenschutzdivision der Ostsee, 10 April 1917," T-1022, Roll 994, PG76893, *RGN;* "Kriegserfahrungen der Küstenschutzdivision der Ostsee," 10 April 1917, T-1022, Roll 994, PG76893, *RGN;* "Verteidigung gegen Unterseeboote durch Hindernisse," T-1022, Roll 1283, PG90406, *RGN;* and TH40, 56.

11. "KTB der IV Gruppe der II S. Halbflottille," 12 April–15 November 1916, 22 and 23 May 1916, T-1022, Roll 250, PG62865, *RGN*.

12. The material on decoys is from "KTB SMS Arkona, 1 bis 15 September 1915," T-1022, Roll 241, PG62790, *RGN;* and "Vernichtung eines

feindlichen U-Bootes am 28 May 1916, Sud Utlängen, durch SMH K,"
T-1022, Roll 4313, PG90321, *RGN*.

13. Halpern, *A Naval History of World War I*, 208.

14. Firle et al., *Der Krieg in der Ostsee*, 2:212.

15. Herzog, *Deutsche U-Boote*, 178; Rehder, *Die Kriegsschiffsverluste der fremden Flotten*, 16–18, 24–25, 28.

16. The material on hydrophones is from "Unterseeboote und Unterseebooteabwehr," 21 March 1929, T-1022, Roll 2100, PG33380, *RGN;* "Kriegserfahrungen der Küstenschutzdivision der Ostsee,"10 April 1917, T-1022, Roll 994, PG76893, *RGN;* and Rehder, *Die Kriegsschiffsverluste der fremden Flotten*, 16–35.

17. "Kriegserfahrungen der Küstenschutzdivision der Ostsee,"10 April 1917, T-1022, Roll 994, PG76893, *RGN*.

18. Ibid.

19. The material on patrol routes and convoys is from Firle et al., *Der Krieg in der Ostsee*, 2:325–36; and "Ansichten von U-Boots-Kommandanten über Handelsschutz durch Gleitzug," T-1022, Roll 1284, PG90406, *RGN*.

Chapter 27   The Baltic and the Helgoland Bight

1. Firle et al., *Der Krieg in der Ostsee*, 1:218.

2. Ibid., 209.

3. Ibid., 211–14.

4. Firle et al., *Der Krieg in der Ostsee*, 2:2.

5. Ibid., 151–52.

6. Michael Wilson, *Baltic Assignment: British Submarines in Russia, 1914–1919*, 71, 126; Firle et al., *Der Krieg in der Ostsee*, 2:100–101, 135, 151, 361; the author's figures are based on the material.

7. Firle et al., *Der Krieg in der Ostsee*, 2:312.

8. Ibid., 313.

9. Ibid., 365; Wilson, *Baltic Assignment*, 94.

10. Firle et al., *Der Krieg in der Ostsee*, 2:313.

11. Ibid., 293.

12. Wilson, *Baltic Assignment*, 111; Firle et al., *Der Krieg in der Ostsee*, 2:323, 366.

13. Firle et al., *Der Krieg in der Ostsee*, 2:324; Wilson, *Baltic Assignment*, 114.

14. Firle et al., *Der Krieg in der Ostsee*, 2:324–25.

15. Ibid., 3:9–11.

16. Ibid.

17. "Kriegserfahrungen des Befehlshabers des Sch.Verbands der mittlern Ostsee," T-1022, Roll 994, PG76893, *RGN;* "O Sache: Allgemeine Gesichtspunkte für die Bekämpfung der U-Boote in der Ostsee Sommer 1916," 26 April 1916, Roll 1284, PG90406, *RGN.*

18. Firle et al., *Der Krieg in der Ostsee,* 3:31; SMH *K KTB,* T-1022, Roll 392, PG63482, *RGN;* "Vernichtung eines feindlichen U-Bootes im Kattegat SO Anholt am 12 August 1916." T-1022, Roll 4313, PG90321, *RGN.*

19. "Vernichtung eines feindlichen U-Bootes am 27 May 1916, 10 Uhr 22 NM SO Häfringe, durch SMH K," T-1022, Roll 4313, PG90321, *RGN.*

20. "Vernichtung eines feindlichen U-Bootes am 28 May 1916, Sud Utlängen, durch SMH K," T-1022, Roll 4313, PG90321, *RGN.*

21. Firle et al., *Der Krieg in der Ostsee,* 3:48.

22. "Auszug aus Kriegstagabuch der Handelsschutzflotilla," 21 May 1917, T-1022, Roll 1284, PG90406, *RGN;* "Bekämpfung eines U-Bootes am 21 May 1917 durch I Gruppe der I Handelschutzhalbflottille S Häfringe" and "Gefechtshandlungen der Handelsschutzflottille," T-1022, Roll 4313, PG90321, *RGN.*

23. U27 KTB, 18 October 1914, T-1022, Roll 89, PG62053, *RGN.*

24. Edwards, *We Dive at Dawn,* 268–69; Tarrant, *U-Boat Offensive,* 184.

25. Edwards, *We Dive at Dawn,* 286.

Chapter 28   The Mediterranean

1. Rehder, *Die Kriegsschiffsverluste der fremden Flotten,* 16–17, 24–25, 28.

2. Edwards, *We Dive at Dawn,* 110; Norman Polmar and Jurrien Noot, *Submarines of the Russian and Soviet Navies, 1718–1990,* 54.

3. Rehder, *Die Kriegsschiffsverluste der fremden Flotten,* 16–17, 24–25; Polmar and Noot, *Submarines of the Russian and Soviet Navies,* 56.

4. Edwards, *We Dive at Dawn,* 111.

5. Navy Department, *War in Turkish Waters,* 217, 243.

6. Ibid., 134, 161, 192.

7. Cowie, *Mines, Minelayers and Minelaying,* 37–40; Tarrant, *U-Boat Offensive,* 149.

8. Corbett and Newbolt, *History of the Great War,* 2: map "The Dardanelles."

9. Peter Shankland and Anthony Hunter, *Dardanelles Patrol,* 56–59; Corbett and Newbolt, *History of the Great War,* 2: map "The Dardanelles"; and Tarrant, *U-Boat Offensive,* 149.

10. Shankland and Hunter, *Dardanelles Patrol,* 183–89; Corbett and New-bolt, *History of the Great War,* 2: map "The Dardanelles."

11. Navy Department, *War in Turkish Waters,* 197, 444–50.

12. Rehder, *Die Kriegsschiffsverluste der fremden Flotten,* 24.

13. Heimburg, *U-Boot gegen U-Boot,* 62–66; Edwards, *We Dive at Dawn,* 170–72.

14. Navy Department, *War in Turkish Waters,* 141–46; Heimburg, *U-Boot gegen U-Boot,* 63.

15. Edwards, *We Dive at Dawn,* 141, 145–46, 161; Tarrant, *U-Boat Offensive,* 166–67.

16. Wilson and Kemp, *Mediterranean Submarines,* 91–92; Heimburg, *U-Boot gegen U-Boot,* 76–77.

17. Navy Department, *War in Turkish Waters,* 136–39; Edwards, *We Dive at Dawn,* 168.

18. Peter Broucek, Direktor des Kriegsarchivs, österreiches Staatsarchiv, Wien, letter to the author, 21 June 2000.

19. Wilson and Kemp, *Mediterranean Submarines,* 29–30; Edwards, *We Dive at Dawn,* 237–38.

20. Rehder, *Die Kriegsschiffsverluste der fremden Flotten,* 17, 25, 28.

21. Wilson and Kemp, *Mediterranean Submarines,* 104–5.

22. Rheder, *Die Kriegsschiffsverluste der fremden Flotten,* 24; Winterhalder, *Die österreichisch-ungarische Kriegsmarine,* 18, 30.

23. Rehder, *Die Kriegsschiffsverluste der fremden Flotten,* 17; Edwards, *We Dive at Dawn,* 238.

24. Rehder, *Die Kriegsschiffsverluste der fremden Flotten,* 24.

25. Ibid., 24.

Bibliography

PRIMARY SOURCES

Technical Monographs and Official Histories

Admiralty Technical History Section. *Technical History and Index: A Serial History of Technical Problems Dealt with by Admiralty Departments,* Part 4 [TH4], "Aircraft v. Submarines: Submarine Campaign 1918," March 1919. Imperial War Museum, London, U.K.

———. *Technical History and Index: A Serial History of Technical Problems Dealt with by Admiralty Departments,* Part 7 [TH7], "The Anti-Submarine Division of the Naval Staff, December 1916–November 1918," July 1919. Imperial War Museum, London, U.K.

———. *Technical History and Index: A Serial History of Technical Problems Dealt with by Admiralty Departments,* Part 40 [TH40], "Anti-Submarine Development and Experiments Prior to December 1916," September 1920. Imperial War Museum, London, U.K.

Corbett, Sir Julian S., and Henry Newbolt. *History of the Great War: Naval Operations.* 5 vols. London: Longmans, Green and Co., 1920–31.

Cowie, Captain J. S., RN. *Mines, Minelayers and Minelaying.* London: Oxford University Press, 1949.

Duncan, Robert C. *America's Use of Sea Mines.* Washington, D.C.: Naval Ordnance Laboratory, 1962.

Elco Works. *Hounding the Hun from the Seas.* Bayonne, N.J.: Electric Boat
    Co., 1919. This is Elco's company account of the building of the British
    MLs.
Fayle, Ernest C. *Seaborne Trade.* 3 vols. London: John Murray, 1920–24.
Firle, Rudolf, Heinrich Rollmann, and Ernst von Gagern. *Der Krieg in der
    Ostsee.* 3 vols. Berlin: Mittler and Son, 1922–64.
Gröner, Erich, *Die deutschen Kriegsschiffe, 1915–1945.* 2 vols. Munich: J.
    F. Lehmanns Verlag, 1966.
Groos, Otto, and Walter Gladisch. *Der Krieg zur See, 1914–1818: Der Krieg
    in der Nordsee.* 7 vols. Berlin: E. S. Mittler and Son, 1922–65.
Hackmann, Willem. *Seek and Strike: Sonar, Anti-Submarine Warfare and the
    Royal Navy, 1914–1954.* London: Her Majesty's Stationery Office, 1984.
Hartmann, Gregory K. *Weapons That Wait: Mine Warfare in the U.S. Navy.*
    Annapolis: Naval Institute Press, 1979.
Herzog, Bodo. *Deutsche U-Boote, 1906–1966.* Herrsching: Pawlak, 1990.
Hogg, I. V., and L. F. Thurston. *British Artillery Weapons and Ammunition,
    1914–1918.* London: Ian Allen, 1972.
Howeth, Captain L. S. *History of Communications-Electronics in the United
    States Navy.* Washington, D.C.: Office of Naval History, 1963.
Marder, Arthur J. *From Dreadnought to Scapa Flow: The Royal Navy in the
    Fisher Era, 1904–1919.* 5 vols. London: Oxford University Press, 1961–70.
Nutting, William W. *The Cinderellas of the Fleet.* Jersey City, N.J.: The
    Standard Motor Construction Co., 1920.
Rehder, Jacob. *Die Kriegsschiffsverluste der fremden Flotten im Weltkrieg,
    1914–1918.* Munich: J. F. Lehmanns Verlag, 1933.
Scott, Lloyd N. *Naval Consulting Board of the United States.* Washington,
    D.C.: Government Printing Office, 1920.
Spindler, Konteradmiral Arno, a.D.. *Der Krieg zur See, 1914–1918: Der
    Handelskrieg mit U-Booten.* 5 vols. Berlin: Mittler and Son, 1932–66.
U.S. Department of the Navy. *History of the Bureau of Engineering, Navy
    Department.* Washington, D.C.: Government Printing Office, 1922.
——. Bureau of Ordnance. *Navy Ordnance Activities, World War
    1917–1918.* Washington, D.C.: Government Printing Office, 1920.
——. Office of Naval Intelligence. *War in Turkish Waters.* 488 pages,
    typed, 8½ x 14, hard bound, register No. 19076-A, Copy No. 6, pub.
    date and translator not given.
Winterhalder, Konteradmiral Theodor. *Die österreichisch-ungarische
    Kriegsmarine im Weltkrieg.* Munich: J. F. Lehmanns Verlag, 1921.

Manuscripts and Documents

"Declaration Concerning the Laws of Naval War, 208 Consol. T.S.338 (1909)" [Declaration of London, 1909]. University of Minnesota Human Rights Library. http://www.umn.edu/humanrts/instree/1909b.htm, accessed June 1999.

The Enemy Submarine, Bulletin No. 2, 1 May 1918. New York: Naval Consulting Board, 1918.

The Enemy Submarine and Kindred Problems, Bulletin No. 1, 14 July 1917. New York: Naval Consulting Board, 1917. This technical bulletin was issued to members of the War Committee of Technical Societies to assist them in devising ASW countermeasures. The bulletin includes information on current U-boat tactics and technology, and current ASW countermeasures.

Records of the German Navy, 1850–1945. Microfilm Publication T-1022, Record Group 242, National Archives, Washington, D.C.

Report on Listeners' School and Hydrophone School: Bulletin 102. New London, Conn.: Naval District Base, November 1918.

The Submarine Sweep as Fitted on Trawlers. London: Vickers Ltd., 1917. This Royal Navy manual was issued to trawlers and contains instructions on how to operate and maintain the explosive antisubmarine paravane.

U.S. Congress. House of Representatives. *The Problems of Neutrality When the World is at War,* Part I, *The Submarine Controversy.* 64th Cong., 2d Sess. Document No. 2111. Washington, D.C.: Government Printing Office, 1917.

U.S. Department of the Navy. *Instructions for the Navy of the United States Governing Maritime Warfare, June 1917.* Washington, D.C.: Government Printing Office, 1918. This contains the U.S. Navy Prize Regulations, based on the Declaration of London, 1909.

Memoirs and Personal Recollections

Bacon, Admiral Sir Reginald. *The Dover Patrol, 1915–1917.* 2 vols. London: Hutchinson and Co., 1919.

Bauer, Hermann. *Als Führer der U-Boote im Weltkrieg.* Leipzig: Koehler and Amelang, n.d.

Belknap, Captain Reginald R., USN. *The Yankee Mining Squadron: Laying the North Sea Mine Barrage.* Annapolis: Naval Institute Press, 1920.

Brodie, C. G. *Forlorn Hope, 1915: The Submarine Passage of the Dardanelles.* London: Frederick Books, 1956.

Campbell, Rear Admiral Gordon. *My Mystery Ships.* New York: Doubleday, Doran & Co., 1929.

Carpenter, Captain Alfred F. B., RN. *The Blocking of Zeebrugge.* Boston: Houghton Mifflin Co., 1922.

Cornford, L. Cope. *The Paravane Adventure.* London, New York, and Toronto: Hodder & Stoughton, 1919.

Crompton, Oberleutnant zur See. *Crompton U-41: Der zweite Baralong-Fall.* Berlin: August Scherl, 1917.

Fisher, Admiral of the Fleet Lord. *Records.* London, New York, and Toronto: Hodder and Stoughton, 1919.

Görlitz, Walter. *The Kaiser and His Court: The Diaries, Note Books and Letters of Admiral Georg Alexander von Müller, Chief of the Naval Cabinet, 1914–1918.* Trans. Mervyn Savill. New York: Harcourt, Brace and World, 1961.

Halpern, Paul G., ed. *The Keyes Papers: Selections from the Private Correspondence of Admiral of the Fleet Baron Keyes of Zeebrugge,* Vol. 1, 1914–18. London: Navy Records Society, 1972.

Hashagen, Ernst. *U-Boote Westwärts!: Meine Fahrten um England, 1914–1918.* Berlin: E. S. Mittler and Sohn, 1931.

Heimburg, Heino von, Oberleutnant zur See. *U-Boot gegen U-Boot.* Berlin: Verlag August Scherl, 1917.

Jellicoe, Viscount. *The Crisis of the Naval War.* London: Cassell and Co., Ltd., 1920.

Keyes, Admiral Sir Roger, RN. *The Naval Memoirs of Sir Roger Keyes: The Narrow Seas to the Dardanelles, 1910–1915.* New York: E. P. Dutton and Co., 1934.

———. *The Naval Memoirs of Sir Roger Keyes: Scapa Flow to the Dover Straits, 1916–1918.* London: Thornton Butterworth, Ltd., 1935.

Millholland, Ray. *The Splinter Fleet.* Indianapolis: Bobbs-Merrill Co., 1936.

Moffat, Alexander W. *Maverick Navy.* Middleton, Conn.: Wesleyan University Press, 1976.

The Northern Barrage: Mine Force, 1918. Edited by all hands. Annapolis: Naval Institute Press, 1919.

Rose, H. Wickliffe. *Brittany Patrol: The Story of the Suicide Fleet.* New York: Norton and Co., 1937.

Sims, Rear Admiral William Sowden, USN. *The Victory at Sea*. New York: Doubleday, Page and Co., 1920.

Spiess, Johannes. *Sechs Jahre U-Boot-Fahrten*. Berlin: Wilhelm Kolk, 1932.

Tirpitz, Grand Admiral von. *My Memoirs*. 2 vols. Trans. unknown. New York: AMS Press, 1970.

Valentiner, Max. *300,000 Tonnen Versenkt!: Meine U-Boots-Fahrten*. Berlin: Ulstein, 1917.

Von Spiegel, Kapitänleutnant Freiherr. *Kriegstagebuch U202*. Berlin: August Scherl, 1916. The boat number 202 is fictitious, but the material covers von Spiegel's command of U-32.

Wemyss, Lady Wester. *The Life and Letters of Lord Wester Wemyss, Admiral of the Fleet*. London: Eyre and Spottiswoode, 1935.

SECONDARY SOURCES

Articles

"Fighting U-boats from Towed Kite Balloons." *Scientific American* (9 February 1918), 129.

Lundeberg, Philip K. "The German Naval Critique of the U-Boat Campaign, 1915–1918." *Military Affairs*, XXVII (1963), 109–13.

———. "Undersea Warfare and Allied Strategy in World War I, Part I: To 1916." *The Smithsonian Journal of History*, vol. 1, no. 3 (autumn 1966).

———. "Undersea Warfare and Allied Strategy in World War I, Part II: 1916-1918." *The Smithsonian Journal of History*, vol. 1, no. 4 (winter 1966).

Santoni, Alberto. "The First Ultra Secret: The British Cryptanalysis in the Naval Operations of the First World War." *Revue Internationale d'Historie Militare*, no. 60 (1985), 99–110.

"Shells That Will Dive." *Scientific American* (9 February 1918), 125.

Books

Beesley, Patrick. *Room 40: British Naval Intelligence, 1914–1918*. New York: Harcourt Brace, 1982.

Chatterton, E. Keeble. *The Auxiliary Patrol*. London: Sidgwick and Jackson, Ltd., and Boston: Charles E. Lauriat Co., 1924.

———. *Beating the U-Boats*. London, New York: Hurst and Blackett, Ltd., 1943.

———. *Danger Zone: The Story of the Queenstown Command.* Boston: Little, Brown and Co., 1934.

———. *Fighting the U-Boats.* London: Hurst and Blackett, Ltd., 1942.

———. *Q-Ships and Their Story.* New York: Arno Press, 1980.

Domville-Fife, Charles W. *Submarine Warfare of Today.* London: Seeley, Service and Co., 1919.

Edwards, Lieutenant Commander Kenneth, RN. *We Dive at Dawn.* Chicago: Reilly and Lee Co., 1941.

Friedman, Norman. *U.S. Naval Weapons: Every Gun, Missile, Mine and Torpedo Used by the U.S. Navy from 1883 to the Present Day.* Annapolis: Naval Institute Press, 1985.

———. *U.S. Submarines Through 1945: An Illustrated Design History.* Annapolis: Naval Institute Press, 1995.

———. *Submarine Design and Development.* Annapolis: Naval Institute Press, 1984.

Gibson, R. H., and Maurice Prendergast. *The German Submarine War, 1914–1918.* London: Constable and Co., Ltd., 1931.

Gilbert, Martin. *The First World War: A Complete History.* New York: Henry Holt and Co., 1994.

Grant, Robert M. *U-Boats Destroyed: The Effect of Anti-Submarine Warfare, 1914–1918.* London: Putnam, 1964.

———. *U-Boat Intelligence, 1914–1918.* Hamden, Conn.: Archon, 1969.

Gray, Edwyn. *The Underwater War: Submarines, 1914–1918.* New York: Scribner's, 1971.

———. *The Killing Time: The German U-Boats, 1914–1918.* New York: Scribner's Sons, 1972.

Halpern, Paul G. *A Naval History of World War I.* Annapolis: Naval Institute Press, 1994.

Hart, Albert B., et al., eds. *Harper's Pictorial Library of the World War.* 12 vols. New York: Harper and Brothers, 1920.

Humphreys, Roy. *The Dover Patrol, 1914–1918.* Gloucestershire, England: Sutton Publishing, 1998.

Krause, Günter. *U-Boot-Alarm!: Zur Geschichte der U-Boot-Abwehr, 1915–1945.* Berlin: Brandenburgisches Verlaghaus, 1998.

Lambert, Nicholas A. *Sir John Fisher's Naval Revolution.* Columbia: University of South Carolina Press, 1999.

Langsdorff, Werner von. *U-Boote am Feind: 45 deutsche U-Boot-Fahrer erzählen.* Gütersloh, Germany: Verlag Bertelsmann, 1937.

Macintyre, Captain Donald, RN. *Wings of Neptune: The Story of Naval Aviation.* New York: Norton and Co., 1963.

Mantey, Eberhard von. *Auf See unbesiegt.* Munich: J. F. Lehmann, 1922.

Marshall, S. L. A. *World War I.* New York: Houghton Mifflin, 1992.

Masters, David. *I.D.: New Tales of the Submarine War.* London: Eyre and Spotteswoode, 1935.

Maxwell, Donald. *The Naval Front.* London: A. & C. Black, Ltd., 1920.

Messimer, Dwight R. *The Merchant U-Boat: The Adventures of the Deutschland, 1916–1918.* Annapolis: Naval Institute Press, 1988.

Moore, John, ed. *Jane's Fighting Ships of World War I.* New York: Military Press, 1990.

Mowthorpe, Ces. *Battlebags: British Airships of the First World War.* Phoenix Mill, Great Britain: Alan Sutton Publishing, Ltd., 1995.

Polmar, Norman, and Jurrien Noot. *Submarines of the Russian and Soviet Navies, 1718–1990.* Annapolis: Naval Institute Press, 1991.

Price, Alfred. *Aircraft versus Submarines.* London: William Kimber, 1973.

Ritter, Gerhard. *The Sword and the Sceptor: The Problem of Militarism in Germany.* Vols. 3 and 4. Trans. Heinz Norden. Coral Gables, Fla.: University of Miami Press, 1972–73.

Shankland, Peter, and Anthony Hunter. *Dardanelles Patrol.* New York: Scribner's, 1964.

Tarrant, V. E. *The U-Boat Offensive, 1915–1945.* Annapolis: Naval Institute Press, 1989.

Thomas, Lowell. *Raiders of the Deep.* Garden City, N.Y.: Star Books, 1932.

Van Wyen, Adrian. *Naval Aviation in World War I.* Washington, D.C.: Chief of Naval Operations, 1969.

Wilson, Michael. *Baltic Assignment: British Submarines in Russia, 1914–1919.* London: Leo Cooper, in association with Secker and Warburg, 1985.

Wilson, Michael, and Paul Kemp. *Mediterranean Submarines.* Wilmslo, U.K.: Crécy, 1997.

Correspondence

Peter Broucek, Direktor des Kriegsarchivs, Österreiches Staatsarchiv, Wien. Letter to the author, 21 June 2000.

French Navy Historical Service, Chateau de Vincennes, Paris. Via Evelyn DeBernado, Embassy of France in the United States. Letter to the author, 13 June 2000 with enclosure, Document Code #1, No. CC 309, "Les Armes."

Index

Aberdeen, Scotland, 32, 53, 183
Adam, Kapitänleutnant, 192
Admiralstab, preoccupied with fleet engagement, 6
Adriatic Sea, 196, 201, 208, 217, 243, 252, 254 255
Aegean Sea, 204
aircraft, 132; effectiveness, 139; and exaggerated claims by aircrews, 136; German opinion of, 130–31, 139; small ASW role of, 130; statistics on, 136
  Austrian, 254
  British: Blackburn Kangaroo, 132, 134; blimp, 133; DH-6, 132, 134, 136; DH-9, 132; FE2B, 136; N2B, 138
  French, 134
  German, 224–25
  U.S., 131; AT-1, 134; H-12, 133; H-12L, 133
airships: British, 137, 129, 137; French, 134, 137; German, 233
anti-shipping campaign:
  British, 234–35
  German: and Admiralstab, 13, 62; Mediterranean operations started, 193; no prewar plans for, 4, 11, 12; started, 18, 94–97; stopped, 69–70, 92, 95; U-boat officers favor, 13; under prize regulations, 68, 69–70;

unrestricted, 13, 62–64, 67, 68
  Russian, 239–40
Antisubmarine Committee, 85, 86
antisubmarine warfare:
  British: capability nonexistent, 5; goals for, 196; organization, 23–24; overestimated by Germans, 4, 21, 23
  Central Powers: goals for, 196, 243; operations areas, 217; statistics for, 243–44
  German: categories, 218; convoy system, 227–28, 238, 239–40; hunter groups, 224, 229–30, 235, 236; operations areas, 217–18; organization, 228, 229, 235
Arabic, 69
Arkö, 239
Army of the Orient, 193, 203
Asia Minor, 204
Auxiliary Patrol, 158; duties, 122; lays nets off Flanders, 87; vessels in, 5, 22, 122; zones, 23–24

Bachmann, Gustav, 7, 17, 67–68, 69
Bacon, Reginald, 40, 55, 57, 58, 59, 89, 170, 171, 180; argument with Keyes, 163–64; quoted, 25, 49, 60, 61, 87; sacked, 163; and Zeebrugge plans, 171
Ballard, George A., 5

294

Pohl, Hugo von, 7, 16–18, 69, 94
Pola, 192, 195, 196, 200, 201, 252; UB-
  and UC-boats assembled at, 194
Port Said, 205
Preusse, Prinz Heinrich von, 225,
  228–29, 231, 235
Prize Regulations, 4, 7, 9, 10; Germans
  operate under, 76, 69–70, 88, 95, 96
Pustkuchen, Oberleutnant zur See, 95

Q-ships. *See* decoy vessels
Queenstown, 40, 150, 177

radio direction finder, 28, 152
radio intelligence, 27–28, 46, 144,
  177–80, 257
Raikes, Commander, RN, 143
Ramien, Oberleutnant zur See, 168–69
ramming, 29; Admiralty orders about,
  31–32, 207; attacker damaged, 54,
  104; Austrian U-3 by *Cittadi di
  Palermo*, 207; statistics on, 102; U-6
  by SS *Thordis*, 31; U-12 by *Ariel*, 54;
  U-15 by *Birmingham*, 30; U-14 by
  Hawk, 33; U-18 by *Dorothy Gray*, 30;
  U-18 by *Garry*, 30; U-29 by *Dreadnought*, 65; U-48 by *East Point*, 103–4;
  U-65 by *Caldonia*, 208; U-87 by P-56,
  104; UB-36 by *Ferdinand*, 104; UC-26
  by *Milne*, 102–3; UC-33 by P-61, 207
rapid vent system, 29, 32, 37
Reimarus, Oberleutnant zur See, 131
Remy, Walter, 166, 169, 131
Riga, Gulf of, 209, 231, 239
Risa, Lt. Ali (*Yar Hissar*), 250–51
Rohrscheidt, Oberleutnant zur See, 144
Room 40, 27–28, 49, 144; capabilities,
  28; daily returns, 28, 177; estimates
  and projections by, 164, 177; UC-44
  ambushed by, 178–80
Rosenberg, Korvettenkapitän von, 229,
  235, 236
Rücker, Klaus, 74
Ruytingen Bank, 45, 48
Ryan, C. P., RN, 113

Saalwächter, Kapitänleutnant, 153
Sage, A. H. 199
Saint Petersburg, Russia, 230, 231, 238
Saint Trojan, 134
Sakaki, IJN, 206
Salonika, 194, 203; landings at, 193
Salonika, Gulf of, 203

Saltzwedel, Reinhold, 153–54
Sanders, W. E., RN, 110–11
Sarrail, Maurice, 193
Saseno Island, 207
Sato, Kozo, IJN, 206
Sauerland, Oberleutnant zur See, 45–46
Scapa Flow, 4, 30, 229
Scheer, Reinhard, 94
Scheldt River, 87
Schiffsmeldepost, 226–27
Schmettow, Graf von, 102–3
Schneider, Rudolf, 15
Schröder, Ludwig von, 66, 67
Schultz, Friedrich, 230
Schwieger, Walter, 66
Sebelin, Kapitänleutnant, 142
Seeburg, Max, 53
Sevastopol, Russia, 191
Shakespeare Cliff, 168
Shetlands, 91
Shipwash Sands, 88
Sims, William S., USN, 140, 151
Skagerrak, 91
Slevogt, Kurt, 185
Smith, K. R., USN, 137
Smiths, Wilhelm, 83–84
Smyrna (Izmir), 193
Somme, 96
sonar, 113, 256, 257
Souchon, Wilhelm, 251
Sound, The, 228, 232, 233
South Goodwin, 52
special service vessels. *See* decoy vessels
Spiegel von und zu Peckelsheim, Adolf
  Freiherr von, 47, 110–12
Spiess, Johannes, 210–12
Spindler, Arno, 27, 29
Sprenganker, 222
Sprenger, Otto, 138–39, 200–201
Standard Motor Construction Company,
  124
Steinbauer, Oberleutnant zur See, 199
Steinbrinck, Otto, 44
St. George's Channel, 123, 140
Stocker, H. G. D., RN, 250–51
Stone, A. J., USNRF, 160
Stoss, Alfred, 44–46
Stöter, Oberleutnant zur See, 166
Strnad, Karl, 207
Studer, H. W., USN, 137
subchaser, 125–26, 147
submarines, 3; ASW role of, 102, 140,
  201–2; equipped with hydrophone,

About the Author

Dwight R. Messimer is a lecturer at San Jose State University, California, where he is a military historian specializing in early U.S. aviation and World War I. His earlier works include *The Merchant U-Boat* and *Escape.*

Messimer served in the U.S. Army (1954–62) and was stationed in Berlin from 1957 to 1959. After being discharged he completed his graduate degree in history and joined the San Jose Police Department. Following his retirement in 1988, he began his teaching career.

Messimer and his wife live in California. This is his sixth book published by the Naval Institute Press.